Feast OF SOULS

Feast OF SOULS

INDIANS AND SPANIARDS IN THE SEVENTEENTH-CENTURY MISSIONS OF FLORIDA AND NEW MEXICO

Robert C. Galgano

University of New Mexico Press
Albuquerque

10 09 08 07 06 05   1 2 3 4 5 6 7

Library of Congress Cataloging-in-Publication Data

Galgano, Robert C., 1970–
    Feast of souls : Indians and Spaniards in the seventeenth-century
  missions of Florida and New Mexico / Robert C. Galgano.
       p. cm.
    Includes bibliographical references and index.
    ISBN 0-8263-3648-5 (cloth : alk. paper)
    1. Indians of North America—Missions—Florida. 2. Indians of North
  America—Missions—New Mexico. 3. Missions, Spanish—Florida—
  History. 4. Missions, Spanish—New Mexico—History. 5. Florida—
  History—Spanish colony, 1565–1763. 6. New Mexico—History—I. Title.
    E98.M6G35 2005
    975.9′01—dc22
                                                                    2005011381

Book design and composition by Damien Shay
Body type is Minion 10.5/14.
Display is Caslon Antique and Tiepolo.

for K.,
always

CONTENTS

LIST OF ILLUSTRATIONS

Maps

Figures

ACKNOWLEDGMENTS

I am indebted to the community of scholars gathered in Williamsburg, Virginia at the Lyon G. Tyler Department of History at the College of William and Mary, the Omohundro Institute of American History and Culture, and the Colonial Williamsburg Foundation. James Axtell, William R. Kenan, Jr., Professor of Humanities at the College, has shown by example what it means to be a professional historian. His incisive editorial remarks guided this project from its inception. Fellow students John Coombs, Anthony DeStefanis, Elizabeth Kelly Gray, Phil Levy, Dan Matz, Paul Moyer, and Andy Schocket made graduate work an unforgettable adventure. Michael Guasco and Suzanne Cooper Guasco indulged my fanatical enthusiasm for soccer, provided intellectual support and professional advice, and opened their home to a boy and his dog during summer archaeological field school. I consider myself lucky to have their friendship. The archaeologists of Colonial Williamsburg's Department of Archaeological Research tolerated my intrusion into their highly skilled world, and even considered me one of their tribe for a time. Marley Brown III, David Muraca, Amy Muraca, Andrew Edwards, Karen Wehner, Kevin Bartoy, and Jenny Gates taught me to love soil and toil in hot, humid conditions.

Researching and writing is a solitary task, but the assistance of librarians and readers made crafting this work less trying. I benefited from the patient guidance of Bruce Chappell, archivist and paleographer at the P. K. Yonge Library of Florida History at the University of Florida, and the curators of the Anderson Room at the Zimmerman Library of the University of New Mexico. I wish to express deep appreciation to David Weber for his thorough critique. I also want to thank James Whittenburg and Paul Mapp for their careful criticism and evaluation of the manuscript. David V. Holtby, Maya Allen-Gallegos, and the good people at the University of New Mexico Press have been supportive and immeasurably helpful during my first foray into the world of academic publishing. My students both at the College of William and Mary and James Madison University inspired me to write accessible history, and reminded me that research must eventually translate into teaching. They have worked hard for me over the years; I hope this book can begin to repay their dedication.

I have been blessed with numerous familial debts. I am grateful to my mother-in-law and fellow historian, Sally Meyers, who happily watched my daughter so that I could dedicate at least one day a week to writing. My father-in-law, Rick Meyers, provided welcome diversions from work with a steady stream of tickets to UVA men's basketball games. To my mother, Virginia, who instilled in me a passion for learning and a love of teaching; to my father, Michael, who showed me that the pursuit of wisdom through higher education is necessary and honorable; to my brother, David, who reminded me to focus on what is important in life and to laugh at the rest; and to my sister, Laura, who indulged my intellectual predilections, I love you all.

I am eternally grateful to Bogie who patiently waited until it was time to retrieve the Frisbee, to Isabel Katharine who helped daddy "play" on his computer and dispensed snuggles without discrimination, to Evelyn Sophia who kept daddy from sleeping too much, and to Kim for loving me.

INTRODUCTION

Frontiers and Missions

I would like to know what he felt
in that moment of vertigo
when past and present intermingled.
— Jorge Luis Borges

Without the presence of Indians, no Spaniard would have settled Florida or New Mexico. Explorers would have marched
through empty lands in vain attempts to find sources of for-
tune. Their journeys would have been shorter without Indian guides and
sustenance; their expeditions would not have taken slaves or killed inhabitants. No tantalizing tales of pearl-stocked rivers or cities of gold would
have encouraged Spaniards to fund further explorations. Without
Indians, Spanish strategies for settlement would have been problematic.
There would have been no one to construct defensive palisades or municipal offices, no one to plant food for subsistence, tribute, and trade. No
local military structure would have helped protect the colonies. Spanish
colonizers would not have attached themselves to local populations or
reached agreements with local chiefs. Native escorts would not have led
curious Spaniards to new villages or neighboring trading partners; there
would have been little hope of colonial economic profit. Without Indians,
Franciscan missionaries would never have volunteered to preach on the
frontiers. Spain's colonial American enterprises—strategic, economic,
political, and religious—required Indians. Where multiplying English settlers eventually expelled natives from their homelands, relatively few

Spaniards (by 1700 approximately fourteen hundred in Florida and three thousand in New Mexico) purposely sought Indians as laborers, trading partners, military allies, guides, informants, and potential converts.[1] Placing Indians at the center of the story is not an historian's conceit or a device for explaining a forgotten, neglected, and marginal part of America's colonial past. Historical Spanish settlers would have understood the suggestion perfectly. Spaniards who conquered and colonized Florida and New Mexico in the seventeenth century knew that Indians were essential, especially in places removed from densely populated regions. Spaniards were attracted to the frontiers of their American colonies because sedentary Indians lived there. Village-dwelling natives had, by definition, established political, social, and economic systems recognizable to Spanish newcomers. Indigenous populations could provide necessary labor for Spanish economic enterprises, and natives' knowledge of the land could speed the development of agriculture, ranching, and craft production. For Franciscan missionaries, natives offered much more: Indians were lost souls in need of Christianity's salve. For economic and religious reasons, Spaniards risked the journey to unknown lands to settle among unfamiliar people. Yet the newcomers were experienced enough to understand that local Indian settlement did not guarantee colonial success.

By the time Spanish settlers set foot on Florida's shores and New Mexican mesas, the New World had lost some of its novelty. Spanish conquistadors had toppled imperial dynasties in central Mexico and highland Peru, marched through the hinterlands of South and Central America, and decimated the peoples of the various Caribbean islands. A new generation of Spanish explorers had heard tales of mythic riches and empires to the north, and cast their eyes toward the borderlands. As the adventurers saw it, frontiers were places of opportunity for those willing to pawn their lives and wealth. After multiple *entradas*, Spanish settlers eventually agreed to accompany armed soldiers and to relocate to the fringes of Spain's New World empire. The northern borderlands were removed by thousands of miles of either rough, barren terrain or treacherous, violent waters. Their new homes lacked familiar political, social, and religious institutions, were difficult to defend, and held uncertain economic promise. Settling in such places was not a popular, or even a wise, choice.[2] Though Spanish missionaries, soldiers, and settlers considered Florida and New Mexico the extreme edges of "civilization," the native inhabitants saw their lands as the center of the universe. Seventeenth-century Indians would learn the invaders' foreign terms for their land and some would adopt the strangers' tongue. But the Spanish view of Florida and New Mexico as remote frontiers would never be the natives' perspective. Their homelands were more than impermanent settlements. Native lands were hunting grounds, agricultural fields, seasonal home-steads, and habitations for countless spirits. Indians' ancestors emerged into the world from nearby caves or passed to the afterlife by way of local mountains or streams. Spirits mingled with natives in their councils, dur-ing their celebrations, on the trails, and in their dwellings. The Indians had no need of faraway continents or far-off philosophies; the core of the cosmos lay all around them. Regardless of geographical location, eco-nomic circumstance, or population density, Indians never considered the relevance of any other place but their own world. The frontier was the fringe of their territorial hunting grounds or—in the case of large empires or confederacies—their imperial influence. Nothing else mattered.

When Spanish and Indian perspectives collided, the results were pre-dictably turbulent. People with disparate cultural imperatives and dis-tinct economic, political, and religious goals rarely get along. The Catholic missions of Florida and New Mexico were the meeting places for Indians and Spaniards, and the settings for the process of cultural dialogue. Spaniards constructed forts and farms near Indian settlements, but fre-quently only the Franciscan missionaries settled in native villages. Missions were the primary mechanism for the seventeenth-century col-onization of Florida and New Mexico. While religious goals were not the only ones on the Spanish agenda, the circumstances of frontier settle-ment made missions and, by extension religion, a central issue.

Discerning what constituted genuine conversion, adherence to reli-gious doctrine, or rejection of foreign intrusion is difficult at best. Trying to examine the inner workings and shades of individual souls is like try-ing to describe a figure standing just beyond peripheral view. But we are not without means. To decipher the behavior of Indians and Spaniards through the lens of time, scholars read between the lines of Spanish doc-uments, screen the soils of archaeological excavations for architectural, faunal, and material remains, and compare documentary evidence with modern ethnographies and oral traditions. Ethnohistory—combining his-torical and anthropological techniques to try to recover the world of non-literate peoples—gives investigators the best chance of gleaning the

Indians' past. When faced with the trauma of invasion and the ensuing cataclysmic changes, Indians made choices and sought solace in various, sometimes surprising ways. Faith always changes over time; tenets fall from favor, practitioners emphasize certain doctrines over others, religious leaders clarify or denounce particular ideas. The Spanish conquest of the Indians in Florida and New Mexico introduced a new religion and challenged traditional native practices. Indians attempted to handle those changes as they came, but the process tested natives' faith deeply.[3]

Historians, anthropologists, and archaeologists have revealed just how profoundly contact with Spanish newcomers affected native communities and have thoroughly analyzed the specific cultures of natives in the Southeast and Southwest. John H. Hann, Amy Turner Bushnell, Clark Spencer Larsen, Bonnie G. McEwan, John E. Worth, and Jerald Milanich for Florida, and France V. Scholes, Elsie Clews Parsons, Alfonso Ortiz, John L. Kessell, Ramón A. Gutiérrez, Andrew L. Knaut, and Carroll L. Riley for New Mexico, have traversed some of the trails before. Each expanded our vision of the Indian past in lands that became Spanish frontiers for a time. But the tendency of current studies to focus on one group or one region misses the bigger comparative picture that leads to greater insights and reveals new patterns. Local and regional analyses of Indians' reactions to Spanish frontier colonization cannot show whether natives' experiences were unique or common. They fail to explain the dynamic variations of Spanish colonization schemes. Narrowly focused histories fail to see broader designs in the negotiated coexistence between natives and newcomers.[4]

While scholars have examined Spanish relations with Florida's natives and New Mexico's Pueblos independently, few have treated Spain's seventeenth-century conversion and colonization of these Indians together. Hindering comparative studies of the two frontiers is the disparity in document collections. Florida scholars enjoy substantial archives of letters, reports, investigations, trials, visitations, and accounts. The relative paucity of documents from New Mexico—most originals did not survive the Pueblo Revolt in 1680—makes comparison more arduous. The most common way to compare the history of different regions is through edited volumes that gather the work of several scholars over large geographic and chronological space. Editors David Hurst Thomas, Erick Langer and Robert H. Jackson, and Donna J. Guy and Thomas E. Sheridan have compiled articles from a variety of scholars of the Spanish frontiers of both North and South America.[5] Nicholas Griffiths and Fernando Cervantes, and Christine Daniels and Michael V. Kennedy have cast wider nets, uniting works on French, British, Portuguese, Dutch, and Spanish America under single titles.[6] Edited volumes include several perspectives under one cover, but only superficially relate one to the others.

There are few who genuinely compare two or more Spanish frontiers and their people in one scholarly work. José Rabasa skillfully examines surviving sixteenth-century expedition accounts of both frontiers to construct an analysis of Spanish violence. But David J. Weber is the only scholar to systematically analyze and compare the history of seventeenth-century Florida and New Mexico in one volume. Broad in scope, Weber's magisterial *The Spanish Frontier in North America* surveys the colonial history of Florida, New Mexico, Arizona, Texas, the Gulf Coast, the Plains, and California. While Weber admirably treats Indians and Spaniards as equal participants in the frontier drama, his "chief purpose is to broaden our understanding of the American past by illuminating its Hispanic origins."[7] The scope and design of Weber's work differs from my own. My pedagogical goal is not to champion the often ignored Spanish past against an Anglocentric American history, but to emphasize the central roles Indians played, and their reactions to Spanish missionization in Florida and New Mexico. Designed as an accessible history especially for undergraduate use, *Feast of Souls* shifts our perspective to observe what the colonies looked like from the vantage point of the missions, not the colonial capitals. Though I am most interested in natives' views, the Spanish perspective is equally important.

Despite the unproven prospects, Spaniards voluntarily moved to the northern frontiers in the seventeenth century. The settlers' approach differed from that of their sixteenth-century predecessors. Both colonizers and the royal government rejected the conquistadors' "war of fire and blood," and established relationships with local inhabitants. Nevertheless, Spanish settlers benefited from violent frontier antecedents. Indians in Florida and New Mexico suffered from a series of invasions by less scrupulous Spaniards over the course of a hundred years. Their physical, demographic, and psychological scars were not quite healed when colonizers Pedro Menéndez de Avilés and Juan de Oñate arrived on the scene. While the intentions of the Spanish leaders may have been benign, some of their number wandered down an infernal path. Soldiers extracted tribute from resource-poor Indian villages, mistreated natives, and threatened the

Spanish colonial chain of command. Fearing that the latest incarnations of bearded newcomers were turning as abusive as previous visitors had been, Indians rebelled. Spaniards definitively suppressed native efforts to expel them, and secured their hold on the frontiers through military action.

As the Spanish conquest of Florida and New Mexico ended, the religious component of colonization came to the fore. The Franciscans worked most closely with and lived nearest to Indians. Their efforts to convert natives were the driving force of Spanish colonial operations and held the key to the colonies' success. Borrowing from their missionary experiences in Europe, Central and South America, and the Caribbean, Franciscans attempted to mold natives into God's servants and loyal Spanish subjects. Not permitted to preach in more thoroughly accultur-ated parishes, mendicant orders went to the frontiers to bring wayward souls to the Christian faith. The outskirts of new world settlement pro-vided a place for friars to ply their trade; Indian missions sustained Spain's colonial enterprises in both Florida and New Mexico.[8] But the Spanish Franciscans did not approach their charges uniformly, nor did they resolve some of the problems concerning the conversion of Indians in a colo-nial context after decades of contact. Missionaries had precedents to fol-low from Europe, the Caribbean, New Spain, and Peru, but they learned quickly that local conditions required flexibility to convert the natives. How far religious negotiation went was difficult to determine, and for nearly a century friars failed to reach a consensus.[9]

The clash of cultures introduced by Spanish invasions of Florida and New Mexico created several crises in native communities. Epidemiological, political, material, economic, and religious changes came with dizzying speed, and Indians had to adjust rapidly to being colonized. There was no formula to native responses; each individual, clan, and community faced an altered world and decided on a course of action according to par-ticular circumstances.[10] But when we take a broad perspective and step back from atomized studies of individual native groups or local geographic associations, patterns in natives' reactions emerge. In some cases Indians responded by embracing what their conquerors brought. At times they accepted novelties, but only on their own terms and in their own ways. Sometimes they rejected foreign ideas and goods alike. Periodically natives fled to avoid the more detrimental effects of colonization and, occasion-ally, Indians rebelled. In every case the native peoples of Florida and New Mexico sought to control their own destinies.

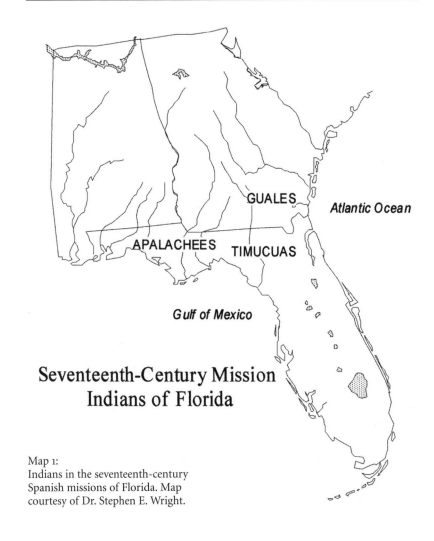

**Seventeenth-Century Mission
Indians of Florida**

Map 1:
Indians in the seventeenth-century
Spanish missions of Florida. Map
courtesy of Dr. Stephen E. Wright.

Missionization and colonization affected not only intra-Indian relations but also the negotiated terms of coexistence between natives and
Spaniards. Indian wars reflected the different ways natives coped with
their changing world. Indians usually revolted in an effort to expel the
newcomers early in the colonial relationship once they discovered what
Spanish colonization meant. These revolts were isolated events designed
to redress degrading conditions in local villages and, specifically, chiefs'
fears over lost authority and influence. But after fifty years of contact with
Spaniards, native revolts changed. In the case of the Timucua revolt of
1656, Indian leaders did not wish to expel the Spaniards entirely, but rose

to reestablish the terms of colonial cooperation that secular Spaniards had neglected. For Pueblos, the 1680 revolt adopted a millennial flavor. Rebels attempted simultaneously to rid the Southwest of all things Spanish, co-opt Spanish technologies and materials that natives deemed beneficial, and resurrect local spiritual traditions that expanded to meet pan-Pueblo concerns.

The Spanish colonial enterprise also underwent changes over the course of the seventeenth century. At first glance, Spanish colonial structures and methods appear rigid. Wherever they went, Spaniards appointed governors and local governmental councils and recruited missionaries, privileged settlers, and soldiers. Governmental palaces, municipal buildings, missionary churches, haciendas, and garrisons stood in every Spanish colony. In an ideal world, state and church worked in tandem to create a cohesive, efficient, and peaceful Spanish settlement. In reality, Spanish secular and ecclesiastical officials vied for control over Indians, tested the limits of their jurisdictions, and recklessly exercised their power over others. Spain's colonial design was actually more fluid than its structure suggested. Some colonizers emphasized secular expectations, others religious ones. Spaniards fought with each other as they decided to stress military, economic, or religious endeavors. What had been conceived as a coherent colonial system, protected from potential abuse by institutional checks and balances, devolved on the frontiers. Governors and churchmen were mutually suspicious and, at times, pursued conflicting imperatives and carried out their responsibilities independently of their colonial partners. Contradictory political, economic, military, and religious goals made the contest for native muscle and native souls heated, to say the least. Spanish colonial ventures were bold in geographical scope and in ideological optimism, but often lacked administrative cooperation. Success of one goal sometimes seemed possible only at the expense of another.

Intra-colonial squabbling found ideal environments in Florida and New Mexico. Frontiers were less economically viable than their more settled, more populated counterparts. Florida was the more "profitable" of the two, boasting shorter, faster trade routes, complex native societies used to mustering large labor forces, and comparatively rich soils for agriculture. New Mexico was hindered by long, desolate trails, geographically isolated settlements, smaller and poorer native villages that suffered from excessive Spanish demands for tribute, and an arid climate. In order

Seventeenth-Century Mission Pueblos of New Mexico

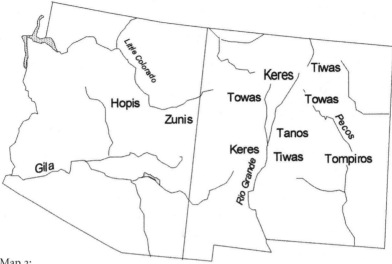

Map 2:
Indians in the seventeenth-century Spanish missions of New Mexico. Map courtesy of Dr. Stephen E. Wright.

to squeeze any profit from these frontiers, secular and ecclesiastical Spaniards had to have access to Indians. Sources of wealth were scarce, so control of Indians became the only way to make the colonial enterprise financially or spiritually solvent.

Despite violent conflicts during the first years of settlement, most initial relations between Indians and Spaniards in the late sixteenth and early seventeenth centuries were negotiated accommodations. Indians clung to their own conceptions of cooperation with the newcomers and Spaniards realized that they could not indiscriminately dictate the terms of colonization to the inhabitants. Governors had to acknowledge the power of the chiefs, settlers had to rely on native workers, and friars had to preach within the confines of Indian life. Indians and Spaniards established the terms of coexistence during the first decades of the seventeenth century, but by the 1640s several things had changed. Disease decimated native populations and Indian communities suffered from ever-increasing Spanish demands for labor and loyalty. Spanish colonizers became less sensitive to the terms of cultural negotiation and more concerned with discharging their administrative responsibilities, even to the detriment of their colonial partners. While Spaniards in

Florida recovered a balance between secular and religious programs and between Spanish and Indian needs, their New Mexican counterparts never effectively resolved their disputes. Florida seemed prepared to meet the future, but outside forces created turmoil in the missions and tested the bonds of Indian-Spanish relations. New Mexico, on the other hand, appeared ready to implode, though Spanish officials appeared either ignorant of the warning signs or incapable of repairing a decayed Pueblo-Spanish relationship.

In Florida and New Mexico, the story of Indians' and Spaniards' navigation of their unpredictable and sometimes violent world is an account of cultural negotiation. The dialogue between Indian leaders, native peoples, Spanish settlers, and Franciscan friars was complicated, and revealed moments of conflict and occasional confluence. Spaniards had many advantages but did not possess all the power. Indians decided for themselves whether to accept, adapt, or reject what their conquerors offered, and while their choices were not always pleasant, they had decisions to make. By comparing the options Indians and Spaniards took in two different places over the same century, we can achieve a deeper understanding of Indian responses to conquest, religious conversion, and Spanish imperial goals. When the strategies of cultural negotiation break down and when people cannot establish a framework for dialogue, the world becomes less safe.

The following chapters compare native cosmologies and religious practices with Spanish theology and Franciscan Catholicism, the establishment of colonial frontier mission systems, Indians' reactions to conquest and conversion, struggles between Spanish secular and religious authorities, and the disintegration of the frontier missions. Before examining what happened when Spaniards and Indians met, we should understand the cultural perspectives of each group. The precontact cosmologies of Indians in Florida and New Mexico and Spaniards and Franciscans in Europe reveal the hopes and expectations that each held and help explain how those anticipations became reforged in New World encounters.

CHAPTER ONE

Different Paths

each man is saved according to his own religion.

— proverb proscribed by spanish inquisition

Before local scouts tracked the hairy-faced, metal-clad beings on American shores, before mariners stocked vessels to search for undiscovered sea passages, before robed and tonsured men uttered the first incantations of a foreign faith to native audiences, Indians, Spaniards, and Franciscans had evolved in separate worlds. Despite cultural differences including custom, social complexity, and language, Indians in both the Southeast and Southwest practiced flexible, inclusive religions that readily absorbed new spiritual concepts to augment traditional practices. Lay Spaniards and Franciscans, on the other hand, followed an increasingly exclusive, evangelical religion that united countrymen against foreign invaders, distinguished Christian "faith" from others' "superstition," and sometimes forced dissenters to convert. When these distinct cultures—Timucuas, Guales, and Apalachees in Florida, Pueblos in New Mexico, and Franciscans and settlers from Spain—met, their cosmologies and perceptions of spiritual power concussed. The collision of worlds led to a protracted, often violent, negotiation over whose approach to faith would predominate. In the process Indians and Spaniards forged a new world.

Discerning a people's cosmological beliefs is delicate and difficult work. Deciphering the beliefs of people in the past is exponentially more complicated. Each native culture practiced particular traditions, recounted unique versions of origin stories, and cultivated independently derived conclusions about human relations to the world. Many of the minute details that characterized and delineated one culture's beliefs from another are lost. But by culling ethnographic interviews, sifting archaeological evidence, scouring ethnohistorical documents, and applying ethnological analyses, a general native perspective emerges.

The key to Indians' views of the universe lay in their surroundings. The Guale, Timucua, and Apalachee Indians of Florida, and the Tano, Tewa, Tiwa, Keres, Piro, Zuni, and Hopi Pueblos of New Mexico, lived in close contact with the landscape. Whether hunting, farming, fishing, cooking, crafting, building, or dancing, Indians spent nearly all their time outdoors. Their wooden huts or mud houses were places to sleep or to seek shelter from winter frost or summer storms. The lands encircling native settlements were as familiar as their kith and kin. Passing the majority of their time along riverbeds, in miles of wilderness, or atop mountain ridges, Indians did not consider themselves divorced from, or opposed to, their environment; they saw themselves as important players in their universe. They encouraged the continuation of life and the passing of seasons through their rituals. They also appeased powerful spirits that animated and articulated their world. Natives were an essential part of their environment.[1]

But Indians knew that they lived in lands that could take as easily as they could give. Florida's coastal and riverine environment that provided abundant fish and lush, varied vegetation was also pocked with sinkholes and swamps. Warm year-round temperatures encouraged fierce thunderstorms; nearby Atlantic and Caribbean shores were targets for hurricanes. Lightning could create an inferno if it struck dead trees or native structures made from dried wood. Persistent rains could flood a season's plantings and drought could wither fertile fields. Animals also posed perils for negligent Indians. Treacherous alligators lurked in the swamps where natives fished and gathered canes, while poisonous snakes slithered among the reeds, in rivers, and in forests. Staggeringly high humidity bred countless mosquitoes and other parasitic insects that feasted on human blood.[2]

Although ecologically different, New Mexico posed equally perilous conditions for its inhabitants. The Southwest was a study in extreme contrasts. Mesas, buttes, and mountains rose in solitary nodes or in powerful, snow-capped ranges, while treacherous canyons cut deep into the earth.

The Rio Grande, Colorado, and San Juan drainage systems provided lush vegetation near their main waterways but most of the landscape was a sparse, desert-like plain covered with sagebrush and cacti. Water was the rarest resource; the Southwest's annual rainfall of twenty-five to thirty centimeters parched the land and its inhabitants. Thunderstorms between July and August and snows from December to March provided almost all of the region's moisture. Summer temperatures in the 90s, winters that could last through April, and average elevations of 1,524 meters above sea level made the Southwest an inhospitable place to live.[3]

Yet for thousands of years people came to these two places, remained there, and found ways to survive. Despite harsh climates, Florida and New Mexico could be fruitful. Soils, grasses, and trees gave native architects the mud, thatch, and timber they needed for their structures. Local game granted their bones, tendons, and furs for artisan's tools and Indians' clothes. Shrubs provided several kinds of edible fruits and the clouds delivered enough rain for agriculture. Corn, beans, and squash—the trinity of Indian cultigens—were the staples of natives' diet. People made the most of their environmental predicament and carefully monitored the skies to mark changes in the moon's phases, the sun's progress across the horizon, and the weather. It was essential to know when to plant and when to harvest. Learning which places supported specific crops, where nuts and berries grew, where water might be found during droughts, what various elevations meant for vegetative life, and when storms were likely was vital. Unforgiving environments required, even demanded, an intimate knowledge of their secrets and resources.[4]

From their experiences in difficult conditions, Indians in Florida and New Mexico arrived at similar conclusions about the universe, even if they expressed their beliefs differently. The dual power of the land—to sustain or destroy—was expressed in the spirits that controlled those lands; they, too, could nurture or ruin life. Moreover, spirits trod the same earth the Indians walked. Native peoples in the Southeast and the Southwest made no distinction between the "natural" and "supernatural" worlds; these two places were one and the same. Indians may have needed heightened awareness or formal ceremonies to see or to speak with spirits, but they did not have to await death or to reach a "heaven" to be with the gods. Spirits protected the land by guarding and inhabiting Indians' geographical boundaries; spirits made the land sacred by living within its limits. Any place outside the natives' region was alien space, territory unprotected by and unrelated to the spirits. The relationship natives had with spirits was personal and they properly propitiated them to mitigate life's risks. The Indians' universe was a seamless tapestry linking what Spaniards would call the "visible" or "tangible" and the spiritual. Natives willingly fulfilled obligations to the spirits to acquire nature's benefits.[5]

To create stability in their inconstant world, and to safely negotiate potential pitfalls, Indians relied on strictly arranged patterns of practices and beliefs to direct and protect them. While each group had its own rituals, values, and political autonomy, the native peoples of Florida and New Mexico—who numbered approximately between thirty thousand and seventy-five thousand souls in each region—shared general cosmological concepts. Guales living in small, independent villages along the coast of Georgia and South Carolina were as susceptible to the whims of their environment as the various Timucua towns in the northern half of Florida's peninsula and the paramount chiefdom of the Apalachees in northwestern Florida. The wildly varied and geographically isolated Pueblos—from the Tiwas in northern Taos to the Zunis and Hopis in the west and the Piros in southern Quarai—all faced the daunting prospects of living in a dry, barren climate. Native spirituality in Florida and New Mexico was, at heart, an effort to achieve balance or harmony between the people and their surroundings. Those who were not vigilant in their religious observances courted disaster.[6]

Peer pressure was a significant force in native towns. Although many Indians were part of larger political associations and all were members of extensive, exclusive clans, most natives were born into settlements of three hundred to six hundred people. They relied on their fellow villagers in these close-knit, face-to-face communities for their survival. Indians defended themselves against numerous neighboring enemies and depended on each other to secure game and raise crops. Internal dissent and discontent could destroy villages. Native townspeople relied on shared responsibilities and common goals; agreed-upon religious practice was the key to maintaining village organization. Certain rituals and procedures conciliated the spirit world and bound it to bettering native conditions. However, an improperly performed rite could take a person's life or endanger an entire village; each ceremony had repercussions on both individuals and the society at large. Even incantations meant to inflict harm on a rival could have unintended or broader consequences for the community or region. Spiritual power was no plaything.

To secure agreeable weather and to assure plenty for the future, all natives, not just their religious leaders, observed a litany of rites and sacrifices. Many Indians' farming and gathering customs involved primary events. Indians prayed when farmers dug a new field for sowing, harvested the first maize, collected wild foods, opened storehouses, or removed food from their stocks. Before they gathered nuts and palm berries, natives performed ceremonies. Ever mindful of their precarious existence and their dependence on local flora, natives put aside first fruits for either ritual offering to the spirits or reserved them for the elite to consume. Indians of status prayed before eating the first fruits cut from the vines or the first crops gathered from the fields; common Indians did the same before they ate each meal. Leaving nothing to chance, the natives prayed during the preparation of food and before consuming the flour they made from their stores of grain. Natives in both Florida and New Mexico thanked the animal spirits in advance of hunting trips so that local fauna would allow themselves to be captured. If an animal was not killed with the proper respect and used with appropriate humility, future hunts would be barren. Natives were cautious about the spirit world because it had the power to withhold their means of survival.[7]

Native religion was also intimate. Every native person, regardless of age, gender, sex, or station, had some access to spiritual power. All Indians could recognize the signs evident in the world around them and could adjust their behavior accordingly. In Florida, hearing an owl's call or encountering a snake on trails, fields, or houses portended evil. Interrupting the song of a woodpecker or an owl could bring harm. Indians discovered other omens by observing each other. Eye twitches could be a sign of happiness or a prognostication of sadness. A trembling mouth suggested that something bad was eminent, that one was being talked about, or that food was coming. Natives considered belching both a sign of wanting to die and evidence that there would soon be an abundance of food. By combining augers in their environment and consequent human behavior, the Indians gleaned more information about the future. For example, when a blue jay or another bird sang and the native listener's body trembled, it meant that either people were arriving or that something important was about to happen. Some practices may have been poetic reminders rather than ontological predictions. Florida's Indians believed that a crackling fire indicated the coming of war, but perhaps firewood was drier in the heat of summer—the season of war—and the association of popping hearth fires and battle created an apt maxim.[8]

In New Mexico, Pueblos also practiced a personal faith. When planting they sowed under a waxing moon so that the crops would grow along with the celestial orb. Farmers planted wild mustard seeds with corn so that heartiness of the mustard plant would pass its strength to the corn stalks. Small offerings given in any context were meant to magically increase for recipients, while extreme generosity indicated the giver's hope of receiving a far greater return. Pueblos were fluent in spiritual language and knew that offerings or decorations conveyed specific messages. Colors had particular significance: turquoise represented maleness, yellow femaleness; black was the hue of the spirits, while purple was the pigment of war. Appealing to the spirits required both an appropriate gift and the proper mindset. Pueblos carefully performed their rites to meet both criteria, watching for any indication of their pleas' fate. Damaged offerings meant that someone had harbored ill thoughts and had caused the prayer to be rejected. However, animal tracks discovered around an offering usually meant a warm reception from the spirits. The conditions of any prayer, the attitude of each supplicant, or the position of any offering "meant something."[9]

Indians were not passive observers of spiritual power; they were active participants in the spiritual world. Their faiths were practical. When Florida natives crossed sandbars or other obstacles in a canoe, they whistled so they would not turn over. They also whistled toward storms to make them dissipate. Pueblos in New Mexico built shrines on frequently traveled routes to appease spirits and to ensure safe passage. Spanish explorer Antonio Espejo noted that "as the Spaniards have crosses along the roads, these people set up, midway between their pueblos, their artificial hillocks (*cuecillos*) built of stones like wayside shrines, where they place painted sticks and feathers." There the natives' spirits rested with and comforted those on the trails. Decorated prayer sticks were special offerings to the spirits; creating them curried spiritual favor and allowed Pueblos to properly commune with sacred forces around them. Corn meal and pollen possessed tremendous spiritual potency for the Pueblos. Indians sprinkled them to demarcate sacred space and to control foreign influences. But Indians' most potent connection and most direct access to spiritual power were dreams. In dreams, spirits revealed truths, made requests, suggested courses of action, cautioned other

Figure 1:
Reconstructed Apalachee council house (foreground) and chief's house at Talimali.
Photograph courtesy of Christopher R. Versen.

endeavors, and threatened punishment. While asleep, Indians conversed with the spiritual world and could act independently on what their dreams meant. Natives also believed in truth revealed though the words of the possessed. They understood that spirits could choose to speak through any of their fellow villagers, and that what European observers might have defined as "madness" or some grotesque "contortion" was a revelation of spiritual insight.[10]

Indians concerned about the affairs of their own lives actively courted spiritual powers to solve their problems. Like human beings throughout history, native Americans dwelled on matters of the heart. With herbs and incantations, natives compelled their loved ones to amend their amorous behavior. Women bathed in herbs to get wayward husbands to return, while others ensured that their husbands would not stray by perfuming themselves and their garments with incense. Similar herbal salves enticed potential lovers, and fasting or the nocturnal preparation of certain foods or drinks attracted desired paramours. Men could seduce women from their husbands with sung charms or by placing herbs in their mouths. Any person, regardless of station, could induce the spirits to work for them.[11]

The Indians' beliefs formed an active religion. In all the uncertainty of their world, natives' practices afforded them the opportunity to alter their conditions. It was an empowering religion that gave Indians the ability to compel the spirit world to conform to human desires. Native ceremonies purified spirits that had strayed from right behavior or that had been tainted by evil, rejuvenated society in rites of renewal, or wrapped communities in somber acts of remembrance and reconciliation. Indian rituals ushered people, seasons, weather patterns, and spirits from one state of being to another. In that sense, Indian religion was assertive.

⟨⟩

Local religion in Spain was remarkably similar to natives' faith. Like their American counterparts, Spaniards' devotion was deepest in times of crisis. Periodic epidemics, recurrent warfare, agricultural pests, and poverty made life uncertain and fragile. Towns collectively bargained with patron saints to secure a brighter, more productive, and safer future. Individuals made private vows to direct God's influence in their favor. Also like the Indians, Spaniards expected divine intervention in their everyday lives; heavenly forces simply required incentive. Local confraternities—religious associations dedicated to particular saints or organized to provide particular community services—held processions, sponsored festivals, and hosted feasts in the honor of a town's patron saint. They raised funds to do good works in the saint's name. Individuals offered food, candles, clothing, crafts, alms, and good works as advance payment for spiritual requests. But the competition for human affection was stiff, and Spaniards could be fickle, discerning followers. Saints who failed to deliver their ends of spiritual bargains found themselves abandoned for saints with better promise. Hopeful Spaniards chose their patrons by interpreting signs, assessing the value of saints' accumulated favors, or casting lots. Lotteries were providential. Over time, saints showed their preferences by intervening on behalf of particular people or aiding in specific situations. Gregory effectively combated locusts, while Mary was the logical choice for fertility.[12]

Christian devotion was in perpetual flux. Spaniards constantly adapted to new spiritual agents, applied spiritual power to broader concerns and interests, and co-opted official church tenets for local purposes.

Local faith was potent among Spaniards because it was tied to the landscape, just as natives' spirits animated their shared environment. Spaniards left gifts in caves, by rivers, and along roads. They urged the saints to mediate between Spanish communities and the forces of nature and traded human prayers and offerings for divine action. Miracles and answered prayers not only enhanced the saints' reputations but made their shrines, and the surrounding territory, sacred. There heavenly power mingled with earthly creatures to help humankind. Each community clung to local traditions and to particular patron saints.[13]

Unlike natives in America, not all Spaniards believed that these local practices were appropriate. Between 1545 and 1563, Catholic leaders met to discuss ways to reform their church and the practice of their religion. The Council of Trent brought uniformity to Christian rites and more stringent education to both "wayward" priests and "misguided" laity. Prompted in part by the growing Protestant Reformation and in part by the diversity of Christian practices, the Tridentine reforms attempted to co-opt and control what was sacred, and reaffirm the priesthood's superiority over lay spirituality.

The change was gradual and often unwelcome. Over the course of the sixteenth century, the new Catholic Church asserted its power over matters of religion and enforced its views on the substance of faith. Generally, Spaniards who once embraced ecstatic visions, personal deals with saints, and a proliferation of holy relics and sacred shrines found the religious mood changed. The clergy was more cautious about individual claims of personal revelation and the creation of cults; they wanted relics authenticated and miracles investigated. Skeptical church leaders reserved the right to determine which claims were genuine divine intercessions. They discouraged traditional expressions of personal religious commerce, such as vows and community oaths. They dismissed bargained supplications as popular superstition and indications of simple-minded vulgarity. Priests seized control over church sacra and imposed restrictions on traditional practices, such as blessing fields and crops. Prelates did not automatically ban every local feast or regional cult, nor did they turn their backs to miraculous incidents. Instead, they progressively limited the number of community festivals, commandeered the dispensation of sacraments, captured the authority to validate supernatural phenomena, and wrested power from local lay professionals who offered their spiritual services to any who could pay.[14]

The Catholic Church, therefore, encouraged the faithful to turn their spirituality inward. Church fathers urged faithful Christians to examine their own consciences and to rely on the wisdom and power of the established religious hierarchy. They emphasized the seven sacraments—baptism, communion, penance, confirmation, marriage or holy orders, and unction—administered by parish priests, and dampened community traditions that smacked of "paganism." Theologians reemphasized the cosmological concepts of heaven, purgatory, and hell. Priests reminded Christians of humankind's sinfulness and its need for redemption and forgiveness. But mostly they demonstrated the Church's power to bestow or withhold God's salvation. In practice, Church reformers taught Spaniards to pray to Christ, refocusing individual spirituality on the religion's founder. No order was more adept at preaching these lessons than the Franciscans.[15]

Francis of Assisi established the Order of Friars Minor (OFM) in the early thirteenth century as a monastic brotherhood under the aegis of the Roman Church. It followed the example of Jesus of Nazareth and the apostolic life of poverty, preaching, and penance. Francis's first Rule directed his followers to observe the three vows of poverty, chastity, and obedience and called them to practice a simple existence of prayer, of zealous service to the poor and sick, and of wandering evangelism. Wherever people would listen, the friars preached simple sermons that were intelligible to even the least educated Europeans. The early brothers practiced what trades they knew, and when they lacked necessities they begged alms. In the increasingly secular world of medieval Europe, St. Francis and his mendicant Friars Minor focused on religiosity and spirituality, and observed the founder's four pillars of the order: poverty, humility, prayer, and simplicity. The Franciscans quickly attracted thousands to their ranks.[16]

The Franciscans changed the way Christians approached their God. They described a tender deity who was so full of love that he created the world and put his people in it. They emphasized that God's love led him to sacrifice his son to redeem the sins of humankind. By stressing the centrality of Christ in Christianity, the friars deflected spiritual attention away from the saints. Francis himself was fixated on the worship of Jesus and concentrated his private spiritual investigations on the Nazarene's birth and death. At Christmas, Francis erected manger scenes in front of local churches, and in prayer he tried to imagine Jesus's suffering on the cross. Focusing on Christ's earthly existence highlighted his humanity and made God more comprehensible. The Son of God subtly changed from High-Priest and Arbiter of the Last Judgment to Jesus, son of Mary, who expressed human emotion and lived among the people, sharing in their joys and sorrows. The friars made Christianity more tangible to the masses.[17]

For their own edification and training, the Franciscans observed a starkly compact Rule that encouraged them to literally follow Jesus's example. Francis himself cited the Gospel instruction that "If thou wilt be perfect, go, sell what thou hast, and give to the poor, and thou shalt have treasure in heaven; and come, follow me."[18] Those wishing to enter the Franciscan life had to forfeit their possessions and donate to the poor before embarking on a year-long novitiate. Once they took the vow of obedience, the order issued them a habit with a hood, a cord, and trousers. Every day the clerics said the divine office: a catalog of psalms, hymns, prayers, and biblical and spiritual readings for chant or recitation at particular times of the day. At eight times during the day—beginning shortly after midnight and concluding after the evening meal and before retiring—the friars recited particular sequences of the *Creed*, *Our Father*, and *Glory be to the Father*. Additionally, the Franciscans prayed for the faults and failings of the friars, for the souls of their deceased brothers, and for all the dead. Mindful of the power of prayer, Francis's friars took their responsibility to beseech God on behalf of the world seriously and solemnly.[19]

Apart from their duty to pray for the world, the Franciscans also felt an obligation to emulate the Apostles' example by spreading Christianity. Francis gave specific instructions about the manner in which his followers were to serve as missionaries among North African Muslims and other nonbelievers. He quoted biblical verses to prepare his friars for what they would face, cautioning them, "Our Lord told his apostles: 'Behold, I am sending you forth like sheep in the midst of wolves. Be therefore wise as serpents, and guileless as doves.'"[20] Besides keeping their wits about them, the missionaries were to "avoid quarrels or disputes and 'be subject to every human creature for God's sake,' so bearing witness to the fact that they are Christians."[21] The friars' model life was the lure for wayward souls, and Francis admonished his preachers to "proclaim the word of God openly so they might get listeners to accept baptism and become Christians."[22]

Franciscan missionaries faced acute danger during their wanderings, and Francis was aware of the risks he and his followers took. He urged the friars to embrace the opportunity for martyrdom: "No matter where they are, the friars must always remember that they have given themselves up completely and handed over their whole selves to our Lord Jesus Christ, and so they should be prepared to expose themselves to every enemy, visible or invisible, for love of him." He then rallied the power of Scripture to prepare them for the daunting task of converting those who had ignored or eschewed the Christian way of life. He quoted extensively from the Gospel and assured the friars that "'Blessed are they who suffer persecution for justice's sake, for theirs is the kingdom of heaven.'"[23]

To further ready themselves for their evangelical task, the Franciscans denied themselves worldly comforts and observed a severe relative to other communities of mendicant monks. Francis strictly forbade the ownership of property and took the vow of poverty literally. But he also insisted that the friars leave the security and seclusion of monasteries to work in the world, armed with little more than the habits on their backs and the zeal in their hearts. The Franciscans wandered throughout Italy and soon Europe, preaching, ministering to the sick, and begging food and shelter during their travels. If no one offered them sustenance, the preachers went without. As their souls and bodies weakened from their strenuous labors, they retired to secluded places to pray and rejuvenate their energy. The apostolic life was hardly an easy path.[24]

And yet the basic tenets of the Franciscan monastic life—poverty, humility, obedience, and simplicity—were subject to the realities of religious life in the Middle Ages, and became points of tension throughout the history of the order. Poverty was the most problematic issue. The founder's call to embrace extreme poverty was difficult to heed for even the most dedicated Franciscan. The order's responsibility to provide basic security for its members compromised the Rule's demand that the brothers own nothing. Poverty became a less literal requirement as the order bowed to the need to feed, clothe, and shelter its friars. Humility, too, was not an easy dictate to follow. Surely the friars understood Francis's command to always take the lowest place and to refuse personal glory or recognition. Nevertheless, in practice, living humbly was not as straightforward a regulation as it might have seemed. Preaching and converting were central services the Franciscans provided; without some level of authority the friars' sermons would fall on deaf ears. Francis's directive that the friars lead a simple life became increasingly difficult in an age when education became important. For friars to proselytize effectively, they had to thoroughly know theology and Scripture. As Francis's order grew, it attracted more intelligent students and men of higher station who demanded a more rigorous intellectual foundation for the Franciscans. Like it or not, the Friars Minor had to curry some status to achieve their goals.

Obedience was also an ambivalent directive. The Franciscans had to be obedient to the Church they served and to remain separate from parish priests and bishops whose job it was to administer the sacraments to the faithful. Monastic orders in the Roman Church were special; they did not fall under the normal Church hierarchy. Those who followed a rule, in Latin *regula*, were "regular" clergy, and obeyed the strictures of their own brotherhood and fell under direct jurisdiction of the pope. They were removed from the hierarchy of the "secular" clergy that included parish priests, bishops, archbishops, and cardinals. The secular clergy had pastoral responsibilities in established Christian towns and cities. Unlike the regular clergy, the secular hierarchy followed no particular rule and obeyed the dictates of those above them in rank. Regular and secular clerics formed two separate branches on the Christian tree. Francis wanted his brothers to facilitate the Church's work, but often the tools of the trade that friars and priests plied were the same. The Franciscans encroached on the hierarchical clergy's duties, despite the saint's intention that his friars respect separate jurisdictional spheres. The minor friars often vied with parish priests for followers and alms. Yet the Franciscans, who owned nothing and controlled few churches, depended on the generosity of their parochial counterparts for the instruments of the mass and the implements of the faith. The relationship between the regular and secular clergy was always contentious.[25]

From the late thirteenth to the sixteenth century, the Franciscans gradually embraced a more practical monastic life. The friars adopted a modest security in buildings established for their order, accumulated libraries of learning, and enjoyed the benefits of money even if they did not handle the finances themselves. Poverty was less important than security, simplicity bowed to learning, and humility yielded to privilege. Franciscan poverty remained a particularly divisive issue that could have forced the order to run afoul of the Church itself. The medieval Church had become quite wealthy throughout Europe, and the pope was more theocratic prince than religious leader. The Church owned its places of worship, monasteries, burial grounds, holy relics, religious accoutrements, and gifts from penitents, ranging from huge land tracts to gold. Parishes and dioceses—local and regional organizational districts under the direction of individual priests or bishops respectively—collected tithes from both the Catholic faithful and the general citizenry, regardless of religious predilection, to pay for Church expenses. For the Franciscans to reject all forms of property ownership seemed a criticism of the greater Roman Church if not simply impractical.[26]

The early history of the Franciscan order was largely an attempt to resolve the tension between the strict standards St. Francis himself set and the exigencies of being a monk working in the world. Ever mindful of Francis's hopes and expectations, the friars attempted to make their founding father proud. To their credit, the Franciscans generated significant internal reforms and consistently debated the means and methods of following Francis's way. Their willingness to periodically reject wealth and return to a severe and simple Rule endeared them to lay Christians and royal crowns alike. In Spain, they became trusted holy men.

Those with heightened access to spiritual power were influential people in their societies. Religious leaders in Florida and New Mexico were as significant to community faith as their counterparts were in Europe. While Indians individually intervened in the spiritual world to affect their own lives, they could not wield every tool of spiritual power. The surest way to manipulate the spiritual realm was to enlist the services of Indians who had been chosen by the spirits themselves to keep and use the knowledge of the spirit world. Each native group recognized a variety of holy people. Chiefs of various offices, shamans, herbalists, medicine men, clan leaders, and elders all had specific duties in native towns. Generally, native spiritual leaders served their people as physicians, spiritual guides, clan headmen, and keepers of sacred knowledge. Like mendicant friars and Christian priests, native shamans were the middlemen between Indians and mysterious spiritual power, and they exercised extensive influence over indigenous life. Their responsibilities, however, were more expansive. Shamans prescribed medicinal herbs to ill patients, prepared spells, breathed prayers of blessing, peered into the future, procured lost items, and presided over communal ceremonies. They uttered prayers and blessings to ensure favorable weather, bountiful harvests, successful hunts, and harmonious relationships with the landscape. Native holy men conjured rain and thunderstorms or forced them away by blowing into the sky. Shamans were significant enough in native society to affect everyday decisions of villagers and the course of community social and political life. They prepared native warriors for battle against enemies, conducted ceremonies for entire villages and confederations, and advised chiefs on village policy.[27]

Spiritual power was double-edged in the Indians' world; power could cure as well as kill. But only those who deliberately abused spiritual power could create evil. Indians understood that native priests could manipulate medical-spiritual power to enhance life, but they also acknowledged that shamans could wield spiritual powers in harmful ways. To win spiritual favor and to secure benign results, Indians paid shamans for their services in kind and willingly parted with their prized possessions. Timucuas offered the first deer killed on a hunting expedition to shamans, and both Timucuas and Apalachees planted special fields for native priests so they would not have to spend time tilling the soil. Common Indians reserved the first crops, the first fruits from each collection, and the first supplies removed from food stores for ritualistic purposes and gave them to native priests, political leaders, or the spirits directly. Pueblos paid shamans for administering cures, performing marriage ceremonies, and interpreting messages conveyed in medicine bowls. However, shamans at times extorted villages for more pay, threatened communities with deadly spells, and refused or delayed their services to achieve more agreeable conditions. They could even induce spirits to harm native clients if the terms were not acceptable or a payment was tardy.[28]

Indians engaged shamans to harm as well as heal. Shamans cast spells for natives who wished to induce other villagers to fall in love or ill. They bewitched rivals with doses of water, moss, animal skins, and plants. Spells were potent manipulations of the spirit world, and Indians understood the dangers involved in tapping into such power. As part of the bewitching ceremony, natives abstained from eating fish, from painting themselves, and from sleeping with their wives. Once their spell was successful and took the life of the desired target, Indians bathed to ritually cleanse themselves of the evil spirits and resumed their lives as normal. Should the bewitched person survive, however, the spell would turn its deadly force back upon the one who cast it. In this all-or-nothing endeavor, the risk of counter spells and spiritual retribution was serious business.[29] Shamans and medicine societies were, therefore, dangerous wielders of double-edged spiritual power.

Indians believed that spiritual health and bodily fitness were identical; soul sickness had physical symptoms and vice versa. Shamans, therefore, were practicing physicians who looked after the well-being of the community in formally orchestrated, carefully timed rites, and cared for individuals during house calls. Medicine men had an impressive arsenal of sacred items to deploy for cures and ceremonial rituals. Pueblo shamans invested elaborately constructed and decorated prayer sticks, prayer feathers, corn meal, pollen, shell, tobacco, and pigments with the hopes of native supplicants. They sprinkled powders over altars in formal rites or in everyday places during life's routines to cast the proper spiritual mood for Pueblo endeavors. Dolls and fetishes in wood or stone and beautifully carved masks represented powerful spirits in household shrines, clan altars, and community dances.[30] Herbal remedies varied from simple exchanges of a medicine pouch for goods in kind, to complex rites that took days to perform. Medicine served diagnostic purposes, found lost items, strengthened Indians' ability to conduct their daily tasks, and prepared them for special events. They were well acquainted with the applications and properties of a variety of herbs, roots, plants, powders, and therapeutic concoctions. Native physicians prescribed a variety of items as pharmaceuticals, such as ingested charcoal, dirt, pottery shards, fleas, or lice.[31]

The most potent medicine, however, was conjured in community-wide ceremonies.[32] In Florida, one particular herb played a central role in several of the natives' most important communal rituals. *Cacina*, the "black drink," had medicinal, social, and political significance. Indians put the leaves of the yaupon holly (*Ilex vomitoria*) in ceramic jars and roasted them over a fire. Then they broke the dried leaves, ground them, and poured water into the jar. They boiled the water and the steeped leaves made a tea that smelled like lye and looked like a frothy beer. They filtered the beverage and drank it hot.[33] Its effects were dramatic. French explorer René de Laudonnière observed that "assoone as they have drunke it, they become all in a sweate, which sweate being past, it taketh away hunger and thirst for foure and twenty houres after."[34] Native councils consumed cacina during deliberations, dancers drank it before, during, and after feasts, and sportsmen imbibed before ball games. Beyond its ceremonial import, the drink's ability to stave off hunger for a day made it valuable for hunting and war parties absent from their homes and without food for periods of time. Before they went to battle, Indian warriors drank the black liquid. It also had medicinal value. Fray Genaro García noted that natives at times consumed great quantities of black drink, "whereupon their bellies became like kettle drums and as they drank their bellies grew and swelled up." García then declared that "we saw each one of them opening his mouth with much calmness, throw out a great stream of water as clear as when he had drunk it, and others on their knees on the ground, scattering the water thus made in every direction." Its purgative properties made cacina a notable "benefit against the [kidney] stone," swore fray Genaro, but the remedy was no soft drink. Despite its flavor, "it cannot be used as a dainty like chocolate," warned the friar.[35]

According to the English adventurer John Sparke, the medicinal value of another native herb was less certain. He remarked in 1565 that when the Indians traveled they had a kind of dried herb that they put in a cane with an earthen cup in the end and lit with fire. Florida's Indians sucked smoke through the cane. Sparke suggested that the smoke satisfied their hunger and that they could go four or five days without meat or drink. But he also observed that it "causeth water & fleame to void from their stomacks."[36] But sharing a tobacco pipe was pivotal for establishing the correct mood and the proper atmosphere for native rites and ceremonies.

In New Mexico, community rituals were controlled by medicine societies that gathered resources to sponsor ceremonies and feasts. Medicine societies were the collective keepers of sacred knowledge and provided service to the community by exercising their spiritual muscle to help the sun's progress across the sky, bring rain, or make hunts profitable. Dances, accompanied by song and drum, were the most articulate and powerful form of spiritual communion. Elaborately decorous and exquisitely executed rituals beseeched the spirits even as they bent powerful forces to natives' will. Song was as important in the supplication of the spirits. Winter dances invigorated the sun, redistributed foods and goods to needy villagers during lean months, and guaranteed that animal spirits would permit fruitful hunts. Spring rites welcomed the return of life to regional flora, urged the spirits to bring rain, and ensured the proper beginning to the sowing season. Summer rituals brought more rain and gave continued strength to the sun to nourish native crops and to ensure the orb's

Figure 2:
Hlauuma (North House) in the Northern Tiwa Pueblo of Taos.
Photograph by the author.

return across the sky. Harvest ceremonies celebrated autumnal bounty and offered prayers of thanksgiving to the fertility spirits and prepared Indians for the approaching winter. Whatever the ritual, Spanish chroniclers were impressed. Dancers "performed at the beating of a sort of leather container [jicara] sounding like the beating of a drum," explained historian Baltasar de Obregón in 1584. Natives sang "without anyone getting out of tune. It is very pleasant due to the excellent harmony of the song, for it sounds as if only one were singing."[37]

Native medicine did not rely solely on herbal remedies or complex community feasts. It included cures, prayers, and spells. Curers based their practice on the theory that the appearance of foreign objects inside the body caused physical pain. Foreign objects were introduced into native bodies or on their legs and feet through incantations or from angering the spirit world, and medicine men removed them by "operating" on their patients. One European observer in Florida wrote: "They have the custom that when they feel ill, whereas we would have ourselves bled, their doctors suck the place where pain is felt until they draw blood."[38] Pieces of coal, small lumps of dirt, little insects, or tiny rocks were common offending objects. At the end of the operation, native doctors showed their patients what they had extracted as proof of their diagnosis and evidence of their successful treatment. In other cures, medicine men and their native charges followed careful protocols before and after their operations. Florida shamans sometimes placed white feathers, a new chamois (a kind of soft hide), the ears of an owl (possibly the feathers from around an owl's ear), and arrows stuck into the ground in front of the sick person before removing the sickness. Afterwards, patients made cakes or pap or some other food and invited their physician to share the meal. If patients neglected this ritualistic meal, they risked the return of the illness and courted death.[39] Pueblo breathing rites and spitting or spraying water imparted the properties of the medicine to the patient. Rubbing snake oil on the skin made people fear the patient as they would fear a serpent. Pulverized stones made warriors arrow-proof. If patients suffered from foreign contagion or contamination, medicine men cleansed their bodies and spirits with water, corn meal, or pollen. Pueblos endured ritual whipping to increase strength or to curry fortune.[40]

Caring for native women and midwifery were equally serious. Indians appreciated the power inherent in women's capacity to bring new life into their world. In fact, native societies feared the awesome spiritual potency of women's menstrual periods and pregnancies. Florida Indians observed strict taboos to temper women's heightened power during pregnancy and childbirth. During menses or after childbirth, women abstained from eating fish or deer meat for fear that their increased spiritual power would hurt those who shared those foods with them. They carefully regulated their diet during pregnancy and observed restrictions on the kinds of foods they consumed. Menstruating and pregnant women monitored the company they kept and were careful to avoid food stores and hunting parties. French settlers knew that the Indians were careful with women's power: "After the husbands learn that their wives are pregnant, they stop living with them. The men do not eat anything the women have touched while they have their menstrual period."[41] Pueblos also recognized women's increased power during their childbearing years and observed strict taboos that forbade premenopausal women from male rituals. While Pueblo men and women struggled with each other for spiritual control—women through their biological cycles, men through ceremony—both recognized the occasional necessity to temper women's particular spiritual potency.[42]

In the natives' minds, spiritual power was not divided into dichotomous, mutually exclusive halves. Power was good *and* evil. The Christian conception of cosmological power was similar to the Indians' view in that it recognized good and evil spiritual forces. But the difference in interpretation created wildly different results. Doctors of the Christian faith taught that God was the embodiment of all that was good, while Satan was the personification of all evil. The two were diametrically opposed, if theologically unequal, and vied with one another in a cosmic war for supremacy. God was omnipotent; Satan was a wily, but ultimately doomed, adversary. Christians saw the earth as a battlefield where God and the Devil fought for human souls. God enlisted human allies to assist in his struggle against evil and rewarded his loyal servants with a place in paradise after death. Spanish Christians did not have to search too far to find examples of this cosmic contest. For nearly eight hundred years, Muslims had governed parts of Iberia. The metaphor of a universal battle was appropriate for the medieval history of Spain.

⸎

Between the early ninth century and the late fifteenth century, Spanish Christians gradually reconquered their lands and re-Christianized the inhabitants. In the process, Spain became intimately associated with the Christian Church and later the Roman Catholic Church. The *reconquista* followed episodic spurts. Like Indian cultures in the Americas, Spaniards were isolated geographically and culturally from one another. Each region boasted its own dialect, nurtured its own economy, adhered to its own institutions, followed its own traditions, and obeyed its own governments. Spanish regional leaders did not cooperate, but vied with one another for territorial, strategic, and diplomatic gains. Peoples' lives followed the rhythms of provincial existence, not the beat of monarchical pretensions.[43]

Over the course of eight centuries, the various segments of Spanish Christian society united in a loose affiliation to affirm their control over political and religious affairs region by region. From the start the anti-Muslim alliance was militantly Christian and fiercely determined to win independence. The reconquest of Spain was as much a crucible for the creation and consolidation of kingdoms as it was a holy war against the "infidels." Nevertheless, it was the religious mythology of the reconquista that resonated for future generations of Spaniards and helped the monarchs of Castile and Aragon to gradually create a somewhat united Spain in the fifteenth century. However, few Spaniards, if any, harbored a fully developed notion of a united peninsula or of a religious war for control over Iberia. That took centuries to develop.[44]

Bolstering the burgeoning Spanish ideology was the ninth-century discovery of a tomb in central Galicia. The tomb's contents, according to authorities in the kingdom of Asturias-León, included the remains of the Apostle, St. James the Great. Legend held that St. James had gone to Hispania to preach the Gospel and to undertake the conversion of its inhabitants, despite the fact that little evidence that James ever tread on Spanish soil existed. The people adopted James as their patron and protector and soon embellished the saint's role. James became *Santiago Matamoros*, St. James the Moorslayer and the anti-Muhammad. In the spiritual struggle against the Muslims, the Christian resistance had its symbol and its source of divine sanction. James's shrine at the Church of *Campus Stellarum*, or Compostela—the field of stars—eventually became one of the most visited religious sites in Christendom. The spiritual cachet Santiago bestowed on the Spaniards also fed their darker impulses.[45]

Many Spaniards were suspicious of non-Christian religion and thought that Islam and Judaism "contaminated" Iberia. By the sixteenth century, Spanish religious intolerance reached its peak. According to

Christians, both Muslims and Jews denied that Jesus was the Messiah, the one promised by God to redeem the sins of the world. Muslims, Christians believed, followed a false prophet in Muhammad and the Jews had killed Christ. Although all three faiths worshipped the same God, their different approaches seemed too great a chasm to bridge.[46] Contributing to Christian Spaniards' growing intolerance was a more concerted effort to convert Jews and Muslims in *España*. Zealous mendicants gained influence during the cessation of open war in the fourteenth century. They advocated an evangelical war against the "infidels." Traveling in pairs, they preached to Christians, Jews, and Muslims alike and performed services to all.[47]

Dependant upon the favor and patronage of the Spanish royal houses, the Franciscans became instruments of crown policy and counterpoints to non-Christian elements in the peninsula. Most of the Spanish friars came from the middle classes, for the most part were educated men, and served as advisors and emissaries in secular circles of power. Admitting these representatives of the middle sorts to positions of influence allied merchant and urban families with the crowns of Spain and ensured greater commitment from Spanish Christians to embrace political and religious orthodoxy. As the Spanish royalty of Castile and Aragon consolidated its control over Spain, the Friars Minor became minority shareholders in a partnership of power.

The reconquest of Spain meant resettlement of Christians in territories formerly dominated by Muslims; the Franciscans' presence encouraged Christians to relocate to the Iberian frontier. There the friars ministered to the new settlers and tried to convert local Jews and Muslims. The *custodias* (Franciscan convents in locales too sparsely populated to be provinces) were the front lines of the conversion movement, and not only provided a place from which the *doctrineros*, or evangelical missionaries, propagated the faith, but also stabilized the less settled and potentially volatile borderland territories that Christian kings had yet to secure through force of arms. Friars serving in underpopulated areas also ministered to Christian settlers who had no parish priests to provide them the sacraments of the Church. The network of Franciscan doctrineros, preachers, and diplomats provided a bulwark against non-Christian faiths, and helped win frontier settlers' compliance with royal objectives and policies.[48]

The Franciscans' relationship with the royal houses of Spain was symbiotic. The friars' success depended upon the generosity and favor of the wealthy and powerful kingdoms, and the monarchs' ability to gain the loyalty of its subjects required the work of the Friars Minor and the support of the Catholic Church. Spanish rulers gave more than ample funds and land grants to the order for constructing houses, feeding, clothing, and supplying friars, and for undertaking conversion efforts in the hinterlands. Since the Franciscans observed a vow of poverty, rulers provided the friars with supplies of water, salt, grain, and other food-stuffs, and permitted their use of royal mills. They rebuilt friaries destroyed by fire and came to their rescue during natural disasters and economic emergencies. The kings of España also provided the Franciscans with protection against Muslim reprisals, from brigands' attempts to rob them or do them harm while they conducted their holy business, and from the jealousies of rival orders and secular priests. Rulers designated the friars as royal messengers no matter what duties the friars were conducting, and crimes against Franciscans were pun-ishable in royal courts of justice where stiffer penalties were expected. Members of royal families and courts trusted the friars with secret cor-respondences and with their confessions, and named them as treaty nego-tiators, ambassadors, and executors of their wills. The Spanish kings also exempted the order from taxation, allowing it to amass a substantial for-tune.[49] In exchange, the Spanish monarchs gained a more loyal and pacified populace through the friars' preaching. They also won lever-age with the powerful papacy, and became leaders in the European strug-gle against Islamic rivals. The Spanish rulers procured papal support and Christian sanction for the reconquista by characterizing their mil-itary efforts against the Moors as part of a greater holy war intended to secure Jerusalem from Islamic control.[50]

The Friars Minor rapidly became a fully operational clerical organ-ization with the ability to perform the duties of parish priests and the right to collect fees for performing the sacraments. Ironically, it was the Franciscans' initial rejection of materialism that convinced faithful Christians that the order was worthy of trust. Once earned, however, the people's trust came in the form of valuable goods, property, and money. The Franciscans' reputation for genuine faith and honest works attracted lost souls from every region of Spain, and grateful con-gregants recognized the friars' efforts by bequeathing large sums of money and property to the Friars Minor rather than to their local churches. Friars proved their trustworthiness by performing countless acts of service with discretion and love. They diffused potentially embarrassing conundrums, forgave mortal sins, and attended to the needs of the community. With each service rendered, the friars' reputation grew. Soon local people entrusted delicate matters to the Franciscans who had proven themselves up to the task. They also entrusted important religious matters to the Franciscans. The Spanish faithful contended that the "gray robes" were closer to God, and therefore prayers they said for the dead, for the ill, or for those souls laden with sin were more likely to be heard and granted. People paid for the saying of masses to limit the time souls languished in purgatory. People paid for repairs to Franciscan friaries and churches. They even gave large sums to the order to gain some concession in their afterlife. Lay Spanish generosity continued and grew through the sixteenth century.[51]

Local merchants allied themselves with the friars to advance local control. Both groups were members of the middle classes and had familial ties. They also had vested interests in cooperating against local traders and shopkeepers who adhered to non-Christian faiths. Jewish and Muslim merchants were direct competitors with their Christian counterparts, and cooperation with the Franciscan preachers could limit the "infidels'" influence in the marketplace as well as in the battle for souls. The two theaters were becoming one and the same. By courting both popular and royal support, the Friars Minor insulated themselves from the vagaries of loyalty. When they overstayed their welcome or became embroiled in local conflicts, the centralized royal authorities supported their position. When the friars ran afoul of government policy, the people zealously defended their holy men.[52]

The marriage of Isabella of Castile and Ferdinand of Aragon effectively united Spain, and ushered in a new era of increased political and religious energy in the peninsula.[53] The two monarchs summoned a national synod at Seville in July 1478 to reform the Catholic Church in their kingdoms. By including Spanish clerics in the process, the royal couple secured widespread support for cooperation between church and crown and cleared the way for greater autonomy from Rome. Through their social and religious policies, Isabella and Ferdinand encouraged the emergence of a Spain that rejected the pluralistic spirit of *convivencia* (Jews, Muslims, and Christians "living together"), and embraced the culture of the Old Christian majority. Repudiating their Muslim and Jewish past, Spaniards adopted Christianity as a cultural prerequisite for citizenship. The royal couple rejuvenated the war against the Moors by adopting and professing themes of the reconquista and Christian hegemony. Isabella and Ferdinand repaid growing Spanish zeal by completing the centuries-long reconquest. From 1481 the Spaniards attacked the last Moorish holding at Granada, which fell to the Christians in 1492. The successful conquest of the Moors in Spain prompted Pope Alexander VI to bestow upon the royal pair the title of *Los Reyes Católicos* (the Catholic Kings); their preeminent status, and through them Spain's role in Christendom, was expanding.[54]

The year the reconquista ended was also the year the Catholic Kings expelled Judaism from their territories. All Jews had to either convert to Christianity or accept exile. Queen Isabella had instituted the Holy Office of the Inquisition in 1480, not to indict and punish non-Christians but to investigate Christians and especially converts. *Conversos*, Jewish converts, were the particular targets of the Inquisition's effort to root out heterodoxy. *Moriscos*, Christianized Moors, were also subject to Spanish scrutiny. In both cases, Spanish religious zealotry had been enflamed by Christian propaganda and fostered over centuries of reconquista. In both cases, Spaniards viewed converts suspiciously. Isabella and Ferdinand came to power at a time when millenarian ideas of Jesus's Second Coming were commonplace. People believed that the unification of Spain under a Christian monarchy foretold the coming of the Last Judgment. Many Spaniards believed that they were preparing not only for the end of the world but also for the triumph of Christ over his enemies.[55]

When the Friars Minor reached the New World frontiers of Florida and New Mexico, they carried with them habits formed and lessons learned during the reconquest of Spain and the ensuing conquests of Mexico and Peru. While Spain's invasion of the heavily populated New World empires set the tone for subsequent frontier policies, circumstances in the northern borderlands forced Spanish settlers and friars to adjust their strategies. Frontier friars could be initially flexible, but their battle-inspired approach to "otherness" dictated that only Christianity could survive the clash.

CHAPTER TWO

Conquering the Spirit

a voice cries out in the desert,
prepare the way of the Lord.

— isaiah 40:3

Spaniards' New World conquests were extensive by the end of the sixteenth century. They had toppled the Aztecs of central Mexico in 1521, had deposed the Incas of highland Peru in 1533, and thirty years later had spread their influence over tens of thousands of square miles in Central and South America. Following patterns developed during the fifteenth-century reconquista of Hispania and fine-tuned on the Canary Islands in the Atlantic Ocean, Spaniards settled the islands in the Caribbean.[1] Conquistadors gathered supplies, assembled bands of soldiers, and set off in search of vast treasure, secret trade routes, and people to subdue. Once they subjugated native people, colonial officials granted use rights of native labor to Spanish settlers (*encomienda*), and arranged work drafts for public improvement (*repartimiento*). Those holding titles to native labor were responsible for defending the work force and providing religious instruction.

When natives lived in highly complex, sedentary societies, Spaniards dominated their subjects. Indians less tied to agricultural or urban settlements were more difficult to congregate. Spanish expectations were set by their early successes in Mexico and Peru. The magnificence of the Aztec and Inca empires convinced the Spaniards that still more fantastic kingdoms remained to be discovered. Utopian rumors, fountains of youth, cities of gold, rivers clogged with pearls, and stores of opulent wealth captured the imagination of would-be conquerors, and whetted their hunger for earthly power and heavenly glory. Each *entrada* or exploratory venture into regions beyond Aztec and Inca influence went under the assumed sanction of the Christian deity and with the stated purpose of bringing salvation to the "heathen." Representatives of the Roman Catholic Church were oftentimes participants in Spanish incursions. Secular and regular priests from various orders served the religious needs of the conquering armies, blessed their endeavors, and, ostensibly, initiated the conversion of the natives they met.

By 1565 Spanish soldiers had penetrated the Amazonian jungles of South America, climbed the rocks of northern Mexico, and traversed the spine of the Andes. In each case the invaders established Spanish governments, imperial economic systems, and Christian missions and churches. Governors enforced Spaniards' use of Indian labor to mine precious metals, plant marketable crops, erect the edifices of Spanish settlement, and exploit local resources. In many cases, missions were the best means of controlling native populations who were less sedentary than Aztecs or Incas. Doctrineros, missionaries from regular religious orders, lived among native populations to create liaisons between Spaniards and Indians. While they filled political, diplomatic, and economic roles, the doctrineros were primarily concerned with spiritual matters. Mission theory suggested that "pagans" could be saved if they became "civilized" (adapted to Spanish customs, dress, and language) and were converted (embraced Roman Catholicism).[2] The friars' hope for success was based on their belief that the Indians were capable of discerning and voluntarily embracing Christianity. On the whole, missionaries did not subscribe to opinions of Indians' inherent barbarity, but agreed with the argument that the Dominican Bartolomé de las Casas championed between 1530 and 1550 concerning the nature of Indians' intellect. The doctrineros had seen the natives' capacity for impressive architecture, and admired their tremendous skill in crafting weapons and tools, hunting wild game, and planting extensive fields. Surely people who could create the great cities of Tenochtitlan and Cuzco were soul-filled human beings with artistic talent and organizational acumen.[3]

As Spain's American holdings expanded, Spanish colonists demanded novel sources of income and labor. They also needed more certain defenses against the imperial pretensions of Spain's European rivals in

Portugal, the Netherlands, France, and England. But access to the promise of wealth and status faded for new generations of Spaniards; to make
their fortunes, they turned their eyes to new frontiers. The triumvirate
of New World conquest—the search for riches, the desire for new sources
of labor, and the duty to spread Christianity—justified the ambitions of
late sixteenth-century explorers. Religion was a tertiary goal, subordinate to the desire for wealth and labor. But in the Spanish mind, religion could not be divorced from economic or political concerns. They
were intimately entwined.[4]

Attempts to conquer New Mexico and Florida continued over the
course of the sixteenth century. Entrepreneurs (*adelantados*) who had
or could raise the necessary capital and supplies secured royal grants and
contracts, and sought fortunes in the unknown northern frontiers.
Uncovering mineral or material wealth could win explorers power, land,
and noble titles.[5] Streams of hopeful Spaniards negotiated New Mexican
mesas and rounded the Florida peninsula in their drive to discover new
Tenochtitlans and Cuzcos. Instead, they found small, mobile Indian settlements whose warriors vigorously defended their territories. The
entradas into the northern limits of Spanish America were numerous and
not always official: three trips to Florida and seven to New Mexico. By
the time Hernando de Soto and Francisco Vázquez de Coronado had
returned from their explorations, or had died in the process, their targets had proved to be remote frontier regions with little promise. Each
venture brought violent conflict with the indigenous peoples, reinforc-
ing the Indians' conclusion that the newcomers were destructive but distracted visitors. They soon moved on to other lands and other peoples.
The Spaniards who reached New Mexico and Florida in the final decades
of the sixteenth century were different; they had come to stay. In both
cases, expedition leaders asked Franciscans to join them.[6]

Convinced that previous explorations had missed New Mexico's hidden riches, Governor Juan de Oñate was determined to settle the territory and procure the assistance of the local people. Indians' acute
memories of the damage Coronado, Espejo, and Castaño de Sosa had
wrought during their marches through the Southwest decades earlier
worked in Oñate's favor. From 1598 to 1599, he secured obedience from
initially acquiescent Pueblos, and went about searching the surrounding country for sources of wealth. Southwestern natives bore the scars
of previous Spanish invaders and chose to grant the latest visitors the

tribute they demanded. But the Pueblos lived in small, autonomous villages with relatively few resources; Oñate had to search farther afield to recoup his investments. Amicable relations between Pueblos and Spaniards were short-lived. Some Spanish soldiers, angered by the dearth of mineral resources and chafed by Oñate's firm command, abused Pueblo hospitality. Armed with guns and steel blades, rogue Spaniards demanded extra tribute from Pueblos and plundered native food stores. Oñate meted stiff penalties to mutinous men who either mistreated Pueblos or tried to abandon the colony. But he was equally resolute when avenging an uprising against his *maese de campo* (in this case, adjutant) and nephew, Juan de Zaldívar, at Acoma. Zaldívar and a band of thirty soldiers extracted supplies for themselves and horses from reluctant Acomas. The following day, a Spaniard named Vivero stole two turkeys and assaulted an Indian girl. The Acomas rose against the newcomers and killed eleven. After consulting his Franciscan advisors about the legalities of a "war of fire and blood" on the Acomas, Oñate sent Zaldívar's brother, Vicente, to exact retribution. The Spaniards killed eight hundred Acomas and captured over five hundred. Oñate tried and found the Acomas guilty of murder. He ordered that soldiers cut off one foot of every male over the age of twenty-five and sentenced all adults over twelve to twenty years of servitude. The girls he entrusted to the discretion of the father commissary and the boys to his *sargento mayor* (major) so that they might learn Christianity. The governor similarly ravaged rebellious Tompiros in Abó and Jumanos in eastern New Mexico.[7]

Spanish military might forced colonial governance on the Pueblos but did little to seduce them to the Spaniards' faith. As fray Francisco de Zamora observed, Spanish behavior discredited Christian teachings and undermined the friars' attempts to convert the Pueblos. Spanish settlers "took away from them by force all the food that they had gathered for many years, without leaving them any for the support of their women and children, robbed them of the scanty clothing they had to protect themselves…and took many other valuables from their homes."[8] Violently subduing "recalcitrant" Pueblos encouraged the Indians to resent and to mistrust Spaniards and their faith.

Armed Spaniards also invaded Florida but under quite different circumstances. In June 1565, Governor Pedro Menéndez de Avilés sailed with a punitive force of over two thousand men to Florida's northeast Atlantic coast to expunge a fledgling colony of French Protestants and to establish a permanent Spanish presidio in its place. Menéndez needed the indigenous people as allies, or at least as neutral bystanders, to combat the French interlopers and to provide safety for his settlement. Timucuas and Guales who had alternatively aided and fought the French observed the Spaniards' complete destruction of Fort Caroline and wisely chose to ally themselves with the victors. The Indians took advantage of the Europeans' enmity to secure exotic trade goods from the Spaniards, who generously offered beads, cloth, and iron goods as tokens of esteem and solidarity. Collaborating with Menéndez also won more favorable defense agreements for native towns over neighboring rivals who neglected to side with Spain. While the new Spanish-Indian alliances were not always free of violence or native revolts, Timucua and Guale chiefs understood that association with Spain was a strategically attractive option in the long run. Florida's Indian leaders welcomed the newcomers and voluntarily accepted the missionaries in their towns. In fact, native requests for friars from the late sixteenth century to the early decades of the seventeenth century outpaced the number of available Franciscans.[9]

By performing lavish gift ceremonies when chiefs came to the garrison at St. Augustine to pledge their allegiance, Florida's governor secured native alliances and fortified Spain's hold on the geographically vital Florida peninsula. Philip II was concerned with the safety of Spanish ships in the Caribbean and worried about European rivals' renewed ambitions in the region. He subsidized Menéndez's efforts to ply Indian alliance, while he left Oñate in New Mexico to his own devices. Conquered Pueblos in New Mexico paid Spaniards tribute; the Florida Indians received wondrous trade items for their friendship and cooperation.[10]

The amicable beginnings in Florida, however, did not last. It took the Spaniards just over a decade to alienate their new allies. As in New Mexico, Florida's Spanish settlers took advantage of Indian resources and cooperation. Unruly soldiers disobeyed orders and raided native supplies and injured Indian villagers. Guales revolted in 1577 to avenge the execution of a leader who had killed a baptized rival, and rebelled again in 1597 after a Franciscan denied a polygamous heir's right to assume the rank of chief. Both uprisings nearly destroyed Spain's hold on coastal Florida.[11] Retaliatory Spanish forces burned nearly every Guale town and killed hundreds of people in 1577 and repeated their stiff punishment two decades later. In each instance, the insurrections failed to spread to

Timucua where the friars retained their positions as respected emissaries in native villages. The interruption of missionary work in Guale, however severe, was brief. When the rebels returned to their villages, the doctrineros joined them. This time, however, the friars were emboldened by the violent Spanish suppression of the natives' attempts at rebellion.[12]

By the start of the seventeenth century, indigenous peoples in both frontier territories had seen the destruction Spanish anger wrought and understood that the threat of Spanish violence was neither vague nor hollow. Despite the emphatic establishment of Spanish hegemony, the frontier colonies stood on weak legs. In Florida, the Franciscans knew that the successful harvest of souls depended upon the seed money and the support of the Spanish crown. The sorry state of the colony's financial affairs, however, threatened the future of the missions and compromised the friars' ongoing conversion efforts. The colony faced a litany of obstacles. Florida was a swamp-ridden territory that hindered agricultural production and commerce; providing food and supplies for the colony meant that Florida was a drain on royal funds rather than a productive contributor to the Spanish empire. Attempts to find the rumored city of Tama, with its unparalleled stores of gold and pearls, had failed, and few Spaniards held out hope for the discovery of bountiful mineral deposits. The peninsula was also difficult to defend, so its position along the Atlantic trade routes proved less strategic than Spanish organizers had expected. The cumulative effect of these worries forced King Philip III to consider abandoning the fledgling colony and moving the newly baptized Indians to Española in 1606.

But there was more to Florida's value than could be determined by accountants. Frays Francisco Pareja and Alonso de Peñaranda urged the monarch to "shelter and help to defend" Florida. In a desperate letter, the Franciscans alerted the king of the folly of his plan. "With regard to removing from their natural state the Christian Indians (who are more than six thousand) they will not do it by any means," the clerics warned. What was more, renouncing the newly converted was beneath "so great a Catholic King as Your Majesty." If for no other reason than the salvation of native souls, Spain had to maintain its hold on Florida, no matter the financial cost.[13]

Two years removed and thousands of leagues west of Florida, the Franciscans in New Mexico were bedeviled by similar concerns. Reconnaissance had not found Cíbola, the fabled Seven Cities of Gold, and had not discovered plentiful veins of ore to exploit. The list of New Mexico's shortcomings was equally long and discouraging. The poverty of the land, its distance from Mexico, its parched climate, poor roads, disenchanted settlers, hostile Indians, and paltry numbers of native converts were insufficient returns for a decade of effort. While friars in Florida had established lasting missions among the Guales and Timucuas, their New Mexican brothers had failed to maintain a consistent presence among the Pueblos. Without converts, New Mexico's economic and political value to the Spanish empire was suspect. The Council of the Indies recommended on July 2, 1608, that the king consider forfeiting the New Mexican enterprise. The colony's fate appeared sealed; the friars needed a miracle, and they got one.

Two Franciscans visiting the frontier from Mexico City, frays Lázaro Ximénez and Ysidro Ordóñez, reported that "more than seven thousand persons had been baptized and so many others were ready to accept baptism that it seemed the Lord was inspiring them to accept Him to gain salvation."[14] The clerics also hinted that some recently discovered metals seemed potentially profitable. The reports of precious minerals were exaggerated and the number of conversions spurious, but the news made the colony viable again in the minds of Spanish authorities. Christian natives could work and pay tribute while they made their spiritual journey to heaven.

Originally, the Spanish monarch had envisioned uniting Florida and New Mexico into one jurisdiction, a defensible buffer zone along the northern border of Spain's New World territories. His plan proved illusory. Investigations revealed that while "it was assumed that the distance from Florida to New Mexico was not less than from [Mexico City] to New Mexico" the span was much greater.[15] Maintaining two far-flung frontier colonies was not what the king had in mind, but Philip and his counselors understood that transplanting so many converted Christians was impractical, and that abandoning the new catechumens was a betrayal of the evangelical achievements purchased by Franciscans and safeguarded by soldiers. The heir to the title "Catholic Majesty" felt responsible for the baptized Indians in Florida and New Mexico. Knowing full well that colonies built primarily on missions might never become profitable, the king promised ample funds and supplies to the Franciscans, and urged his governors to find ways of turning the financial fortunes of the frontier enterprises around.[16]

Both the real and putative conversion of thousands of natives saved Florida and New Mexico, and became the primary justification for continued colonization, even if not its sole purpose. The Franciscan order, chosen to convert the frontier inhabitants, played a vital role in the establishment of both colonies. While the royal authorities expected the frontier settlements to become self-sufficient and prosperous, the friars' missions were the means by which the Spaniards attempted to achieve stability and solvency. Before they could become productive subjects of the Spanish crown and peaceful participants in Spanish culture, New World natives had to first embrace *Dios*, the Spanish God. The fate of the frontier colonies depended upon the Franciscans' abilities to reduce the natives to Christianity.

Getting the native inhabitants to adopt a new faith was no simple task. Imposing exclusive religious ideas on conquered peoples required delicacy and tact. Each friar was responsible for the conversion, instruction, and civilization of his assigned charges. The attitude of the individual missionary had a major impact on the success of the mission effort. The friars must have been apprehensive as they entered their posts. But their own training had encouraged them to temper worldly trepidation with otherworldly confidence. Recruiters told them that should they die professing the Catholic faith, they were assured a heavenly reward.[17] In the Franciscans' logic, they could only win: either the friars would save native souls or reach paradise themselves. But applying this calculus of salvation in isolated frontier locales was a difficult step.

Spanish missions in Florida and New Mexico were practical mechanisms designed to render Indian villages obedient and submissive, and a way to place Indians under Spanish and canon law; they gradually evolved into centers of Christian religious indoctrination. Doctrineros had to establish a rapport with their native congregations, construct churches with Indian labor, teach neophytes Christianity, enforce Catholic doctrine, and raise support and funds for their missions. The missionary program sought to work significant changes in Indian life, and the Franciscans' approach was calculated to ease the missionaries into the native world and consolidate spiritual authority.

Despite the different origins of the Spanish frontier settlements in Florida and New Mexico, the Spanish settlers adhered to the same hard-line ideology concerning colonization and the conversion of indigenous peoples. Legal-minded and intensely bureaucratic, the Spaniards relied on formal ceremonies, meticulously performed and carefully constructed according to rules of European international law, to stake their claim to new colonies. On both frontiers, promulgating an "Act of Taking Possession" justified and legitimized the capture and rule of foreign peoples, just as it had in Mexico and Peru in the previous century. The significance of the Spaniards' ritualistic declaration was lost on native listeners; though the orations were directed·at the Indians, they were not intended for their comprehension. The formal language was meant for the Spaniards, who believed that their conquest of New World peoples had a sacred purpose that unequivocally voided any other country's claims and specifically charged the Spaniards with the responsibility to save pagan souls.[18]

Indian-Spanish alliances on both frontiers were conditioned by the Spaniards' imperative to convert. While Timucua and Guale chiefs initially believed that their agreements with Florida's governor were alliances between equals, the Spaniards considered their relationship with all Indians tutelary. "The Act of Obedience and Vassalage" that Oñate's notary read in unintelligible Spanish to the chieftains of seven Pueblo villages on April 30, 1598, for instance, asserted Spanish hegemony over conquered peoples. "The Christian aim," declared the notary, "is the baptism and salvation of the souls of so many children among these heathens, for they do not acknowledge or obey their true Father, God, nor can they, spiritually speaking, know Him except through these means." Accepting the waters of baptism was merely a part of the natives' salvation. To secure lasting grace, the Indians had to change their entire lives, for "they cannot preserve their faith or preserve in it if they remain among idolatrous and heathen people who oppose this undertaking. Moreover, the will of God is that they shall all be saved and that the aim and purpose of His word and death shall reach everyone."[19] Again, the words' meaning to the subjugated natives was irrelevant. Spanish suppression of native uprisings provided all the explanation the Indians required and left little room for interpretation. The Indians knew they were accepting foreign domination, even if the conditions of their surrender were as yet unclear.

Although they seemed oblivious to Indian perceptions of their actions, the Spaniards were quite calculating when native comprehension was essential. The Spaniards had learned during their frontier experiences in the sixteenth century that friars striking out on their own without military escort did not return and failed to convert any of the indigenous population. To bring the Indians to God, the Spaniards needed to deliver the friars to the Indians. Cognizant of the fragile position friars held among people who were forced to accept them, Spanish authorities tried to foster affection for the churchmen. King Philip III himself charged his representatives with seeing that the friars were "respected and revered, as ministers of the gospel should be, so that, with this example, the Indians may attend and honor them and accept their persuasions and teachings." The king also warned the people in the governor's company that setting bad examples or injuring the Indians would cause the natives to "adopt an unfriendly attitude toward the faith."[20]

In theatrical performances choreographed to ensure the safety of vulnerable doctrineros among potentially violent and resentful natives, the Spaniards found ways to make their desires known, despite the barriers of language. Spanish soldiers either marched into a village or paraded before a gathered collection of chiefs in full military regalia and with banners flying. The governor or the highest-ranking officer present knelt before the friar assigned as the town's minister and either kissed his hand or received a benediction from him. Demonstrating fealty to the missionaries showed that the Spaniards held them in esteem and were concerned about their welfare. The Indians knew that the friars held special rank and that the soldiers, who had the strength to level their homes, paid homage to these strangely robed men. The show of force, with armed soldiers witnessing the performance, indicated wordlessly that the friars were not to be harmed. Governors and soldiers also conducted elaborate ruses to suggest that the friars were defenders of native interests. When Oñate ordered the attack on Acoma, he told his soldiers that "if you should want to show lenience after they have been arrested, you should seek all possible means to make the Indians believe that you are doing so at the request of the friar with your forces." As Oñate explained to his men, the Acomas "will recognize the friars as their benefactors and protectors and come to love and esteem them, and to fear us."[21]

While Spanish theatrics were perhaps more appropriate for the public stages of Madrid, the Franciscans needed the performances to secure their foothold in mission towns. They required secular support to save "wayward" souls. The doctrineros genuinely considered themselves the Indians' advocates; they were responsible for educating, training, and ultimately redeeming the natives, so they were sympathetic to native

predicaments. The friars' dependence on the implied and actual violence of Spanish soldiers to enforce mission discipline was not awkward in their estimation. For the Franciscans, Christian salvation and
force were not necessarily incompatible. Saving "pagans" from eternal
damnation was serious business. Nothing less than the victory of good
over evil was at stake.

The missionaries were the Indians' protectors but also instruments
of Spanish colonization, bearers of Spanish religion and culture, and brokers of Indian labor and produce. Governors regretted the influence that
friars held over native populations, and the antagonism between the secular and religious components of the Spanish government was a constant source of strife. Each tried to weaken the influence of the other,
and yet each understood that the relationship was symbiotic; they needed
one another to make colonization work. On the northern fringes of
Spain's New World, the need to pacify mutinous natives through the
teachings of the Christian faith had political and economic significance
as well as religious import. Disorderly and undisciplined Indians threatened the crown's ability to extract profit from its colonial endeavors;
Spanish steel purchased Indian compliance through fear. Friars relied on
Spanish military might to secure a modicum of safety, and to ensure that
the Indians remained sedentary. Only Indians who came to church could
be taught the ways of Dios.[22]

Missionary installation ceremonies subtly started the conversion
process itself. One of the first things the Spaniards did in any new town
they entered was to rename it. Christening Indian villages with Catholic
saints' names staked a Spanish claim on the territory and gave religious
sanctity to the Spaniards' conquest by invoking the protection of God's
holy intercessors. Assigning patron saints to native towns also incorporated the inhabitants into the Church calendar and imposed Spanish
meaning on older native traditions. A patron saint automatically designated a feast day—a celebration of spiritual significance associated with
the arrival of the missionary—for the Indians and provided them with
a spiritual defender and sympathizer to pray to and to adore. Native craftsmen decorated the mission church and native homes with paintings and
statuary dedicated to their patron in New Mexico, and it is easy to imagine Florida's artists doing the same. Indians were interested in the
Spaniards' peculiar practice. In at least one case, a messenger from a
Timucua town tracked down Father Commissary Luís Gerónimo de Oré

during his 1616 tour of Florida "to ask the name of the saint they would have to employ in naming the town when they became Christians."23

The elaborate Spanish ceremonies also introduced the primary component of the Catholic conversion process to the native peoples: imitation. After the Spaniards had shown fealty to the friars, they instructed the natives to do likewise. When Spaniards blessed themselves with the sign of the cross, they taught native observers how to do the same. Once they erected large wooden crosses in villages, friars told the Indians to place similar symbols in their homes, along roads, and in meeting halls. Mimicry was key to conversion. If the Indians could copy Spanish gestures, they could memorize the requisite prayers and learn the catechism.24

Before the doctrineros began instructing the natives of Florida and New Mexico on the finer points of Christian doctrine, they first had to have a place to perform mass, to teach catechumens, and to live. Franciscans directed the Indians in larger settlements to build church complexes that served as the bases of missionary operation. From the central *doctrinas*, the guardians traveled to smaller *visitas* to administer the sacraments and to preach to dispersed populations. Friars followed blueprints adapted from Spanish parishes but made allowances for local materials and local limitations. More often than not, the friars in Florida had to bend their architectural aspirations to fit the frontier environment, and quickly accepted the prudence of varying their church designs to accommodate native labor restrictions and constraints of landscape. Working around native agricultural, hunting, and gathering responsibilities, friars coordinated the construction of the best structures they could manage. Some were coarse in appearance, but others were impressive edifices, and stood as silent testimony to the friars' architectural knowledge and Indian artistry.

Unlike the Spanish doctrineros in New Spain or Peru, the frontier friars of Florida and New Mexico rarely usurped native sacred space by erecting churches on the ashes of destroyed native temples. The Franciscans' position among the natives was precarious. Guale and Pueblo acquiescence had come through force of arms, and Timucuas succumbed to disease at alarming rates. Each situation was potentially volatile. For lone missionaries to destroy native places of worship in such tense circumstances would have risked violent reprisal.25

Initially, Indians built open chapels with enough shelter to protect the altar from inclement weather. Once a reasonably functional place of

Figure 3:
Reconstructed church at San Luis de Talimali. Photograph courtesy of
Christopher R. Versen.

worship was complete, laborers erected a *convento*, or friary, in which
the missionary lived. After they housed the newcomers' religious paraphernalia and the friars themselves, the natives went to work on a more
permanent *iglesia*, or church. If the mission survived, friars supervised
the addition of new structures: kitchens, workshops, and, in the case of
larger settlements, livestock pens and guests' rooms. The Franciscans were
interested in long-term construction projects, and as the friars rotated
through mission assignments, they stamped church complexes with new
annexes and architectural features.

Mission churches in Florida were mostly wattle-and-daub structures formed around hand-hewn posts. Their roofs were thatch woven
from palm branches and were steeply sloped to deflect Florida's frequent rains. While San Juan del Puerto boasted an ornate bell tower
crowning the roof, many churches made do with one or two brass bells
hung from a wooden frame planted in the church courtyard. Large villages had churches able to accommodate hundreds of worshippers,
including those who traveled from neighboring towns; visitas served

Figure 4:
San Augustine in the pueblo of Isleta, built 1612. Photograph by the author.

more modest numbers and were intended for local congregations' use. Completed mission churches in Florida resembled rectangular wood barns that stood in sharp contrast to the natives' rounded huts and circular council houses. Because Florida's timbered mission churches were easily degradable, only archeological shadows survived the centuries.[26] Pueblo Indians had material advantages over Florida's neophytes. The Southwest's arid temperatures, sparse rainfall, and traditions of adobe brick and stone architecture meant that their mission construction might last. Pueblos were master masons who built upon many of the same linear principles that the Spaniards used. Introducing new architectural forms for church elaboration, Spanish friars expanded the Pueblos' building techniques.[27] Sandstone and clay were readily available to erect more impressive, more permanent complexes for mission work. All New Mexico's churches reached at least two stories and appeared taller with grand facades arching over the main portals. They were also more elaborately crafted than their counterparts in Florida and included an apse, separate sacristy, transepts, a nave, a baptistry, a choir loft, and a campo santo (cemetery) as European parishes did. Pueblos also built numerous workshops and storage rooms, a kitchen, a refectory (dining room), and a garth (patio or open courtyard surrounded by a cloister). Some even maintained stone corrals to keep livestock for both church and village use.[28]

According to the dictates of the Council of Trent and the Franciscan order, churches were sacred spaces reserved for the celebration of holy rites. Thus the churches' interiors were crucial to the propagation of the faith. Native painters whitewashed the structures' interior walls, and painted Catholic images along the nave and behind the altar. Friars usually lacked imported religious statuary or images, so local craftsmen under the friars' guidance carved wooden icons to adorn their churches. Insufficient funds and infrequent supply shipments forced mission churches to supplement the décor with local materials: clay and lead cups for silver chalices, natural light for candlesticks, coarse cloth for linens. Despite the extreme conditions and the periodic lack of sufficient sacra on the frontier, mid- and late-century inventories indicate that friars did not always want for the apparatus of their trade. Linen altar cloth, numerous varieties of vestments, silver patens, monstrances (for displaying the consecrated host), banners, *retablos* (religious paintings on wooden boards), candle wax, rosaries, and dozens of religious statues were common stock for a frontier mission. As doctrinas, mission centers possessed a greater number of sacred artifacts, but even small congregations had enough holy objects to enliven the celebration of mass.[29]

Religious apparatus were numerous and impressive for friars claiming extreme poverty and paucity of funds, but their complaints had some merit. Some of the sacred paraphernalia they had assembled in the frontier missions they had secured through their own means. To supplement the crown's donations, Franciscans solicited wealthy patrons in the Americas and Spain, sought the aid of family members, and applied proceeds earned from native labor to purchase lavish church furnishings. Native confraternities, organized to fund and supervise special feast days or to provide services for mission churches, contributed to the doctrineros' collection of vestments, banners, and statues. The friars understood that beautifying the church attracted Indians to Christian services. The friars collected church sacra as a bulwark against native traditional religion, and as evidence of Christianity's splendor.[30]

Two symbols more than any other signified the Christian missionary endeavor and represented a Spanish presence in Indian country. The first was the cross, which denoted salvation to the baptized. Catechumens learned to cross themselves as a blessing and as a means of warding off evil. They made its mark on their foreheads, lips, and hearts before hearing the Gospel during mass to ready themselves for the words of God. They helped erect crosses in the church courtyard or on the church roof, and buried their dead beneath its outstretched arms. The emblem created an aura, marked sacred space, and staked a symbolic claim on native life even after death. Even for new Christians, the cross served as a protector or talisman. When Spanish patrols marched through native towns, the Indians pled for peace by making the sign of the cross. To ensure the safety of their homes, Zuñis left the Spaniards' wooden crosses along roads and in their plazas.[31]

The second most identifiable symbol of the Spanish missions was the bell. It indicated the status of a mission as a doctrina rather than a visita in the mission hierarchy, and marked a town's close relations with Spanish colonists. Standing either in front of the church or on top of its façade, the mission bell had more direct influence on native daily life than the esoteric significance of the cross, and had many practical uses beyond its symbolic meaning. The bell indicated the location of the church complex to visiting natives, much like a shopkeeper's shingle. Most important, its toll was a form of communication for dispersed dwellings, a signal of approaching danger, and a timepiece regulating daily labors and hours of worship. It was the means by which the friars called the native population to action and beckoned the faithful to the church's sacraments.

The accoutrements of conversion—symbols, paintings, candles, rosaries, and robes—provided the foundation on which the doctrineros constructed the message of Catholicism. Friars had planted crosses throughout the Indians' world but had yet to hang Christ on them; attempting to teach "heathens" Christian doctrine was delicate work. Spaniards believed it was sinful for those who heard the gospels to disregard its message and to reject its covenant. Even those who never received Christianity's evangelical message endangered the fate of their souls. But the natives of the New World lived unaware of their spiritual peril. The Franciscans taught natives about the risks of their unrepentant and undisciplined lives, and guided them toward the religion that would, they believed, save them from perpetual hell.

The native peoples perceived things differently. In their cultures, "sin," in the Christian sense, was foreign. Like their Christian counterparts, Indians had strictures against certain behavior, complex conceptions of morality, and mature ethical and punitive systems, but they did not adhere to the Christian notion of deliberate transgression against a law of God. Since the Indians did not know the laws of Dios, they could not know that they lived contrary to them, could not know that God was offended by their behavior, and could not knowingly choose to reject God's grace. Although God offered Christian salvation to all people, Christian and non-Christian alike, the Indians lived outside the Christian covenant with God. Before the friars could wield any spiritual authority, they had to instruct the Indians in God's laws.

Once natives learned the laws, they were subject to their restrictions, punishments, and forms of reconciliation. According to Catholic doctrine, priests possessed the power to bestow or deny Indians the blessings of God. The Franciscans introduced nothing short of an entirely new cosmological conception of the universe. They created a new spiritual power among the natives and secured their own status as mediators between the new power and the faithful. Of course, the friars' pretensions to spiritual power brought them into direct conflict with native shamans. In fact, doctrineros sought conflict with their Indian counterparts; they had to supplant the shamans and medicine men who competed for natives' spiritual loyalty. They watched the services traditional holy men rendered and co-opted them. Missionaries suddenly claimed that they could command or predict the weather, foretell the future, or cure the sick by interceding with Dios. After Spanish priests won captive audiences, they introduced the tenets of Christianity. But native holy men did not easily surrender their spiritual territory. When shamans realized that the friars were trying to replace traditional beliefs with new ones, they "become so resentful that they stir up all the people and draw them away so that they may not become Christians," noted fray Alonso de Benavides in 1630. "Not only this, but they also try to induce [the Indians] either to drive the priest out of the pueblo or to kill him."[32] Friars were equally determined to best their native opponents, and one friar considered the defeat of a local religious leader a victory over "a demon who was fleeing, confounded by the power of the divine word."[33]

It was not enough to mimic native holy men and women. Friars had to put the native spiritual leaders out of business. For that, they launched a two-pronged attack. First, the Franciscans had to prove to potential Indian converts that they provided not just the same religious services as traditional shamans, but that their spiritual power was greater.

Doctrineros preached the "superiority" of their "one true God." They illustrated Christian and Spanish power through works of art and technology. Metal tools, domesticated animals, and literacy all became evidence of Christianity's potency.

Second, the friars had to weaken the hold shamans and medicine men had upon native peoples. Franciscans belittled them, challenged them to debates, and mocked their abilities. They claimed that native "superstitions" were "abuses" of the Devil and suggested that shamans were "agents of the demon."[34] Fray Alonso de Benavides described a battle between the forces of good and evil for Tompiros' souls, claiming that Satan, "enemy of souls" saw the friars freeing natives "from his clutches" and "by means of Indian sorcerers," he spread the word that they should move away from there."[35] With customary hyperbole, the friar claimed that a vision appeared to the natives and convinced them to remain with the missionaries. Such accounts indicated to neophytes that the Franciscans possessed access to tremendous spiritual power and could elicit the aid of heavenly hosts against the shamans' "specters."

Missionaries made every effort to insinuate themselves into native relationships and Indians' daily life. They observed the transfer of chiefly power from one generation to the next. They challenged Indian polygamy, and insisted that converts obey the requirements of Christian marriage. They hired natives to work in the churches, tend Spanish livestock, manufacture decorative images for Christian services, and trade crops and goods for mission coffers. As political advisors, counselors, and boss men, the Franciscans became deeply involved in the workings of Indians' communities.[36] As they had with native holy men and women, friars identified Spanish settlers and non-Christian Indians as "bad influences" in order to draw neophytes into closer associations with the missionaries. Friars chastised mission Indians for working too closely with vulgar ranchers or apostate governors. They cautioned them about leaving mission villages for extended periods, and convinced them to work in mission fields rather than settlers' farms. Friars attempted to become indispensable to mission Indians.[37]

The key to winning the native populace was through its leaders. If the chiefs and their families accepted Christianity, the people would follow. Native chiefs were not only political leaders but also cultural trendsetters in their villages. The Indians expected their chiefs to discern what changes were acceptable for the entire town, and regarded a chief's reputation as partially subject to his or her ability to materially better their lives. Chiefs distributed trade goods to followers and favorites, and the ability of the friars to provide wonderful items for their doctrinas' chiefs straightened the path to conversion. Chiefs were also instrumental in helping friars broaden local sources of economic growth in agriculture, crafts, and herding. Bringing Indians to God and bringing wealth to villages were mutually beneficial endeavors, and chiefs retained positions of power in both. While a leader's adoption of Christianity did not automatically ensure the conversion of his or her entire domain, it was a significant determinant.[38]

Even more vital for securing long-term conversion of a native village was convincing the younger generation to embrace the new faith. Should the heirs to chiefly posts adopt Christianity, the Franciscan evangelists could win generations of souls in perpetuity. Converted native youths also weakened the influence of skeptical older villagers who were less receptive to the friars' message and more suspicious of the missionaries' growing prestige. As the younger generations rose to assume positions of authority among their people, the friars, as religious advisors and spiritual guides, rose in status as well. The authority of the friars and the converted youth supplanted the influence of the older leaders and weakened any native attempts to counter the Franciscans.[39] Most of the friars' early catechizing focused on native children, who were the hope for successful conversion and creation of perpetual faith among the Indians.

The essential change the Franciscans attempted to work in the Indians' minds was to instill a concern for the individual over that of the group or community. Sin was particular to the sinner's soul, and damnation was specific to the unrepentant. Friars had to convince Indians that they were individually culpable, that they had to feel remorse for their own evil behavior, and that they had to seek God's forgiveness for their own transgressions. The sacraments—baptism, communion, penance, confirmation, marriage, and extreme unction (holy orders were forbidden for Indians)—were mostly focused on the progress of an individual's spiritual journey, not the achievement of the village at large. One's sins were one's own.

Doctrineros employed allegory to explain the nuances of Christian doctrine to natives who lacked a European concept of sin. Francisco Pareja likened human shame to the toilet habits of felines and to physical illness.

"Cats will hide their excrements and cover them well (so that they do not
stink nor smell bad to others)," he explained, "and people who have any
ugly infirmities conceal and hide them from others' sight, except from the
physicians who are to heal them." The Franciscans were "spiritual doctors"
who were privileged to "see" the secret pains of their patients and who honored the inviolate bond that sharing the burden of ills created.[40]

Allegory failed to convey more esoteric concepts like the nature of
the deity. Catechists reasoned that God was called God "because he sees
all things, and ministers to them, he being the powerful ruler of all things
in heaven and on earth." That the Christian God was omnipotent, omnis-
cient, and active in the affairs of humankind was fundamental to explaining the importance of conversion. A disinterested God, unable to observe
the secret passions of each individual soul, could hardly make demands
on human behavior. But if God existed and was as the friars described,
becoming a Christian paid homage to this powerful lord and secured a
place in paradise for the believer. The theological change was considerable because it required native catechumens to abandon the belief that
baptism was purely a declaration of political and economic affiliation
with Spaniards and to adopt a faith that brought a person's soul to salvation. Once natives accepted this vague concept, they were well on their
way to becoming Christians.

But converting was arduous. The Christian doctrine included various prayers and devotions ("Our Father," "Hail Mary," "Creed," and "Act
of Contrition"), fourteen articles of faith, ten commandments of God,
five church commandments, seven sacraments, seven virtues, seven mortal sins, and fourteen works of mercy. Indian neophytes also had to learn
the answers to lists of questions that the missionaries posed to examine
their understanding of the new faith. At least one ambitious Franciscan,
Francisco Pareja, wrote his own doctrina (book of Catholic doctrine) in
both Spanish and Timucuan to speed the religious education of Florida
catechists.[41] While portions of the Christian doctrine may have been
expressed in Latin, natives certainly learned the Spanish, and in some
instances Indian, translations of the catechism. Since friars frequently
failed to learn the various dialects spoken in Florida and New Mexico,
they relied on native sacristans to instruct converts. Friars tried to advance
the instruction process by consolidating the doctrine into digestible parts
or by chanting or singing the doctrine. Aware that nonliterate natives
might have difficulty with the catechism's size, clerics taught Indians as

they had European illiterates: by rote memorization. Once native converts committed the prayers to memory, the friars instructed them on
the meanings behind the words, usually after neophytes had transgressed.
When Indians sinned, they suffered corporal punishment from either
Indian *fiscales* or the friars themselves. Missionaries employed the same
techniques in Europe, where they found that physical punishment was
an effective means of encouraging Christians to obey church doctrine.[42]
In the frontier missions, whipping was the choice method of correction,
though some friars were overzealous in their efforts to purge natives of
sin. Fray Diego de Parraga ordered every Tompiro in Tajique to carry a
large cross on their shoulders during Easter Holy Week. Fray Salvador
de Guerra, guardian of Shongopovi pueblo, once burned disobedient
Indians with lit turpentine.[43]

Instruction was livelier when missionaries used decorative artwork
to convey their religious teachings or when frontier priests held church
services. The pageantry of Catholicism made the new religion palpable
to Indians and made it attractive to potential converts. Richly painted
retablos depicting Christ crucified and saints' heroic deeds, decorous statues of angelic Mary welcoming worshippers with outstretched arms, the
smell of candle wax, the rhythmic cadence of Latin incantations, and
plainchant charmed native witnesses. Music, a form of communication
that required no translation, was an essential component of the missionaries' attempts to win converts. The friars conducted native choirs to sing
polyphonic choruses accompanied by trumpets and shawms (an ancient
oboe-like wood instrument). New Mexican missions may have acquired
as many as seventeen organs by the 1640s.[44]

The seventeenth-century Catholic liturgy was a feast for the senses,
and shared with traditional native rituals a discernable structure punctuated with music and artistic iconography. The Catholic mass was an
ordered pattern of motion, not unlike a native dance, and contained similar elements to Pueblo kiva ceremonies and Timucua rites. There were
incantations and responses; worshippers participated by praying,
singing, or reading while the priest recited the liturgy; the congregation
alternately stood, knelt, and processed, performing each act at specific
times and in deliberate turn. Once natives learned the prayers, the familiar words and phrases followed, in comforting, rhythmic sequence. Adding
to the sensuousness of the services, the mass was sung in plainchant during the seventeenth century, rather than spoken; this, too, was familiar

for those used to native rites that included chanting or singing rather than casually recited syllables.[45]

Apart from the foreign concepts expressed in Christian observances, the greatest difference in the performance of Christianity for the Indians was the recitation of prayers in Spanish. Celebrating the Mass and even observing the other daily rituals would have required participation from the Indians, which encouraged involvement from all, not just from certain members of specialized clans. In native ceremonies, speaking parts were reserved for persons of a certain rank or politico-religious status. In the Catholic sacraments, each member of the congregation had to participate. Christianity personalized faith in a different way from the natives' traditional religions. To be sure, religion and cosmology did not take on a personal or individual meaning with the advent of Christian missions. Native spiritual practices were absolutely dependent upon the individual's participation and observance of sanctioned dictates. But ceremonial words, as spoken symbols of sacred ideas, had heightened meaning in oral cultures. To allow any individual the power to utter the holy prayers in a religious ceremony was liberating, and might have been an attractive component of Christian faith for prospective converts. It almost did not matter that the significance of the prayers or the ideological concepts they expressed were, at best, unclear to novitiates. Mere incantation conveyed tremendous spiritual power, and the inclusion of even the lowest ranking and youngest member of native society, men and women alike, regardless of clan affiliation, was revolutionary. While Christianity attracted numerous Indians to the missions of Florida and New Mexico, the Franciscans grossly exaggerated their successes in letters to family, friends, and to the royal authorities in Spain. In a concerted publicity campaign, doctrineros described their "successes" in miraculous terms. It seemed that God had blessed the friars' efforts by working wonders among the native inhabitants. When recalcitrant natives belittled Christian marriage, clerics claimed that lightning bolts struck the offenders dead. The results, according to fray Alonso Benavides, were immediate and definitive: "All who had been secretly living in concubinage married and accepted firmly everything taught by the priest."[46] Apparently, thunderstorms were a popular instrument. During a tour of three Timucua villages, fray Martín Prieto met a jeering crowd at Santa Ana. The town's *cacique* had been a boy captive of Hernando de Soto and told his people to reject the missionary. Prieto went to the chief's home, and the moment the chieftain refused audience to the friar, a thunderclap shook the land and a strong wind toppled several buildings. Prieto later explained that "so great was the fear that this brought upon all, that the next day the cacique called for me in order that I might instruct him." Six days later, he received baptism and his townspeople followed.[47]

God worked other "miracles" directly through his Franciscan agents, who began to seem eerily Christ-like. Fray Juan Ramírez, minister of Acoma, saved a dying one-year-old girl with the sacrament of baptism. "As he was pouring the water and pronouncing the words," related Benavides, "the child instantly arose, healthy and sound."[48] While some performed wonderful cures, others became prophets. Fray Pedro Ruíz warned a Guale chief who had abandoned his Christian wife and moved in with his sister-in-law: "I tell you in the name of God that if you do not amend, I will have to bury you or this woman within thirty days." Twenty days later the woman died and the chieftain returned to the Christian fold.[49]

The tone of the friars' accounts suggested that miracles were commonplace. But in reality, the Franciscans wrote their accounts with specific audiences in mind. The missions remained viable because Spain paid for their operation and ordered governors to cooperate with the doctrineros. But the friars were well aware that the colonies' secular authorities did not always appreciate the importance of the mission program. Fray Francisco Pareja angrily complained that "it seems to [the governors] that the soldiers are the necessary ones and that we are of no use; but we are the ones who bear the burden and heats, and we are the ones who are subduing and conquering the land."[50] The friars felt pinched by gubernatorial interference and secular demands on mission Indians. It seemed to the Franciscans that they were undervalued. Fray Lope Izquierdo complained that the friars "are under constant obligation, more so than others, to labor in the cause, exposing our lives to whatever we may meet in the service of God, the propagation of the holy Catholic faith, and the service of our king."[51]

With governors and settlers conspiring to weaken the Franciscans' role in the colonies, the mission priests sent a steady stream of glowing reports across the seas to curry royal favor. Friars wrote ebullient accounts of dedicated and faithful Indians who readily embraced Christianity, intentionally crafted to keep the king and his ministers satisfied with their investment. Fray Francisco Pareja suggested that "Many persons are found, men and women, who confess and who receive Holy Communion with tears." The guardian's rave also subtly praised the ministers' ability to teach the natives Catholic doctrine. "I shall make bold to say and sustain my contention by what I have learned by experience," Pareja averred, "that with regard to the mysteries of faith, many of them answer better than the Spaniards because the latter are careless in these matters."52

Pueblo converts were equally dedicated to the Spaniards' faith, or so professed fray Alonso Benavides. "As soon as the bell rings for Mass and catechism," he wrote, "they all come with the greatest cleanliness and neatness and enter the church to pray." The boys and girls dutifully attended daily lessons in the morning and afternoon, and the cantors "sing in the church every day at the hours of Prime, High Mass and Vespers." In hopes of securing a bishop's mitre, Benavides made astonishingly bold statements about the conversion program in New Mexico. "They are so well instructed in everything, especially in what pertains to the Faith and Christianity," he boasted, "that it is wonderful to consider that ever since they began to be baptized less than twenty years ago . . . they have given the impression of having been Christians for a hundred years."53

By the third decade of the seventeenth century, the Franciscans had, despite their inflated rhetoric, spread Spanish influence over hundreds of square miles and over thousands of people. In Florida they had founded sixty churches distributed over thirty-two doctrinas, and ministered to over two hundred villages and fifty thousand baptized or catechized souls. Friars in New Mexico over the same period preached to sixteen Pueblos and claimed thirty-four thousand baptized Indians.54 But upon further reflection, wise Franciscans were wary of their missions' achievement. Fray Francisco Pareja warned, "What pertains to faith and belief, God is the One who can judge. We can judge only by a person's exterior manifestations, who by the actions he performs presumably shows forth the workings of faith."55

CHAPTER THREE

Braving
the Storm

*father, as yet we have
no power with god.*
—— a tompiro indian

By the first decades of the seventeenth century, the Indians' world
had begun to look vastly different than it had a generation before.
Where once moccasined feet had trod silently on the dirt paths
between settlements, galloping horses' hooves punctured the trails and
wooden wheels rutted the roads. Armed men, even some overly dressed
women and children, marched to the natives' homes to construct forts,
haciendas, and ranches in the hinterlands of the Indians' larger towns.
Domesticated sheep, goats, chickens, pigs, and cows gorged on local flora
and trampled the underbrush where berries and nuts had flourished. Even
the robed Spaniards, who lived next to the freshly wrought churches that
stood within the confines of the Indians' villages, regularly walked a cir-
cuit to neighboring camps to preach the strangers' faith.

But the newcomers were not the only ones on the move. Indians
packed supplies and a few cherished belongings to take to the trails.
Ordered to walk to the colonial capitals or to settlers' plots, native men
provided the muscle for the construction of municipal buildings, military facilities, and expansive agricultural fields. Others toiled on farms
or among the herds of Spanish livestock. The demand for native labor
and the business of the Florida and New Mexico colonies made frontier
byways conductors of perpetual motion.

The ebb and flow of humanity along Indian trails might have made mission villages bustling hubs of social interaction, commerce, and spirituality. But for native inhabitants of the doctrinas and visitas, the world was eerily quiet. Invisible microbes had silently killed thousands of natives who had no acquired immunities to diseases born from centuries of human interaction in the Eastern Hemisphere. The morbid speed and stealth of the epidemics—alternatively smallpox, influenza, whooping cough, bubonic plague, typhus, dysentery, scarlet fever, and measles among others—ravaged native communities and left survivors with reduced resources and depleted populations. The Pueblos were less affected than the Indians of Florida, losing only half their population over the seventeenth century to disease. The Southwest's dry climate and sparsely settled landscape hindered the spread of European diseases. Humid and crowded conditions in Florida made for a different story. The Timucuas' numbers were halved in four years, between 1613 and 1617, and continued to plummet over the course of the century until only 1,370 souls remained. Apalachee suffered a precipitous drop in population from twenty-five thousand in 1600 to eight thousand in 1704. Recurring epidemics efficiently depleted chiefdoms, villages, clans, and households; entire towns were wiped out.[1]

The extensive demographic cataclysm and its attendant disruption, dislocation, and anxiety wreaked havoc on Indian cultures. Native communities that had carefully divided tasks between men and women, distributed certain responsibilities among clans, and invested power in its leadership and its priesthood found that the epidemics left the social fabric in shreds. Those who had kept ritual knowledge for the perpetuation of the cosmos and those who passed on the practical skills needed to survive the changing seasons died too quickly to impart their life lessons to their progeny. Indeed, Indians who survived decimation by disease had difficult choices to make in their search for stability. Some joined with cousins who shared their language and customs. Others risked confederating with foreign groups. Both options were perilous; neighboring kinsmen probably suffered equally from mysterious illnesses, and strangers could be unpredictable. But at least they found security in familiarity and safety in cultural similitude. Still others chose the most terrifying route, and took to the roads as individuals or in small bands with no particular destination in mind. It was no wonder that in light of such insecure times, many Indians decided to welcome the Spaniards to their villages and, perhaps, to find explanations in Christianity for what was happening around them.[2]

No matter how native people reacted to life in the missions, to the message the friars taught, and to the gray-robed doctrineros themselves, they were in a defensive posture.[3] The Spaniards had come across oceans and through jungles and deserts to the peoples in Florida and New Mexico, not the other way round. The conquerors had compelled the Indians to submit to a foreign power and had introduced them to new diseases, technologies, animals, plants, and ideas. Certainly the indigenous peoples taught the Spaniards new things as well, but they did so only after being forced to contend with the invaders among them. Despite their unfavorable position, Indians responded to the Spaniards and their religion in ways calculated to ensure their survival and to best provide a future for their loved ones.

Attempting to stabilize their lives by accepting Spanish missionaries proved an ironic choice, and may even have seemed so at the time. If Indians recognized at least some common elements between Spanish culture and their own, they saw little that was familiar about the friars themselves. For native observers, the Franciscans hardly looked like trustees of Spanish spiritual power. They were tonsured and dressed in long robes cinched with knotted rope. More confusing was the friars' sexual disinterest in native women and their utter lack of weapons. The Spanish priests were unlike any men the natives had seen. Moreover, they spoke a strange tongue, punctuated their speech with unfamiliar gestures, eschewed the privileges of native men, and seemed devoted to the symbol of two crossed pieces of wood. Natives could more easily identify with the Spaniards stationed in garrisons in larger native communities than with the lone, unarmed religious who settled among them. Welcoming the friars in their towns was a calculated response. Caciques and village councils accepted Franciscans because they were forced to, because they received material and political advantages from the move, and because they hoped that Spanish religion would benefit their towns as it had the Spanish conquerors.[4]

Soon the Indians realized that the missionaries wielded significant spiritual influence and had a profound effect on their people. That the Spaniards had access to some unknown power was obvious. The technology the friars employed, the weapons and instruments they manipulated, the strange beasts they commanded, and the plants they coaxed from the soil proved their power. Books, steel, and most domesticated animals were wondrous novelties. But the newcomers also demanded native labor, manipulated Indian behavior, and disrupted the normal rhythms of daily life in the villages. Mission Indians had to come to terms with a rapidly changing new world. There were countless ways that the natives of Florida and New Mexico reacted to Spanish missionization, but the responses fell into five general categories. Indians incorporated Spaniards in traditional ways, they attempted to repel the interlopers, they joined the newcomers and accepted novel modes of behavior, they discriminated between which foreign concepts to adopt and which to reject, and they avoided entangling relations with the Spaniards as best they could. The Guales, Timucuas, Apalachees, and various Pueblo peoples had difficult decisions to make, but they were active participants in the drama that unfolded in the seventeenth-century Spanish missions.[5]

Despite the spread of alien goods, beasts, microbes, and beliefs that irretrievably altered native existence, many Indians initially sought to fit the Spaniards into customary forms of life. The most direct way to incorporate Spaniards was to adopt them into a clan. After Guales from Ospo and Tulafina took Fray Francisco de Avila prisoner in 1597, they attempted to make him an Indian. Avila had to survive a lengthy torture that tested his worthiness while it purged the community's need for revenge. The pain Avila experienced merged with the anguish the Guales felt over the loss of their kinsmen and the upheaval wrought by the Spaniards. Mourning Indians mocked, beat, and burned their captive before treating his wounds and nursing him to health. The Guales then had to tear down Avila the Spaniard so they could build a new, and native, man. Chiefs ordered Avila to carry water and wood—what Guales considered women's work—to till fields, to guard crops, and to sweep the charnel houses. Children taunted him and commanded him to do all sorts of demeaning chores, while others repeatedly threatened his life. Once he had contributed his labor to the Indians and had shown his resilience during this lengthy symbolic purification, the Guales began the final stage of Avila's adoption. Leaders of the town urged him to "leave your law" and to "enjoy what we enjoy." One night an Indian girl brought decayed palm leaves from the woods and made a bed for the Indian novice. Then she prepared a meal for him. The Indians wanted the friar to take a wife and to join the native community as a full-fledged Guale.[6]

Adopting the Spaniards bodily usually failed, but Indians did incorporate European trade goods more readily. Often the first tangible things to reach native communities (undetectable disease microbes usually won the race to native settlements) were Spanish glass beads, metal tools and weapons, fabrics, bells, Catholic rosaries and medallions, and European clothing. None arrived in native hands with instruction manuals for their use. Indians absorbed these items by attaching native functions and meanings to them. At Jémez pueblo a warrior took a paten, a dish used during the consecration of bread in the Catholic mass, "drilled a small hole in the middle," and wore it "suspended from the neck." It became a symbol of his status and a fashionable addition to his appearance. But the Jémez man was not too attached to his prestigious accessory, and soon exchanged the paten for hawk's bells.[7] No doubt the bells proved a more impressive decoration than the silent metal plate had.

Yet native approaches to Spanish material items ran deeper than appearances. Indian political leaders knew that their offices depended on their ability to control and wield power. The arrival of the Spaniards brought Indians in contact with strange and new forces that escaped easy explanation and threatened to tip the balance of power to rival chiefs or to opportunistic usurpers. It was essential for chiefs to gain access to trade goods that could then be redistributed among advisors and important clan members. That Spanish items were wonderful (steel weapons and tools, glass beads, and cloth), mysterious (religious sacra and domesticated animals), or magical (books and clocks) added to chiefs' prestige. Bringing these things to villagers encouraged Indians to remain loyal to their leadership and to trust in the chiefs' capacity to handle whatever changes came their way. For native leaders, controlling the traffic of novel luxury items, distributing goods among their followers, and winning military alliances increased their own status and power, and brought technologically advanced items to their people even if European goods were measured by Indian values.[8]

Indian leaders also handled Spanish requests for labor in ways that reinforced native priorities and philosophies. Indian leaders granted Spaniards access to networks of native labor that the chiefs controlled. They released townspeople to build forts, churches, and farms; to plant and harvest crops; to bear the fruits of their work to markets, wagons, and ships; and to trade with both the newcomers and non-mission peoples in the Greater Southeast and the Plains. Mission commerce benefited the conquerors primarily, but it also guaranteed chiefs the reins of power in their jurisdictions with the aid of Spanish enforcement.⁹

Incorporating Spaniards' spiritual power held especial meaning among people whose loved ones were dying with alarming regularity. The invisible evil magic that seemed to strike without regard for age, gender, or social rank did not harm the newcomers with the same ferocity or frequency. It was clear to the Indians that the Spaniards' god and his priests, the Franciscans, were privileged and knew strong medicine. But for the Guales, Timucuas, Apalachees, and Pueblos, even foreign spiritual power could be co-opted and employed to meet Indian needs. Though Spaniards claimed that the Indians were "clamoring for baptism," the natives had their own reasons for accepting the Franciscans' rite with enthusiasm.¹⁰

The water of baptism seemed to have curative powers, and became more medicinal prescription ceremony for the Indians than Christian initiation. Worried parents and concerned chiefs brought sick children to the friars for baptismal healing. In other instances, natives treated the Christian rite as an item for barter. In New Mexico, a starving woman and her eight-year-old son offered to accept baptism in exchange for food and shelter.¹¹ Some natives understood that the rite was a step toward a greater acceptance of foreign beliefs. But with little or no instruction beforehand, few could have fully comprehended the religious significance of the act and what it meant to the Spaniards. Florida Indians' warm welcome of Juan Cabezas Altamirano, bishop of Cuba, during his 1606 visit proved that converts valued Christian ceremonies in Indian currency. The bishop confirmed more than 2,333 native catechumens during his twelve-week tour, but performed a number of masses in the same locales and chris-tened many natives more than once. Indians concerned with strength-ening their spiritual defenses against evil magic believed that repeated blessings improved their chances of survival. Doctrineros had described the bishop as a religious leader greater than the friars themselves. Therefore, natives reasoned, oils from the visitor packed more spiritual punch than the missionaries' water. The arrival of such a potent holy man was cause for celebration and justification for the Indians' eagerness to gain his benediction as many times as possible.¹²

Mission Indians not only participated in Christian rites for their own purposes, but also communed with Catholic ideas and saints as they would with their own pantheon of spiritual beings. Pueblos included Christian characters in kachina dances to bring the new sources of spiritual

Figure 5:
Altar room in the friar's
convento at San Luis de
Talimali. Missionaries conducted religious instruction
here. Photograph courtesy
of Christopher R. Versen.

power under Pueblo modes of comprehension and communication. They
became part of the Pueblo spiritual consciousness on Pueblo terms. The
Pueblos incorporated Spanish invaders and friars into their own spiritual perception by mocking them in dances of the sacred clowns. Natives
vented their frustrations about village inequalities, gender roles, chiefly
arrogance, and arbitrary spirits through these spiritual pranksters. The
sacred clowns eased the burden of natives' tightly ordered lives; their face-
to-face communities made few other allowances for expressing deeply felt
hostilities toward their leaders, gods, and each other. The cathartic purpose of the clown dances was lost on Spanish observers, who did not recognize themselves being lampooned, but rather focused on what they
considered violent performances. Fray Nicolás de Freitas dismissed the
sacred clown dances as "consisting of watermelons and the Indians beating each other." He failed to understand that the clowns symbolically battered those whom Indians could not physically strike. The clown dances
socially sanctioned "violence" against what the community found distaste-
ful or irritating.[13]

Other attempts to incorporate foreign spiritual concepts and ideas were less obvious. Tantalizing hints about the ways in which Indians deciphered and digested Christian concepts appeared in a series of conversations between unconverted Timucuas and fray Francisco Pareja, recorded in 1614. A group of chiefs wandered into the mission village of San Juan del Puerto and approached the doctrinero. Pareja asked the visitors what they were looking for, and the chiefs told him that they sought his blessing and wished "to see the church and your house and that of our relatives." Impressed by what they had seen, they returned to Pareja days later. The friar recalled their request: "Father, we have a house for you and a church; come and instruct us for the Christians [mission Indians] have already told us it is of prime importance for us to go and see the *Utinama* who is in heaven above." Utinama signified "the powerful one" or "the all-powerful one," and was applied to certain native chiefs as well as a particular town in Potano. But in Pareja's conversation with the Timucua chiefs, it indicated the Christian god, suggesting that the natives conceptualized the friars' triune deity as a paramount chief. The visitors' desire to woo Pareja to their town also seemed more inspired by the Timucuas' improved lot than their Christian salvation.[14]

The reasons for the visiting chiefs' enthusiasm for Christianity may even have been a clever attempt to incorporate Spanish power within Indian religious forms. Pareja continued: "Besides, the caciques there, who are most *orobisi*, which means learned, tell us that they have become Christians." Pareja, expert in the Timucua language, recorded and defined the chiefs' significant word choice, but failed to elaborate on its syntactical implications. Orobisi, or *orobisti*, meant both "wise counsel" and "cunning or sly," which nicely demonstrated the Indians' belief that all things had equal capacity for good and evil. More important, the term applied to doctors or shamans specifically. So perhaps the chiefs came on the advice of their neighbors' spiritual leaders, not the political chiefs or caciques as Pareja suggested.[15] It might be that the Timucuas welcomed Christianity in an attempt to give shamans access to the new and foreign spiritual power.

Pueblo shamans were more assertive in their attempts to control the newcomers and their spirit power. When Coronado's soldiers approached the outskirts of native villages, medicine men armed with corn meal and pollen "drew lines, requesting that our men should not cross those lines toward their pueblos." Forty years later, Hopis greeted

Antonio Espejo and his men with bags of corn meal, "scattering some of it on the road and some over us and on the horses and servants." Drawing corn meal lines in the sand invoked for Pueblos one of three scenarios. First, natives hoped that the corn meal would prevent the foreigners from contaminating their sacred space with outside sicknesses. Sprinkling the Spaniards and the road they traveled delineated the strangers from the "people" and protected the Pueblos' sanctified towns.[16] Second, Pueblos used the corn meal to create a "spirit road" over which the strangers could travel. Road making, in this instance, was an attempt to co-opt and purify the newcomers. Finally, the Pueblos threatened the Spaniards; sprinkled corn meal could close a road as well as open one. Any stranger who dared to cross a prayer meal line forfeited his life to Pueblo warriors.[17] Regardless of their intentions, Pueblo medicine men used spiritual power to manage the initial contacts with Spaniards.

In many cases, however, native spiritual leaders believed that the Spaniards' religious teachings were a dangerous threat, and tried to per-suade their people to violently expel the newcomers from their villages. Native holy men and women among the Tompiros, Picurís, Taos, Hopis, Guales and Timucuas rejected the friars and, on more than one occasion, encouraged faithful warriors to kill the intrusive Franciscans. In attempts to discredit the friars, native priests engaged the doctrineros in debates and passionately stressed the oddities of the strangers' practices. A Tompiro (Humanas) holy man at the pueblo of Gran Quivira angrily accused fri-ars of spreading insanity among the Indians. Having witnessed Holy Week processions of flagellants in a neighboring town, the shaman believed that the Franciscans wanted his people to absent their senses by performing similarly bloody rites. Like their Christian counterparts, native priests chal-lenged the friars to prove the power of their preaching, and demanded that the Franciscans miraculously heal the sick or manipulate the weather. When friars spoke to gatherings of natives, holy men organized hecklers to dis-rupt or to ridicule the preachers. At times, Indians yelled to drown out the friars' words, or physically abused them until they left the town. Others employed more traditional methods to counter the friars. They conducted conflicting ceremonies intended to overpower the Christians' rituals. Taos holy men poisoned a friar's tortillas with urine and mouse meat and refused him shelter. Timucua shamans concocted potions and powders to weaken the friars' spiritual faculties. Those Indians whose loyalty to native cus-toms wavered were vigorously persuaded to cling to native ways. A holy

woman in Taos secreted brides-to-be away from town to convince them
to eschew Christian marriage and to wed according to the natives' ancient
rite. Nubile Guales, certain that traditional customs were better, fled to interior towns to marry away from the missionaries' prying eyes.[18]

When missionaries' demands grew too intrusive and burdensome,
Indians in Florida and New Mexico chose to go to war. Opting to fight
was never a casual decision, and killing friars was particularly dangerous. Natives knew that war courted Spanish retaliation. But conditions
grew so intolerable for some Indians that war was the most effective
way of rejecting the friars and their power, despite the consequences.
Exasperated Indians in Florida and New Mexico rebelled periodically
throughout the seventeenth century in an effort to purge their homes
of Spanish contamination. Florida's friars accurately noted that native
"hatred and detestation against us" was not limited to the human
invaders, but included "the herds we tried to bring into the land."
Enraged and desperate warriors "exterminated [livestock]" as if they were
vermin and did the same to our trees and seeds trying to get rid of all
trace and smell of us."[19]

But other wars specifically targeted the Franciscans and were
resounding rejections of Christianity's intrusion into native life. Zuñis
rose up against their resident friar when "he summoned them to mass
on the day of festival," and Taos rebels danced wearing priests' garments
after killing the town's missionary.[20] In Florida the Guale Revolt of 1597
was a prime example of native rebellion. It sprang from a single power
struggle between a friar and the heir of Tolomato and rapidly spread
throughout the province. Juanillo, a baptized Christian, ignored fray
Pedro de Corpa's protestations when he invoked his traditional and
reserved privilege to take more than one wife. The friar unilaterally
interrupted the town's line of succession and appointed a new heir to
the chiefdom. Denying Juanillo his right was an affront to his status,
and chastising him in front of his future subjects was a direct challenge
to his authority. Angered by the priest's presumption, the youth angrily
renounced Christianity and stormed out of the village to join with other
Guales who had resisted the Spaniards' faith. With his new allies, the
warrior returned to Tolomato, burst into the priest's house, and killed
him with a stone hatchet.[21]

The repercussions of Juanillo's act proved less decisive in other
towns; other Guales had suffered equal humiliations from the

Franciscans but, notably, subsequent rebel attacks were executed slowly and equivocally. Some Indians shared the rebels' ideological conviction and chose to join the uprising, but others were coerced. On Guale Island, the order to kill the minister and the lay brother who assisted him came from Tolomato, not from discontented local headmen. Torn by allegiance to the people of Tolomato and loyalty to his Spanish allies, the island's chief warned the lay brother of the imminent danger. He begged the Spaniard to alert his superior and offered a canoe and guides to take them to safety on San Pedro Island at tremendous risk to his own reputation, if not his health. The lay brother did not believe the headman's admonitions; the friar's silence forced the chief to hold his tongue as well. Three days later, Indians from Tolomato arrived on the island to enforce their directive to slay the doctrineros. They assured the cacique that if he did not kill the friars, he would die himself. Desperate to prevent bloodshed, the *mico* (Guale chief) offered the rebels all he possessed, but his pleas failed to deter them. The rebels sacked the priests' house and killed the lay brother and the guardian. The deed done, Christian natives of Guale Island buried the missionaries at the base of a high cross that the Spaniards had erected in their village. Despite the volatility of the situation, faithful native catechumens and novitiates paid respect to their Christian spiritual ministers.[22]

In Tupiqui the local natives rose against their resident friar, but before they took his life they honored his request to say a final mass. Christian members of the community came to the church to mourn the priest and to be with him before his execution. During the service the minister engaged the baptized natives in a discussion of Christian law. Meanwhile, the rebels desecrated the vestments and church relics and destroyed everything in the friar's cell. They delayed vengeance for two days as they heeded the doctrinero's petitions to spare his life. Finally, an impatient warrior killed him with a stone hatchet and threw his body in the woods. The upheaval made Christian natives wary of burying the corpse, but an elderly man, whose age may have afforded him some latitude or at least diminished his fear, secretly interred the friar's body.[23]

The nature of the revolt demonstrated the Guales' ambiguity over the place Franciscans held in village life and showed the range of concerns Indian communities harbored. Natives recognized the friars' significant spiritual power, and understood their connection to the Spaniards settled in the fort just south of Guale territory. The Indians were not naïve savages in awe of the missionaries' theological arguments, but were savvy, discerning, religiously inclined people who understood the necessity of propitiating spiritual power, whatever its form. When it proved destructive, they acted with equal determination. When the Christians' influence grew deleterious, failed to deliver what it provided the Spaniards, or interfered with sacred native customs, some Indians spurned it. Guale rebels fully understood the consequences of their actions and burned the huts the friars' used as cells and as churches, tore down many of the town's structures, and retreated from their coastal homes and away from the soldiers' reach. Even those who had begun to embrace Christianity went with their less convinced relatives and friends after the friars were killed. They knew that survival meant staying together.[24]

Six years passed before the Guale Indians agreed to peace with the Spaniards and returned to their homes. In the end, they gave up Juanillo and his co-conspirators for the security of settled living, cultivated food, and peaceful trade.[25] The needs of the many outweighed the principles of a few. The emotions, concerns, and fears rebelling natives felt about the Christians were myriad and did not evaporate with the return of Franciscan missionaries to their posts in Guale. Indeed, the presence of these religious strangers and the impact of their teachings forced natives in both Florida and New Mexico to adapt to a rapidly changing world, a world where the negotiation of culture was swiftly tilting in the Spaniards' favor. Indians' cosmology provided them an understanding that all things in life changed. Human action, human choice, played a vital part in the way things moved from one state of existence to another. Through their decisions and their ceremonial rituals, natives attempted to harness or at least to direct the changes that were concomitant with the white newcomers' arrival. Like their perception of the spiritual universe, the Indians' view of all things Spanish was two-sided: the Spaniards brought instruments of change that could prove benign or malevolent.

~~~§~~~

Indians accepted, discerned, and discriminated among what they considered the good and evil aspects of missionization through the seventeenth century. These responses required the most creativity in the Indians' and Franciscans' negotiation of culture.[26] The most noticeable alteration to native life—and the first issue negotiated by friars and

Indians—was the physical appearance of the mission village. As chiefs allowed friars access to native labor drafts to erect temples for the worship of the Spaniards' deity, the savvier among them maneuvered for control by dictating the structures' placement and location. No friar built a church complex in either frontier colony without negotiating the terms of construction plan, location, and labor with local indigenous authorities.[27]

Florida's chiefs attempted to secure their own power or at least to minimize the forfeiture of authority by permitting church complexes to stand on the main plazas near the council houses and their own. Associating the church complex with the towns' existing municipal and religious center won the chiefs home-field advantage and enhanced the local leaders' status. The finished product was a modest addition to the village; even the largest mission complexes paled in comparison to the size of native council houses. Florida's churches used the same wood and thatch, wattle-and-daub construction that the natives used themselves. Despite their rectangular shape, the appearance of these novel buildings was not too jarring to Indians' senses.[28]

In New Mexico the Pueblo leaders thought differently. Most Pueblos wanted to keep the Franciscans at a distance from the town's kivas and from the rituals performed in them. The peculiarities of Pueblo architecture also limited the friars' construction sites. Pueblo apartment houses were stacked on top of each other and were closely clustered for more effective defense. The only space available for the church complexes was on the outskirts of settled towns. As a result, the New Mexican churches looked like architectural afterthoughts in the village plan.[29]

And yet the Franciscans' willingness to allow Pueblos to influence church construction contributed to an intriguing sequence of events in the towns of Abó and Quarai. As the ministers supervised the building of the church complexes, they permitted local natives to excavate large kivas in the patios of the conventos. Each was carefully centered in the courtyard and was in use until the 1660s. The simultaneous operation of Christian churches and Pueblo kivas must have been intriguing. It was unlikely that the friars were unaware of the spiritual importance of the round structures, and thought nothing of the Piros' request to contribute kivas to the complex. Perhaps the recently arrived Franciscans allowed the kivas to be constructed, despite their religious importance, to smooth Christianity's entrance into native consciences. Or the Pueblos may have

Figure 6:
Kiva in the pueblo of Acoma. Photograph by the author.

been more aggressive. Piros might have excavated kivas in the convent patios to try to control the spiritual power conjured in Christian churches. Whatever the intent, the fact that kivas and churches occupied the same sacred space in these two pueblos meant that the friars' preaching was never far from watchful native shamans or suspicious native clans.[30] The negotiation over the construction of church grounds showed great nuance. Friars knew that failing to compromise would court Indian violence. The Piros knew that overtly challenging the friars might provoke Dios or the Spanish soldiers; many Indians decided that it was wiser to respect the Spaniards' power and to direct it to serve Indian concerns.[31]

Natives considered Spanish ceremonies different from their own but not impotent; Christian rituals did not invalidate native practices but added to their spiritual efficacy. In theory, Christians thought differently; their practices and rituals were exclusive and the only proper ceremonies for securing heavenly paradise. But folk religion flowered within the structure of Christian dogmatism and strict ceremonial practice in America as it had in Europe.[32] Missionaries initially encouraged, and Indian neophytes practiced, a Christianity that allowed for local flavor and permitted native expression. Concern with wooing converts made the friars' accommodation expedient and wise. And mission Indians frequently mixed elements of the new faith with attributes of native custom. Timucuas and Guales in Florida conscientiously avoided stepping on the shadow of a cross, and Pueblos held kachina dances on church grounds for Catholic feast days. Towas in the town of Pecos had tried to co-opt the newcomers' power by hiding stone, clay, and wooden figurines behind church altars and beneath the plaza's soil. Some among the mission Indians practiced both Christian and traditional rites, separately. Pueblo mission Indians maintained secretive kiva ceremonies throughout the seventeenth century, while Timucuas and Apalachees continued their ritual ball game with its concordant ceremonies until the late seventeenth century. Kiva meetings, kachina dances, ball games, ancestor worship, and household altars survived alongside baptism, communion, Christian weddings, and Sunday Mass. The line between conversion and selective adoption was thin and permeable. In May 1661, for example, Spaniards discovered an underground kiva near a Hopi mission church. The kiva reverently sheltered eleven figures and masks displayed as any sacred Christian relics would be. "Beneath one of the masks was the offering," noted one Spanish observer. Faithful native traditionalists had arranged "a wreath of flowering grass, and a sort of short petticoat marked with black, having a border ornamented with beads."[33]

Mission Indians' cultural compromise was at its most abstruse where burial practices were concerned. Traditional native mortuary rites were serious occasions that linked the living with ancestors in the spiritual realm. Gift giving, praying, mourning, and commemorating the dead in perpetuity were common burial practices in native American societies. Timucua and Guale death ceremonies were elaborate affairs and included month-long mourning periods, offerings of shorn hair, temporary burial until the flesh had deteriorated, burning what faunal remains there were, and final interment on raised burial platforms or tombs away from villages. Surviving family visited their deceased loved ones every day and offered them a portion of their daily sustenance. Instead of erecting charnal houses or biers, Apalachees constructed burial mounds and included craft items, symbols of office, trade goods, personal effects, and food in the tombs. Grass-covered knolls constantly reminded surviving clan members of their duties to those who had passed on to the spiritual world.[34]

While traditional Pueblo death rites were more carefully guarded, they, too, involved thorough preparations and strict regulations. Pueblos believed that life after death matched life before death, and their funerary rituals guided the spirits away from Pueblos and into the towns of the dead. Most buried their deceased the day or night that "breath" left the body. Each group observed specific rites particular to their ethnic group but, in general, Pueblo clans cared for their own dead. Clan members prepared corpses by washing them with yucca soap, water, or prayer-meal; covered them with sacred corn ears, prayer-feathers, or cloths, and dressed them in their best clothing. All personal items they buried with the dead were slashed or marked in some way to distinguish them from the possessions of living persons. They gathered bread, meat, and prayer-meal and placed the bodies in graves along rocky foothills or in canyons away from settlements. Pueblo peoples observed four days of mourning wherein sacred masks and fetishes used by the dead were buried separately; where clans and societies held prayer services and feasts; and grieving kin shattered ceramics, broke tools, and burned or washed the clothes of the dead.[35]

At first glance, Christian mortuary practices seemed utterly novel: Christians buried the dead on their backs with their legs extended and their arms crossed over their chests. But the mission Indians may not have seen the newcomers' ways as entirely foreign. Indians buried beneath churches' dirt floors or in the campo santo just beyond church entrances went into the ground with prayer medals, rosaries, beads, and crosses. These grave goods were offerings given by the living to the dead to sanctify their spirits' passing, just as ceramic bowls, necklaces, or personal items had done in traditional native burials. Priests' ministrations to the dying—last confession and extreme unction—were similar in appearance to medicine men's preparations for ushering souls to the afterlife. Friars used oils; shamans used pollen, corn meal, ash, and herbs. Florida's mission Indians also adopted Christian practices that had counterparts in native traditions. Some mourners carried the dead to the nearest doctrina—where mass was recited every morning—for burial, insuring daily homage to those who had passed on. Over the course of a year, Indians arranged for the friars to conduct services for the dead and left offerings of food for the ceremony. The Franciscans assumed that the offerings were alms, but the food was as likely nourishment for Indian spirits. Native mourners in Florida and New Mexico faithfully kept November 2, the Feast of All Souls, sacred by bringing more offerings "such as pumpkins or beans or a basket of maize or a hamper of toasted flour." Indians did not have to understand the recondite theory of purgatory, wherein the living made earthly payments to speed deceased souls to heaven, and used Christian ceremonies to help the departed on their journey to the spirit world.[36]

While Indians generally adopted Christian burial practices, they shrewdly exercised their own influence where they could. Cemeteries in Florida missions predominantly contained Christian internments, but several included one or numerous traditional graves. The oval-shaped pits with flexed or bundled bodies were a sharp contrast to the rectangular Christian burials. In other instances, Florida Indians were more subtle in observing traditional rites. Some Christian internments included shell gorgets, chunkey stones (used in the native ball game of the same name), or chipped stone alongside crosses, rosaries, and medals. Pueblos also observed traditional rites in their burials. Acomas wrapped their dead in native blankets and broke ceramic water pitchers over graves. Natives followed Christian burial practices but perceived them through the veil of their own expectations and understandings of what happened to the dead.[37]

Despite some mission Indians' continued efforts to reconcile new Christian ways with traditional beliefs, other neophytes completely embraced Christian teachings. Converted natives in Florida and New Mexico earned praise from Franciscan friars and visiting prelates alike. At the least, new converts performed ceremonies for the most important church holy days like seasoned Christians. Fray Francisco Pareja contended that "they assist at Masses of obligation on Sundays and feast-days . . . they have their confraternities and the procession of Holy Thursday, and from the mission stations they come to the principal mission to hear the *Salve* which is sung on Saturdays." They also used holy water to cross themselves, recited morning and evening prayers, met in community houses to learn singing and reading, and taught each other the catechism.[38] While eager friars certainly had reason to exaggerate the native converts' progress, it seemed that mission Indians performed the outward manifestations of Catholicism diligently and with appreciation for theatrical ceremony. Natives in Florida impressed visiting Franciscans and bishops alike with lavish processions and meticulously executed services. Tompiros in New Mexico put on lush masses complete with choirs singing plainchant for visiting Apache traders. In each instance, neophytes proudly reveled in the pageantry of the new spiritual power they had secured.[39]

Some Indians completely comprehended and adopted Christian mores and learned the catechism thoroughly. Doña María, *cacica* of Nombre de Dios mission on the outskirts of the colonial capital, St. Augustine, embraced Catholicism as a child, married a Spanish soldier, and became the friars' enthusiastic ally. As early as 1600, Doña María had mastered the Spanish language and had written to the king of Spain about the missionaries' efforts in her homeland. She behaved as a Christian queen loyal to the monarch of Spain.[40] Other natives worried less about the bonds that united elite leaders and more about Christian practices. Mission Piros traveled to a neighboring pueblo to confess their sins to García de San Francisco because he knew their language better than did their own resident priest. The native penitents did not want to ask for absolution through an interpreter who might betray their transgressions; they understood that the friars were bound to secrecy and that proper confessions absolved them of sin.[41]

Yet adopting new religious practices was rarely simple. Even after years of indoctrination, natives struggled to learn new modes of worship and suffered through more than a few uncomfortable lessons and theological misunderstandings. Florida Indians found kneeling difficult and "fell on the ground when they doubled their knees."[42] Confessing sins was a particularly confusing ritual for many; its proper performance depended on an appreciation of individual sin, guilt, language, and forgiveness. Not surprisingly, Indians found the sacrament odd and used it in their own ways. Fray Francisco Pareja complained that the Florida natives were devoid of shame and urged them to behave more modestly. In his *Catechism*, Pareja wrote that penitent natives should emulate the seashell that "opens itself every night and every morning to receive the dew of Heaven with which it forms a pearl in itself." The friar explained further that "the shell closes itself to the sun immediately and through most of the day as it becomes heated, and because it might be seen afterwards by all, it closes itself. We likewise must manifest our faults or failings only to the Father Confessor, as the vicar of Jesus Christ, and to no other. There are many who do the opposite, those who boast about doing evil and praise themselves for their sins." Timucuas and Guales treated confession like a war or hunt ceremony in which returning and triumphant men told tales of their exploits and reenacted their adventures for the village. After meeting with the priests, natives divulged "not only the sins which they have confessed, but even the penances which they have endured for them."[43] Admitting faults and withstanding the punishment for them was a test of native strength, and its successful passage was a source of pride, not shame, for some mission Indians.

The traffic of supernatural practices was not one-way. Spanish colonists accepted Indian curing methods and spells for both medicinal and magical purposes. They, like the Indians, discerned something about the others' spiritual power that was valid, and applied it to their own problems. Spanish settlers learned from native domestic servants how to concoct potions and powders to influence lovers and spouses, to find lost items, and to improve their economic situations. Spanish men and women ground special herbs, mixed love potions made with urine or mashed worms, cast "witches' curses, whispered spells to turn themselves invisible, and interpreted revealing dreams. Spaniards who dismissed native practices as "superstition" complained when Indians' prescriptions failed. One disgruntled consumer called a native medicine man "a dog of an enchanter." Spaniards, like the Indians of Florida and New Mexico, expected effective human intercession with the spirit world.[44]

Disparate views of the Spaniards and their religion had more systemic consequences within Indian communities. Traditionally, Indian governments mitigated differences in opinion among their people by striving for unanimity. They strengthened the bonds tying each villager to the others by debating issues until nearly all agreed on a course of action. Cautious decision-making made natives' responses to any issue or event deliberate and thoughtful, not rash or passionate. Indians knew that human actions had repercussions in the harmony of the world, where the natural and the supernatural existed side by side. But native prudence did not mean that each Indian wholeheartedly supported every collective move the town made. Natives held different views about a multitude of issues. Despite the bonds of kinship, language, custom, and familiarity, Indians had individual perspectives. When issues arose, natives formed factions, which created rifts between believers, generations, and those who worked in villages and those who took to the trails. If differences of opinion could not be settled, communities split from one another and started anew. But in Spanish mission villages, factions could not easily quit their homes. Native disputes made settlements periodically volatile. Since there were innumerable ways to both survive and to ensure stability for any village's future, Indians did not act in complete accordance with one another at all times.

Social and religious differences undermined native attempts to form a working consensus. A striking exemplar of native factionalism was Diocsale, a widely feared warrior and the regent principal chief of the Chacato town San Carlos de Achercatane. When Carlos, the rightful heir, came of age, Diocsale stepped aside. Carlos and his wife Elena were devout Christians and permitted Spanish authorities and the Franciscan missionaries assigned to Chacato unprecedented influence over tribal affairs. But when the doctrineros denied Diocsale his chiefly rights to numerous wives, the former regent was incensed. Losing power was humbling, but being forced to accept Christianity against his will was humiliating. Diocsale recruited Carlos' *inija* (second-in-command) Cutca Martín, the young cacique of San Nicolás de Atanchia, Miguel, and others to join him. Theirs was an odd confederation of aged chief and young leaders on the cusp of greater power. Other aspiring native leaders avoided Diocsale's faction and tried to boost their status by doing the Spaniards' bidding. Miguel's own second-in-command, Santiago, personally carried an urgent message to Apalachee from the Chacato friars when word of Diocsale's activities came to light. The wily Diocsale and his faction understood the situation perfectly. Miguel, the cacique of San Nicolás, tried to persuade his impressionable inija to defect to Diocsale's side by taunting his second's sycophancy. "What are [the Spaniards] going to give you for having carried the note to the lieutenant," Miguel chided. Miguel was certain that Santiago "was thinking they were going to make him cacique or a great man."[45]

Diocsale warned Carlos and the other Chacato leaders that if they failed to expel the Spaniards, the neighboring Chicsas would "assemble and they would kill the priest and the Indians who would defend him." Diocsale was half Chicsa and counted the "pagan" and notoriously warlike people as his closest allies. The Chacatos admitted that it was only through Diocsale that "they had peace" with the dangerous Chicsas. But Carlos, his interpreter, and some chiefs from other villages remained loyal to the missionaries despite the gravity of Diocsale's threats. In response, the Chicsa faction attempted a twilight attack on the friar and his protectors. They failed. The conspirators were arrested, tried, and punished with prison terms and labor duties. Even after being sentenced to perpetual exile, Diocsale continued to direct actions against Spaniards and his Chacato rivals. He ordered several Chicsa raids on Chacato towns and went so far as to sanction an attack on his home village.[46]

In some cases, pretenders to village power maneuvered to seize chieftainships. Rivals vied for leverage and tried in any way to secure promotions; the savviest used knowledge of the Spanish language or familiarity with Spanish bureaucracy for personal gain. During a routine provincial visita, Antonio, a Guale sacristan, reported to the Spanish authorities that the chieftainship of Yfulo was vacant. He then claimed that he was the successor to the post. The *visitador* learned from other Guales that Juan Ysape, who was absent from the visita convocation, was the rightful heir. In another case, Osunanca Pedro Garcia convinced a group of lower chiefs to support his bid to usurp the chiefdom of Yfalcasar. Garcia informed the Spanish visitador that the heir apparent was cruel to Spanish settlers' livestock and could not be trusted. But two principal caciques of Guale exposed Garcia's play for power, and the Spaniards permanently banned him from serving as a political leader. Over the course of the seventeenth century, Spanish officials increasingly intruded on Indian political chains of command, both unilaterally and at the bequest of Christian Indian chiefs. One Spanish visitador even threatened villagers with jail time if they continued to disregard their chief's orders.[47]

While Indian communities generally revered age and respected the wisdom of town elders, old and young natives did not always perceive things similarly. Heirs to positions of power chafed under the control of their more senior officeholders. Young warriors, eager to prove their prowess and to augment their power on the field of combat, urged their people into more belligerent stances than did older, world wise counselors. Seasoned natives spent their lives obeying traditions that native youth replaced with newer notions. Like the generational division between political rivals, occupational differences created differences of perspective. Warriors and priests clashed in efforts to secure influence over their town and leverage with the spirits. Those who hunted, fished, and traded spent more time away from their settlements and, by virtue of their business, were more open to foreign ideas and goods. Those who farmed or whose work was more intimately tied to hearth and home were more inward looking. Labor divisions paralleled social stratification, too. Men performed different tasks from women, and powerful officials and shamans had different responsibilities from farmers and hunters.[48]

The arrival of Spanish missionaries in Indian towns exacerbated these community fissures and made native life more contentious. Villagers immediately split between baptized and non-baptized factions. Coinciding with or following severe demographic collapse, the introduction of new goods, flora and fauna, and new governmental arrangements, efforts to convert natives targeted already strained populations. The mechanisms in native communities that helped Indians cope with change—spiritual ritual, the succession of leaders, sufficient harvests—were dangerously weakened by so many native deaths from conquest and disease. Thus when members of a mission village turned to the Spaniards' faith, intra-village relations were further strained.

Every mission town included dissatisfied people or those who had rival interests; not every Indian living in a mission village was a Christian convert. Indeed the proximity of conflicting religious groups made mission demography, and mission religious loyalty, somewhat fluid. Some Indians moved from church to kiva or temple and back again, depending on the prevailing political, economic, or military winds. As factions appeared to gain supremacy, as native or Spanish deities responded to native supplication, so went many native faithful. In times of doubt, many natives left mission towns entirely to join neighboring communities that had resisted Christian influence. Indians were not fickle worshippers but practical believers who expected the spirit world, traditional or Spanish, to perform when propitiated. When Dios ignored their prayers, Indians turned to traditional spirits.

Other Indians fervently clung to traditions or embraced Christianity without compromise or apology. In Florida and New Mexico, non-Christian natives in nearby towns and camps offered quick outlets for discontented mission Indians. The greater distances between mission settlements in New Mexico made the recruiting efforts of anti-Spanish factions easier. Pueblos on the edges of Spanish control—especially Jémez, Acomas, Isletas, Taos, Picurís, Hopis and, Zuñis—challenged Spanish influence more fiercely. But eastern pueblos, like their Florida counterparts, were too close to Spanish military garrisons and the colonial capitals for their people to frequently challenge Spanish conquest.[49]

Generational, occupational, and social factions within mission towns became more fractious after the Franciscans began preaching the new religion. Florida youths, forced to attend daily catechism, began to envision a future Indian spirituality that was different from the views held by non-converted elders. "The younger generation," observed fray Francisco Pareja, "makes fun of and laughs at some old men and women" who observed, and sought to preserve, traditional practices. While mocking was an accepted native method of venting social frustration or relieving the pressure of unbalanced power relations, the ribbing must have inflicted deep pain on the generation that had ruled during the Spanish invasion. The change in their children's religious leanings in the wake of conquest made the spiritual future of their communities frighteningly uncertain. Indeed, traditional power struggles between village factions took on more serious meaning in the mission period. Guale converts, once harassed by traditionalists among them, persecuted non-Christians once Spanish missions had survived two uprisings. Friars claimed that they had to become the "defenders and protectors of the *Hanopiras* (literally 'red human-beings'; 'painted ones' i.e. traditionalists) among the Christian Indians" to avoid bloodshed.[50] Non-converted Pueblos were scornful of Christian Indians because they had abandoned their traditional observances and had spiritually endangered their kinsmen as a result.[51]

Spanish occupation of Indian territories also altered the deployment and employment of native labor. Chiefs released Indians to work in colonial capitals, on private ranches and haciendas, and on mission grounds. Over the course of the seventeenth century, native control over their working populations fell increasingly into Spanish hands. Governors demanded more labor drafts to erect municipal buildings and forts and to staff Indian militias. Private ranchers and farmers hired or stole Indian labor to tend their herds or fields. Franciscans, too, employed natives to care for livestock and to work agricultural tracts. With greater demands on labor drafts, the increased frequency of military or trade sorties, and with more opportunities for work on private or mission lands, many Indians became more mobile than they had been before Spanish intrusion and were absent from their homes more regularly. The changed labor conditions exacerbated factional rivalries and complicated familial responsibilities to clan and hearth.[52]

The missionaries themselves introduced still more occupations for the native population to fill. Friars used Indians as interpreters to translate conversations between Spaniards and natives, convey sermons to native congregations, and explain Christianity to neophytes. Sacristans and acolytes maintained religious paraphernalia, church interiors and grounds, and assisted in Christian services. Fiscales enforced church doctrine and friars' orders, often whipping men and women who ran afoul of the Franciscans' commands. Indians who previously had limited access to political or spiritual power in their communities increased their influence by accepting one of these new positions. Each gained brokering power like that enjoyed by village chiefs. They served as middlemen between Spanish and native cultures. But they also became enmeshed with the conquering authorities. They disseminated Spanish and Christian concepts among Indians by explaining administrative directives from colonial governors and resident guardians, or by teaching the catechism. When Spaniards collected tribute or enforced colonial regulations, natives holding offices in the new regime were collaborators. But at other times they protected Indians from imperial abuses. Interpreters smoothed Spanish-Indian relations through misinformation. The vagaries of translation allowed native interpreters to fudge friars' instructions, soften governor's demands, and edit native responses. By refusing to translate the tone of certain statements or by omitting violent or coarse language, interpreters exercised tremendous power in the negotiation of culture in Spanish missions. Choosing when to use that power was risky indeed. One Jumano translator was hanged because "he did not interpret faithfully what he was told."[53] Despite their close symbolic and actual association with the conquering Spaniards, interpreters and sacristans became respected leaders in their communities. In fact, when natives rose up to expel the missionaries from their lands, they relied on their interpreters and sacristans to betray their former employers.[54]

Individuals improved their personal access to power in their communities by accepting Spanish offices and jobs, but entire clans responded collectively toward the missionaries and their message. Each clan was responsible for specific spiritual performances and ceremonies in the Indians' religious calendar. Clans trained medicine men, kept sacra, and maintained communication with its piece of the spirit world for the community at large. Depending upon how the responsibilities of each clan were affected by Spanish intrusion, clan members either embraced or rejected Christianity. For example, when zealous friars burned native "idols," they rarely destroyed all of a town's religious paraphernalia. The Franciscans may have discovered only some clans' sacra while leaving others unharmed. Natives whose symbols of spiritual power were ruined by Spaniards may have had more reason to resent the newcomers' teachings. Clans whose religious images were left alone may have had more opportunity to "compartmentalize" Spanish practices, images, or ideas they deemed marginal, while retaining the core of their cultural imperatives. Compartmentalization was common among Eastern Pueblos, but does not appear to have been a strategy in Florida. Others practiced a blended, synthesized, faith that combined Spanish traits with Indian ones.[55] The status of each clan also may have determined how a portion of the native community reacted to the invaders. Clans with less religious responsibility, with duties less dependent upon elaborate kachina dances or major village observances, could have been attracted to the Christians' promise of more spiritual power, where those with great spiritual responsibility would be less likely to forfeit their power.[56]

The distribution of Indian political power in Florida and New Mexico also affected different native responses to Spanish colonizers. Timucuas, Guales, and Apalachees formed chiefdoms: organizing more than one community under the auspices of a centralized, hereditary leader.[57] Chieftains exacted tribute, labor, military drafts, political counsel, and religious deference from Indians under their control;

their subjects expected to provide services and loyalty to their leader. Spanish demands for Indian labor, military cooperation, and religious compliance were familiar to natives from southeastern chiefdoms. Pueblos, on the other hand, did not create chiefdoms but independent villages. Spanish demands fell heavier on Pueblos who had less experience with large labor or military drafts and excessive tribute levies.[58] Southwestern missions were more volatile as a result. Pueblos revolted more frequently because rebels only needed to convince their own village to rise against the Spaniards. They did not have to consult allied towns and a network of chiefs and councils before acting, as their Florida counterparts had to do.

When cultural negotiation threatened the integrity of native existence and when violence seemed futile, Indians fled the missions. Escaping oppressive orders, avoiding backbreaking labor, fleeing punishment, or evading tribute collectors, some mission Indians decided that remaining under Spanish influence was untenable.[59] Mission Indians could quickly reach dense marsh jungles or labyrinth-like mountains and canyons to hide. Populations in mission towns fluctuated with periodic episodes of war, disease, labor drafts, drought, and famine. But flight also reduced mission numbers and caused great concern among Spanish authorities. Missionaries worried that fugitives abandoned Christianity and returned to "heathen" practices. Governors and settlers knew that Indians who fled the missions could not be recruited to work or to defend the colony. Conditions had become so dire in several New Mexican missions that Franciscans complained that they had distributed an entire week of rations to parishioners "to keep them from wandering away." Spaniards corrected dwindling populations by combining small villages or supplementing smaller missions with non-Christian, foreign groups. These new *congregaciones* were awkward solutions. Different native peoples did not live together easily before the Spaniards came; they did no better when forced to live side by side, especially when the newly settled group remained unconverted. Ironically, news that the Spaniards planned to move people from their homes to a new town often encouraged mission Indians to flee to avoid resettlement.[60]

The rich variety of responses to the Christian missions and to their friars was a product of the native communities themselves. The Indians of Florida and New Mexico were not nations united but towns of confederated clans; some shared cultural traits and spoke the same language, but each town acted according to the dictates of its people. Just as towns were divided from each other, factions divided individual villages. There was no single united Indian reaction to Spanish missionization, and the variety of responses to the Franciscans and to their teachings created a textured cultural negotiation. Missions were organic places that changed as their populations grew or declined, converted or compromised, submitted or rebelled. In their search for balance and harmony, mission Indians adjusted to the changes in their world as best they could.

CHAPTER FOUR

The Imbalance of Power

the governor acts as if [the indians] were his slaves, that do not belong to the religious, but are his.
— new mexico's provincial fray francisco de san antonio, 1657

The terms of conquest that Spaniards and Indians negotiated over the first decades of the seventeenth century changed after the 1640s. The survival of Spain's frontier colonies was largely dependent on extracting native labor and proselytizing native souls. But recurrent epidemics, raids by non-Christian Indians, and onerous labor demands ravaged indigenous populations. Disgruntled native converts started voting with their feet. The struggle to exercise influence over dwindling numbers of mission Indians became more urgent. With colonial conditions in tremendous flux, colonizers and natives in Florida and New Mexico openly vied for power and sought leverage to control their own, and each others' lives. Governors tried to wrest Indian laborers and warriors from clerics' hands; friars pulled the reins tighter on mission Indians; Indian leaders struggled to maintain a hold on their own people. Pushed and pulled by these competing forces, mission Indians in Florida and New Mexico were in unenviable positions. To decide any portion of their future, Indians had to carefully play one contestant off another. As the demands on native labor, loyalty, and behavior grew more insistent, Indians' choices narrowed and left them with few happy options.

Much of the late seventeenth-century instability in Spain's frontier doctrinas was self-inflicted. Spaniards in Florida and New Mexico, secular and ecclesiastical, shared the responsibilities of colonial government, but their jurisdictions overlapped and frequently opposed each other. When one side gained an advantage in the tug-of-war for mission Indians, the weakened party used all its influence to strike back. For the Spaniards, the issues were gravely serious and worth fighting over. The essence of Spanish relations with Indians—when and for whom natives worked, where the profits went, who had the Indians' interests at heart, and what traditional practices were sacrilegious—was at stake. Disagreements were fierce and the contest between state and church raged in colonial capitals, on private farms, and in missions alike. Far away from colonial *audiencias* and viceroys, the northern frontiers provided the ideal setting for jurisdictional squabbling and abuse. Even the very structure of frontier government encouraged Spanish infighting.

The governor was the highest-ranking official in Spanish frontier colonies. Appointed by the viceroy of New Spain, the men who held the title Governor and Captain-General represented the king's interests and had broad responsibilities. They provided for the welfare of Spanish settlers and native inhabitants, arranged the defense and economic development of the colony, promoted the religious salvation of Spaniards and Indians, and carried out the daily operation of local bureaucratic, economic, and military affairs. For their service, provincial governors earned a salary from the king of Spain, but many expected to earn much more than the allotted stipend. To secure fortunes more befitting men of their assumed status, most colonial governors in Florida and New Mexico exploited local resources and native labor whenever they could. Under the guise of the repartimiento (native labor drafts for civic or public works), governors had Indians harvest crops, salt, piñon nuts, deerskins, corn, and other trade items from the frontiers for export. Using their mandate to explore new territories and defend the colonial borders, governors led frequent trade expeditions and slaving forays beyond mission limits. Accepting a colonial post was a risky way to amass wealth, but governor after governor tried to make his appointment personally profitable. Indeed, the colonial system encouraged governors to find ways to supplement their official salaries. Would-be colonial leaders bought their offices with a half-a-year's salary (*media anata*) and needed to raise capital to bribe their successors who investigated them through the *residencia*.[1]

As the king's agents, governors granted *mercedes* (land grants) and municipal concessions to settlers for their private use. But there were significant differences in the ways the two colonial leaders distributed these plums. New Mexican governors bound elite colonists to their side by issuing encomiendas, permits given to select colonists for the use of Indian labor and the right to collect native tribute. In exchange, *encomenderos* agreed to ensure that their allotted Indians were fed, converted, and defended from attack. The most influential encomenderos served on the capital's *cabildo*, or town council, and represented the concerns of the non-indigenous population. With *haciendas* (large rural estates), *estancias* (land grants for herding livestock), and missions, New Mexico was a borderland plantation of working farms and Pueblo villages.[2]

Florida's colonial structure was different. It was a military colony of missions and presidios, or forts that served as defensive stations and trading depots. The capital was the garrison of St. Augustine, and soldiers, not municipal officers, held all the political posts. Governors, as captains-general, appointed lieutenants to oversee the affairs of the Timucua, Guale, and Apalachee Indian provinces. Each drew a salary from the *situado*, a collection of royal funds for the operation of the colony. Instead of granting encomiendas as their New Mexican counterparts did, Florida's governors relied on military protocol for settler loyalty. If governors needed to win special favor, they could retire officers from active military service. These *reformados* were reserve officers who drew guaranteed pensions from the situado. Payments to special retired soldiers achieved what tribute collection did in New Mexico. What was more, reformados were the governors' trusted allies and frequently led military sorties against mission Indians and enemies alike. They, like the encomenderos, were beneficiaries of and partners in the colonial enterprise, and received land grants and rights to farm and raise livestock.[3]

While the governor was the prime authority in law, the Franciscans held as much, if not more, power in fact. Friars lived among the Indians, and while a few Spanish settlers also dwelt in native villages (*agregados*), the missionaries wielded more power than farmers, ranchers, traders, or officers. Franciscans' efforts to convert Indians created a familiarity with native populations that their secular counterparts lacked. Beyond having the situational advantage, friars had political leverage. Administrations in Florida and New Mexico relied on the mis-sions to congregate and civilize native populations; the two frontier colonies would have been abandoned without the doctrinas' "success," and the Franciscans knew the purchase that that gave them in their quar-rels with governors. Having a religious hierarchy independent of the secular chain of command gave missionaries confidence as well. It bol-stered the friars' willingness to challenge the governors' authority. Friars answered to their own elected officials, to those appointed by their order, and, ultimately, to the pope. The provincial minister lived in the colo-nial capitals and had gubernatorial-like power over the doctrineros. He received advice from a Council of Definitors and a larger body of coun-selors called the *difinitorio*. These bodies met every three to eight years to discuss mission business and to assign guardians to each mission sta-tion. Clerics in the Roman Catholic Church were exempt from secu-lar prosecution and punishment. They had their own courts, and reported directly to the Commissary General of the Indies and the king, not to viceroys or governors. New Mexico's organization was compli-cated further by the presence of the Holy Office of the Inquisition, which had jurisdiction over every Spanish Christian in the colony, including governors. It became a valuable weapon for the friars in their troubles with colonial officials, and exacerbated already strained relations between church and state. Friars were specifically responsible for mis-sion Indians: for their religious instruction, their occupational train-ing, and their moral correction. The Franciscans jealously guarded their positions as "protectors" of native peoples.[4]

Spanish colonizers, secular and ecclesiastical, needed Indian coop-eration or, at least, Indian acquiescence to make the frontier colonies viable. Native political leaders in Florida and New Mexico were the gate-keepers to Indian labor and souls. Despite the Spaniards' violent con-quest of their people, chiefs retained their rank and shared in the operation of the colonies. Indian chieftains sent labor drafts to St. Augustine and to Santa Fé, released craftsmen and guides for Spanish trades, and ordered extra fields planted for the invaders' benefit. They also became captains in the Spanish military and formed Indian mili-tias for the defense of remote mission villages.[5] As years of Spanish occu-pation stretched into decades, Indian leaders found it increasingly difficult to discern the source of their status and power: Spanish bureaucratic sys-tems or traditional native customs. At times, chiefs acted like loyal

Catholic subjects of the Spanish crown; at others, they behaved as revolutionaries biding their time. There was no single "Indian" response to the conditions of foreign conquest. There were multiple native reactions to Spanish invasion that shed light on the pressures placed on indigenous peoples.

Without native populations, the frontier colonies would have had no reason to exist, and no means to survive. But the contest for influence over natives undermined Spaniards' authority, and revealed to mission Indians the chinks in the colonial armor. Spanish governors and missionaries, distracted by their mutual acrimony, seemed less able to confront the dangers of the Indians' new world. Enemies raided mission villages with impunity, food became scarce, and the very climate suddenly seemed to conspire against native survival. Increasingly, Spaniards drew the Indians into their political feuds. In the natives' estimation, the Spaniards were growing increasingly erratic and thus dangerous. The conditions by which Indians had submitted to Spanish conquest had become fluid, and natives were not comfortable with the instability that Spanish infighting caused. Discontented natives shifted diplomatic support from governors to friars and back again, in efforts to secure more stability in their communities or to stop Spanish abuses. When diplomacy failed, they rebelled.[6]

The Spaniards' colonial expansion was the catalyst for change in Florida. The forty-year-old mission provinces of Guale and Timucua suffered from a series of brutal epidemics, and the catastrophic loss of so many souls hampered the development of the colony's missions and economy. Friars and governors alike had cause for concern. They were convinced that the solution to the colony's demographic woes lay in the western territory of Apalachee. Spaniards had communicated and traded with Apalachee chiefs since 1608, but had not established missions in the province until the 1630s. Eight chiefs allowed Franciscans and a small group of soldiers to settle among them. But like nearly every Indian people who initially accepted a Spanish "alliance," the Apalachees quickly soured on the newcomers' intrusiveness. With their Chicsa allies, the Apalachees violently expelled the Spaniards from their lands on February 19, 1647, and later defended their action in an eight-hour pitched battle against thirty-one Spanish infantry and five hundred Timucua warriors. Though successful, the Apalachees were stunned by the Spaniards' swift, coordinated reaction during the Timucuas' planting season. They were equally impressed when interim Governor Francisco Menéndez Márquez quickly rallied a smaller force of twenty-one Spaniards and sixty Timucuas to attack a second time. They agreed to surrender the leaders of the uprising and to accept repartimiento labor drafts from their villages. The Spaniards executed twelve Apalachee chiefs and sentenced twenty-six others to forced-labor details.[7]

Determining what had caused the Apalachee revolt embroiled Spanish governors and friars in hot debate. Secular and ecclesiastical officials accused each other of instigating the violence as both sides maneuvered for supremacy in the post-rebellion Apalachee province. The governor suggested that the friars' abusive treatment of mission Indians, presumptuous demands on native laborers, and impetuous interdiction of traditional native dances, games, and cures pushed the recently converted Apalachees to revolt. The Franciscans responded that governors and soldiers taxed Apalachee lands, crops, and labor by settling too many Spaniards in the region. Missionaries also claimed that the governor unfairly increased the frequency of Apalachee work drafts and made irresponsible, life-threatening demands on Indian cargo-bearers. What was more insidious, according to the friars, was that suspended Governor Benito Ruiz de Salazar Vallecilla had required exorbitant native labor for his own extensive wheat, corn, and cattle hacienda on the province's eastern border. There was truth in each accusation. Soldiers and Franciscans marshaled scores of Apalachees to sow fields of corn and wheat, to construct haciendas and churches, and to carry materials, supplies, and produce between Apalachee and the distant colonial capital.[8] The Spaniards' appetite for Apalachee muscle and sweat grew after the suppression of the 1647 revolt. The province became the land of colonial promise and a place of plenty beyond the spent territories of central and coastal Florida.

While Apalachee's stock soared, the value of Guale and Timucua deteriorated. A generation of intimate contact with Spanish conversion efforts, work demands, military conquests, and germs depleted mission populations. Guale and Timucua failed to staff all their doctrinas, work their community fields, or supply the labor required by Spanish authorities. As the populations plummeted, the older mission provinces lost importance and influence with their conquerors. It seemed to mission Indians that the Spaniards had reprioritized their reasons for settling Florida. Bringing natives to Christianity was suddenly less critical than labor and trade. The evidence was in the Spaniards' behavior.

Officials busied themselves with protecting the overland route to Apalachee and with securing trade with the "heathen" Chacatos, Apalachicolas, and Amacanos beyond the western missions. Guales and Timucuas also suffered diplomatic slights and political injustices with more frequency. Spanish governors rarely fêted Guale and Timucua chiefs when they came to St. Augustine, breaking the protocol that had previously guaranteed relatively smooth Spanish-Indian relations. Governors became unwilling to "waste" gifts and trade trinkets on natives already allied to Spain. A Spanish investigation in 1660 recorded Governor Diego de Rebolledo's refusal to show a visiting cacique the proper hospitality. Rather than welcoming the chieftain into the palace and feeding him at his own table, as native diplomacy dictated, the governor let the chief fend for himself. A Spanish interpreter voluntarily offered the Timucua shelter and a meal. When asked by a Spanish officer why Rebolledo had not provided for him, the cacique bitterly complained "if he were a cacique of Ays, or another infidel, that the Governor would give [shelter] to him." The officer urged patience and the chieftain promised to remain calm "because he was a Christian."[9] The Timucua leader failed to mention if his Spanish faith was any consolation, but other Guale and Timucua chieftains, angered by their own miserable conditions and by Spanish neglect, began to reconsider their arrangements with the invaders.[10]

Hasty actions from Governor Rebolledo brought Timucuan dissatisfaction and resentment to the surface. In 1655, English troops captured the island of Jamaica in the Caribbean. European intelligence indicated that England had designs on other Spanish holdings in the region, including St. Augustine. Rebolledo received news of the English conquest in April of the following year, and knew that his defenses were in disrepair, his soldiers outnumbered, and his supplies few. Since the governor had applied funds meant for colonial defense to personal and economic projects, he realized that he could not repel an English invasion. Fearing the situation desperate, Rebolledo ordered the activation of the Indian militias as part of his defensive strategy. He urged the caciques, *norocos* (native warriors), and principal men to gather supplies, including a month's worth of grain and corn, and ordered them to march—"carrying the provisions"—to St. Augustine. While Rebolledo's panic may have had some cause, his insensitivity to protocol proved disastrous. The governor made no distinction between commoners and chiefs in his directives and, when pressed, he asserted that he expected Indian leaders to bear their share of the food to the capital. The Timucuan chiefs lost their patience.[11]

Both Apalachee and Timucua leaders had legitimate complaints. Apalachee was a great distance from the Atlantic coast and the hardship of traveling so far on foot was considerable. Each province was running low on food stores and did not wish to cripple village resources. But in Timucua the governor's order appeared grievous. He humiliated native leaders by demanding that they forgo their rights by carrying their own provisions. Timucua's highest-ranking cacique, Lúcas Menéndez of San Martín de Ayacuto, assembled the various chieftains of the province at San Pedro de Potohiriba and argued for a general rebellion against the secular authorities. In his declaration for war, Lúcas Menéndez stressed the Spaniards' alarming tendency to neglect diplomatic protocol, to disrespect chiefs, and to requisition ever more native labor, despite the Timucuas' depleted population. The old cacique was so determined to reassert the rights of village chieftains that he was willing to risk the perils of revolt.[12]

The Indians hoped that a rebellion would make the governor in St. Augustine observe the covenant his predecessors had formed with Timucuas decades before. The revolt was not, therefore, a maelstrom of aimless violence. Lúcas Menéndez focused the Timucuas' rage upon people and symbols of Spanish secular authority and specifically forbade any violence against the Franciscan missionaries. In fact, the native chief carefully explained his purpose to one of the friars. "He and the rest of the Indians were not abandoning the law of God, nor refusing to be obedient to your majesty," the missionary recorded, "but were trying to liberate themselves from the offenses and continuous injuries, and that they could not achieve it any other way."[13]

It may have seemed that the Timucuas' stance had foreshadowed colonial Spanish-American revolts against poor governmental administration and those who neglected rooted traditions of political and social negotiation. Those rebels, too, remained loyal to the system, but reserved the right to disregard initiatives or orders that they considered against the interest of good government.[14] The Timucua revolt was, indeed, a demonstration against specific members of the Spanish colonial network, not against all Spanish interlopers. But the Timucuas' action was Indian in conception and implementation. They knew that it was impossible to sever all ties with the Spaniards and understood that a general revolt against every Spaniard could never achieve their goals. Instead, Indian leaders discussed their grievances in council only after they suffered numerous injustices at Spanish hands; they decided unanimously to seek revenge against those who had specifically wronged them. The rebels reasoned that if they attacked only the secular colonists, their purpose would be plain. Violence would poignantly express their concerns and would unequivocally prove to their fellow natives that they were worthy of their chiefly titles. Moreover, if the Timucuas aimed their anger toward those who aggrieved them, like-minded natives in Apalachee, still smarting from their unsuccessful revolt nine years before, might rise to support them. Should Apalachee join the Timucuas' cause, the Spaniards would be forced to correct the intolerable treatment of native chiefs.

The Timucuas conducted the revolt with calculation. While the chief's order was to kill every Spaniard on sight, the mayhem was tempered by stays granted to the Franciscans and to a personal friend of the rebel leader. Chief Lúcas Menéndez tried to forewarn his godfather's eldest son, Don Juan Menéndez Márquez, about the coming revolt. The Spanish owners of the hacienda, La Chua, had been longtime friends of the Timucuas; the rebel leader had no desire to harm those who had showed him kindness or respect. But when the cacique reached the hacienda with a band of warriors, he found Don Juan at home. The Spaniard knew nothing about the uprising. Amid the passions of rebellion, the sentimental Timucua chief dragged his friend out of the house while his companions charged the farm's workers. Don Juan was the only living thing, human or animal, to survive the raid on La Chua.[15] In a few days Timucua norocos had targeted soldiers, settlers, slaves, and livestock; they killed seven people and eliminated all but two non-religious personnel throughout the province.

Lúcas Menéndez had wanted the Timucuan revolt to redress specific political and diplomatic grievances. Spanish neglect had so enflamed natives' frustrations that violence became their chosen form of relief. But the Timucuan leadership had seen Spanish retaliation for Indian violence; the Spaniards had punished their ancestors a generation before and their Apalachee neighbors more recently. They knew that sparing the Spanish holy men would earn them few considerations. But the result was less important than the statement they made. Holding positions of chiefly power in the native world required concern for tradition and hierarchy. The 1656 revolt was a last-gasp attempt to proclaim

Timucuan legitimacy to conquering invaders who had grown selfish and overbearing. Their survival hinged on Apalachee support of their rebellion. The Timucuas retreated to the western reaches of their territory, constructed a fortress to guard rebels from Spanish vengeance, and sent messengers to Apalachee to plead for aid. Whether the Apalachees refused to rally to the Timucuas' cause as retribution for the Timucuas' role in putting down the Apalachee Revolt of 1647, no one recorded.

The Spaniards quelled the Timucua rebellion methodically, given their worries about an English attack. Their eventual punishment of the native instigators—garroting six caciques, including Chief Lúcas Menéndez, and four warriors and sentencing the rest to prison and forced labor—was decisive. Rebolledo ordered the bodies of the rebel leaders hung throughout the province as a gruesome deterrent. The executions of most of Timucua's chiefs hobbled the province and left it in chaos. A month after the Spaniards had passed sentence on the rebellion's leaders, Governor Rebolledo took steps to restructure Timucua. He conducted a rapid visitation of the mission provinces in 1657, and left behind

Figure 7:
Reconstructed *convento* and *cocina* at San Luis de Talimali. Photograph courtesy of Christopher R. Versen.

a regulatory code designed to consolidate his power over the Indians. Successfully halting the revolt gave the governor the necessary leverage to appoint new leaders for decapitated towns and to force the remaining chiefs to relocate their villages along the *Camino Real*. Some depopulated villages aggregated with equally ghostly towns in the process; each relocated village abandoned traditional lands. Timucua became a series of way stations to serve Spanish travelers, traders, and soldiers as they conducted themselves between Apalachee and St. Augustine.[16] Timucua was never the same again.

Sorting out what had caused the Timucuas to rebel, like the fallout from the Apalachee rebellion, strained the already tense relationship between the governor and the missionaries. Each side engaged in an escalating war of words waged to deflect responsibility for native discontent and to cast blame on the other. The recriminations became increasingly venomous after Rebolledo's visita to the conquered provinces in 1657. The governor wished to establish a garrison in Apalachee to better exercise influence on this distant province and to attempt to undermine the friars' hold on the local populations. He sought evidence that the Indians rose against the mistreatment they received from the Franciscans. Rebolledo suggested that the friars took advantage of their position in Indian missions to manipulate labor drafts for their own benefit. He also claimed that the clerics were duplicitous. According to the governor, the doctrineros had ordered natives to deny food and shelter to Spanish soldiers. By encouraging the mistreatment of Spanish colonists, the friars implied that the colonists were not worthy of Indian respect; therefore, the missionaries' attitude had incited the Indians to violence. Rebolledo's tone revealed how virulent the rivalry had become. When he claimed that six missionaries had quit their posts and boarded a ship bound for Havana to escape correction for their abuse of natives, he punctuated his point by suggesting that "by the judgements of God they were drowned."[17] The Franciscans dubiously contended that the three missionaries had gone to Havana on a routine trip to inform the archbishop of conditions in Florida.[18] The governor's injudicious language had stung the friars.

Rebolledo knew he faced Franciscan opposition, so he used Indian complaints gathered in his 1657 visita as evidence of his contentions. The Apalachees, recognizing the delicacy of the situation, performed a precarious balancing act. They noted that the struggle between the secular and religious branches of the colonial government was becoming more heated, and that the outcome could not be predicted. Indian leaders care-fully played one side off the other; they logged complaints against the friars during the governor's visitation, and later asked the friars to inter-vene on their behalf against soldiers' demands. Governor Rebolledo recorded that several chiefs asked for relief from "continuous freight car-rying," and for permission to trade with soldiers.[19] But primarily they remonstrated about the friars' neglect of chiefly rights and their harsh reproofs. The Patales groused to the governor that the missionaries "pun-ish the caciques and leaders in the same fashion as vassals," without exempting them in the case of the degrading punishment of whipping." Friars also failed to consult with the chiefs before beating natives for miss-ing Sunday services or before drafting Indians for church work.[20] Some native leaders saw the heightened tensions between church and state as an opportunity to secure traditional rights. Some asked that the gover-nor give them license to "hold their lawful dances in the principal lodge on the festive days, as long as they do nothing in them in offense of God."[21]

After the governor had returned to the capital, the Indians expressed their concerns about the governor's new regulations, and fueled the fri-ars' caustic responses to Rebolledo's charges. The friars urged the gov-ernor to reduce the number of soldiers he had stationed in Apalachee, which was "against the will" of the Indians and threatened to "pull the religious who work at the conversion" of Apalachee out of the province if Rebolledo continued his plans.[22] But the missionaries had reason to take issue with the governor without native prompting. The Franciscans defended their treatment of the Indians by insisting that the governor's interference made physical correction more "necessary to punish the Indians so that they do not return to their pagan ways." The doctrineros explained that "with the permission that your excellency gives them . . . for their dances," the natives reverted to their traditional rites and therefore required discipline.[23] The missionaries also blamed Rebolledo for fomenting the Timucuan rebellion. He should have known that "the Indians' leading men could not be obliged to travel loaded down," the friars asserted. His haughtiness had precipitated the revolt.[24] They sus-pected that Rebolledo had taken advantage of natives' aroused fears fol-lowing the military suppression of Timucua in his hasty visitation of the mission provinces. What was more, they worried that the governor abused his governmental power to establish an Apalachee garrison not for defense, but to ensure his own influence over the doctrinas.

While the causes of Florida's church-state problems were institutional, their solutions were personal. New secular and religious officers made a concerted effort not to resurrect dormant antagonisms. The pattern of colonial mismanagement, native rebellion, and military suppression had drained the colony's resources and prompted a more thorough residencia—a mandatory investigation of the outgoing administration conducted by the incoming governor—of Rebolledo than previous governors had received. The Spaniards carefully considered the workings of the colonial administration, and urged future governors and clerics to help, not hinder, each other. After the struggle between mission and secular authorities subsided, the tensions created by the rancorous clash of strong personalities calmed with the appointment of a new governor and a new provincial. Florida's administrators worked more harmoniously and provided a united front to mission Indians. Florida's natives found it increasingly difficult to play one side off the other when Spanish governors and friars cooperated.

The post-Rebolledo amity among Florida's colonial authorities allowed for a more orderly handling of the next crisis in the Spanish-Indian relationship. In 1675, the Bishop of Cuba, Gabriel Díaz Vara Calderón, toured the Florida missions to see for himself what the friars had wrought. He noted that the doctrineros attended native festivals "to prevent indecent and lewd conduct," and that the Indians were not, as the more cynical contended, "idolators," for "they embrace with devotion the mysteries of our holy faith."[25] But he expressed to fray Juan de Paiva, guardian of San Luis de Talimali, deep reservations about the Apalachee Indians' sport. The natives played several games, including a form of lacrosse and something like field hockey called *chunkey*. But their most popular pastime was a game that was a cross between soccer and rugby. Its Indian name was never recorded, but the Spaniards referred to it unimaginatively as *el juego de la pelota*, the ballgame.

Villages challenged each other to games that took on the fevered pitch of battles; each side sent up to fifty players, painted with symbolic colors and markings and greased with animal fat, onto the field at once. Starting at midday, games continued until darkness or one team scored eleven points. Players tried to kick a dried buckskin ball stuffed with hair and mud slightly larger than a musket ball against a tall goalpost. Perched atop the post was a nest adorned with seashells and a stuffed eagle. Kicking the ball into the nest earned two points. Games were extremely violent and players were frequently carried from the field with broken bones; some players died in the contest.[26] Bishop Calderón objected to the game's violence and the significant wagering that accompanied its play. Fray Juan de Paiva, sympathetic to the Apalachees' need for recreation and cognizant of their love of the sport, reluctantly agreed to investigate the ball game further. What he learned changed his opinion and set off a campaign to eradicate the pastime from Florida.

Paiva enlisted two Christian Indians who eagerly researched the game's origins, superstitions, and practices. Juan Mendoza, chief of Talimali, interpreter for the mission church, and captain of the militia, and Diego Salvador, an interpreter for the king and sergeant major in the militia, interviewed Apalachee elders and visiting interpreters. As leaders in the provincial capital of San Luis, a town with a large doctrina and a garrison, Mendoza and Salvador were enmeshed in the Spanish colonial regime. They compiled their findings and reported them to fray Juan. According to legend, a rivalry between two mythic chieftains begot the Apalachee ballgame and from them originated the game's rules, practices, and strategies for victory. Game poles had to be raised with special attention to the cardinal directions and accompanied by festive dances and sacred blessings from local leaders. Under the soil at the foot of the pole the Apalachees buried a scalp or a skull. There were prescriptions for every facet of the ballgame. Apalachees shaped a game ball only from deerskin from the "animal's hooves" and filled with clay. They cast spells on the ball and on rival teams by putting hair from those killed by a town's warriors in the ball, building new fires, and drinking the Black Drink, cacina. Towns conducted countermeasures to defend against rivals' witchcraft by boiling the carcass of a turkey, squirrel, or raccoon to form a mush that players painted themselves with before a match. Leaders fasted and smoked sacred tobacco to curry favor and strength for their teams.[27] For fray Juan, the devil was literally in those details.

As if the pagan "superstitions" the friar associated with the ball game were not sufficient to condemn the sport, fray Juan also enumerated the detrimental effects the pastime had on Apalachee communities. The Franciscan bemoaned the game's barbarity, the mistrust it fostered between towns, the license given to players' slothfulness and poor behavior, the irresponsibility of fans who abandoned their homes, fields, and children to attend matches, and the reckless gambling and bribery involved in each contest. The ball game's vices were plain and the Indians' reasons for continuing the game—it was their sole entertainment, it was a cherished tradition, and the "pagan" practices associated with it had fallen into disuse—were unpersuasive to the skeptical missionary. "Nor did I arrive yesterday, as they say," fumed the doctrinero.[28] The friar's bravado was meant to cover his embarrassment. Fray Juan had served in Florida for thirteen years and had never criticized the ballgame until prompted by the visiting bishop. We can only guess whether his myopia was selective or genuine. His fury, however, was sincere.

Fray Juan dismissed charges that abolition of the ball game would cause "the land to rise up" by maintaining that the threat of violence should never deter the Spaniards from their moral obligations. "What have we come to?" he stormed, "to adjust ourselves to their laws and abuses in preaching the evangelical law to them, in correcting their vices, in teaching them virtue?" "God's church would have been in a fine fix, if, out of fear, it had ceased to preach the holy gospel and to correct and to chastise evil," he continued. "There is no other course to follow."[29]

As the guardian of the Apalachee's principal village, San Luis de Talimali, fray Juan carried a great deal of clout. His influence extended to St. Augustine where Governor Pablo de Hita Salazar, his sergeant major Domingo de Leturiondo, and the provincial lieutenant Juan Fernández de Florencia agreed to enforce the missionary's sanction. That the lieutenant of Apalachee was the brother of the Franciscans' president only promoted Spanish unity. Church and state were of the same mind, and the secular authorities took as much pride as their ecclesiastical counterparts in securing the ball game's demise.[30] Leturiondo's 1677 visitation focused in part on the ball game so "that it may be evident how legitimate were the causes for extinguishing it." The sergeant major's inquiry was fair. He told the Apalachees straightforwardly "if [the ball game] should be evil, let it be declared for such and be extinguished for the rest of time. And if it is not a source of troubles, let them play it freely." The Apalachee chiefs agreed to a man that the game should be forbidden.[31] Given the cooperation between the friars and the soldiers, the Apalachees found it difficult to enlist one or the other to their cause. Those who protested the ban, claimed the native leaders, were "the interested players, who had the said game as a profession," and the rest of the Apalachees had "already forgotten about it."[32] While the chieftains exaggerated their conviction that the game was not missed, they knew that there was no way to combat both the missionaries and the soldiers simultaneously.

Not so in Timucua where Indian leaders still bristled from the Spaniards' artless diplomacy. When Leturiondo told the Timucuas that the natives' version of the ball game should cease, the chiefs informed the visitor that "they did not practice such superstitions" like the Apalachees. Having no "other games or entertainments with which to enjoy themselves" and because it was "a very ancient practice," the Timucuas wished to continue playing their sport. For the Timucuas, Leturiondo responded predictably when he argued that the prohibition in Apalachee should extend to their version of the game. The visitor added that the Timucuas "had a greater obligation because of being Christians for a longer time than those of Apalachee." If the Timucuas "continue to play it," Leturiondo explained, "the Apalachee would also want to, and the result would be a discord and a consequence that would lead to unrest." The Timucuas felt little responsibility to provide examples of "Christian" living for their western neighbors and could not stomach being punished for something the Apalachees did. The Timucuan chiefs protested again that "among them there had never been nor were there any bad abuses." Instead, "they played it rather cleanly and plainly without any fraud as there was in the province of Apalachee." To his credit, Leturiondo recognized the determination behind the Timucuas' reluctance and set the matter aside for further investigation by the governor, the father provincial, and St. Augustine's parish priest.[33]

Despite the united front the Spanish colonial authorities showed to Florida's Indians in their attempts to rid the provinces of the ball game, the natives continued playing. The Spaniards had to reiterate their censure of the pastime in a visitation seven years later. In 1694, visitador Joaquín de Florencia asked "all people from caciques to transients . . . whether they observe the orders and prohibitions that have been issues concerning the ball game." Other Indian traditions certainly continued and did not escape Spanish notice. The inspector specifically inquired if natives performed "indecent" dances, cured "after the fashion of heathenism," or practiced "customs and abuses from their past that may result in harm to their souls."[34] By the end of the visitation, the invaders and the Indians reached some compromise. Florencia left orders that no Spaniard "prohibit the natives from performing the dances that they hold customarily, and that they [Spaniards] are not to set the hour or the time for them, except in Lent, which is not a proper time." Only "the indecent and obscene dances" were prohibited.

Presumably, the friars had discretion to determine which rites qualified. But even after decades of Christianization, Florida's mission Indians conducted traditional cures and resorted to shamans. Chiefs continued to allow their people to work fields for the support of "*curanderos* [curers, sorcerers] as is the practice." [35]

By the late 1670s, Florida's Indians no longer resorted to traditional forms of rebellion to make their point. They had become as skilled in European diplomacy as in European occupations and crafts. Indians said the appropriate things when officials quizzed them, but negotiated to secure the right to do many things that native custom dictated. They learned to employ Spanish methods to exercise some freedom of traditional expression. Natives also used Spanish visitations to voice their concerns and to seek justice. They quietly requested secret meetings with the visitador to complain about the misdeeds of Lieutenant Diego de Jaen, and secured his recall to St. Augustine. On other occasions, natives refused governors' requests that villages relocate or take on further duties in the colonial economy.[36] In the aftermath of various Indian rebellions and the ballgame investigation, Florida's Indians and Spaniards renegotiated the terms of cultural engagement. Visitas became more pedantic, methodical, and bureaucratic, fueled less by religious crusades to extirpate "pagan" practices or "heathen" behavior, and more concerned with the everyday logistics of labor drafts, taxation, and chains of command. *La Florida* appeared ready to enter colonial maturity.[37]

⎯⎯ᛟ᷁᠊ᶮᎧᎧᛜᛜᏂ᠊᠊᠊⎯⎯

The acrimony between the colonial representatives of church and state in New Mexico was not so easily quieted. Where personal relationships between secular and religious figures mended old antagonisms and allowed for more cooperative colonial governance in Florida, personal aversions and ambitions among New Mexico's colonial leadership exacerbated disagreements over jurisdiction and influence with Pueblos. Tensions grew so heated in New Mexico that rivals came to blows, arrested each other, and resorted to sedition and espionage. New Mexico's jurisdictional struggle went far beyond Florida's pen-and-paper conflict. The Pueblos' response to the governmental chaos took on a more ominous tenor as well.

Controversy between the Franciscan custodian and the governors started in the earliest decades of New Mexico's colonization. With the survival of the frontier settlement in doubt, determining who held the reins of power in the colonial administration appeared equally uncertain. As early as 1613, friars and governors jockeyed for position. In a bid to secure more power, fray Isidro Ordóñez falsified documents so he could exercise inquisitorial authority and check any sovereignty that secular authorities tried to establish. When Governor Pedro de Peralta requested labor drafts from distant missions to march to the villa of Santa Fé, fray Isidro ordered his missionaries to forbid the natives to leave. On another occasion, the governor sent a military force to collect tribute from the Pueblos during the Feast of Pentecost, so Ordóñez had him arrested and investigated for heresy. The incautious custodian later came to blows with one of his own friars who disagreed with some of his policies. Eventually the Franciscans replaced Ordóñez and hoped that new personnel would settle the situation.[38]

It was not to be. Four years later, two equally stubborn men, fray Esteban de Perea and Governor Juan de Eulate, vied for political supremacy. According to at least two friars, Eulate was fond of saying to anyone who would listen that "the king is my chief," and that the custodian had no jurisdictional authority over laymen. His contempt both for the doctrineros and for their work was evident: the governor insulted the friars "in front of Spaniards and Indians with bad sounding words," and even wished he could give troublesome Franciscans a caning. Eulate discouraged settlers and Indians from assisting in the construction of mission churches, and refused to send soldiers to escort guardians to their posts. In an effort to win Pueblo support and to wrest power from the missionaries, Eulate told the Tewas that "they did not have to do anything that the ministers ordered them to do, neither guard their horses or herds." He absolved them from all duties except going to church "when the friars ring the bell," but paradoxically allowed them to practice traditional rites and promised a royal order permitting the Indians religious discretion.[39]

Eulate's personal treatment of the Pueblos, however, was harsh compared to his lenient religious policy. Convinced that he could persuade Indians to work "without paying them," the governor rounded up natives and deposited them on estancias as free laborers. Against clear royal orders, Eulate tapped Pueblos to carry tribute goods he collected, despite the availability of horses. He led slave raids among the nomadic tribes of the Southwest and sold the victims for profit in New Spain; he also granted his soldiers *vales*, or permits, to snatch orphans in mission villages and bind them as household servants. Exasperated friars also complained that both the governor's estancia and the farms of other Spanish settlers encroached on mission lands and interfered with Pueblo agriculture and herding.[40]

Eulate may have been ruthless, but he was not the only one guilty of abusing Pueblos in New Mexico. Friars also taxed native labor and overzealously punished neophytes for their "sins." Eulate alerted the viceroy in Mexico City to the friars' trespasses on the northern frontier. He claimed that they unduly hindered the governor's ability to effectively run the colony and to collect native tribute. Equally offensive were the friars' tendencies to "send to the mountains a great number of Indians for things of little necessity," and to have sinners' "hair sheared, a punishment from which they suffer very great affliction because it is for them the greatest affront that there is." Some natives were so offended by the missionaries' poor treatment, Eulate claimed, that they fled to Acoma and returned "to idolatry." The clerics inconsistently performed their priestly duties in the missions, and used their sacerdotal power to influence whomever they wished.[41]

Indeed, letters from both *custodio* Perea and Governor Eulate complaining about each other's misdeeds reached Viceroy Diego Fernández de Córdova. In an effort to settle a jurisdictional controversy that had gone on too long, Fernandez convened a junta, or council, on the matter and sent the conclusions to both men. His letters carefully outlined the jurisdictional responsibilities of the secular and ecclesiastical arms of the colonial government, and urged both governor and custodian to maintain "good and courteous relations," and to consult with each other. He ordered abuses on both sides corrected, but ultimately established the authority of the governor, the king's representative, as supreme in the colony. After listening to the opinions of the friars, his council, and other advisors, the governor "alone may decide what may seem to you best for His Majesty's service," Viceroy Fernández explained, "neither the Said father custodian nor any other Religious may interfere."[42]

Cut to the quick by the viceroy's rebuke, fray Francisco Perea wrote independently and secretly to the Holy Office of the Inquisition in Mexico City. Eventually, Perea's complaints about the governor's sacrilegious behavior registered with the tribunal, which appointed fray Alonso de Benavides official inquisitor for New Mexico. Simultaneously, the

Figure 8:
Convento of San Esteban, Acoma, constructed between 1629 and 1640. Photograph by the author.

Franciscans elected fray Alonso their new custodian.[43] With two strokes, the Franciscans secured recognized authority over the governor in matters of faith and circumvented Viceroy Fernández' elucidation on colonial administrative jurisdiction. The friars had raised the stakes in New Mexico's church-state conflict.

Relations between the next several governors and the resident friars were contaminated by decades of rancor, and soon the poisonous atmosphere affected the Indians. Soldiers seized native children and pressed them into domestic service. Other Indians collected and carried food to governors' warehouses, painted or wove blankets, bunting, and hangings, or traveled great distances to trade hides to fill the governor's purse. With scant resources and little economic opportunity, New Mexico's only recognized asset was the Indians themselves. Governors' hope for financial gain conflicted with the Franciscans' influence on native converts. In the ensuing contest for control over the Indians, governors failed to show support for the friars' conversion efforts; their contempt was not lost on observant Pueblos. Fray Pedro de Zambrano warned that the Indians no longer "want to attend instruction or mass," as they were obligated to do. In February 1632 the Zuñis killed both the guardian at Hawikuh and a second friar they were guiding to northern Sonora. No Spanish soldiers were near the distant western pueblos, and a tardy punitive expedition found the Zuñi houses abandoned. Rebel natives remained in Corn Mountain for three years before they quietly returned to their villages. Spanish infighting both delayed the reestablishment of the missions and hampered any attempt to punish the natives responsible for the uprising.[44]

With the death of fray Francisco Perea in the winter of 1638–39, New Mexico's Holy Office became temporarily vacant. Luís de Rosas, a strong-willed governor who resented ecclesiastical intrusion into secular affairs, challenged the Franciscans at this opportune time and was, therefore, less fettered by inquisitorial oversight. He followed the same tactics his predecessors had by enlisting mission Indians to weave *mantas* (woolen or cotton blankets) and other textiles, or to plant crops for sale in New Spain and forcing natives to toil in his personal workshop in Santa Fé. Rosas also violently encroached on the Apache and Plains trade with the eastern pueblos. The governor brazenly arrested the friar posted at Pecos, promised the mission Indians that they could revert to traditional practices if they produced more hides and mantas for shipment south, and invaded neighboring Apache camps to supply his burgeoning slave trade.[45] With alarming regularity, Apaches exacted retribution for the governor's slaving on mission Pueblos.

Conflicts with Governor Rosas became more openly antagonistic when the governor accompanied a 1636 expedition to northern Sonora. Ostensibly, the trip was to establish five missions among the Ipotlapiguas and Zipias, but the governor seized the opportunity to plunder native homes for potential trade goods. The friars protested without result. Finally, a sermon delivered during daily mass erased any pretense of cordiality between the friars and the governor. Fray Antonio de Arteaga, head of the band of Franciscans assigned to the Sonora expedition, preached the responsibility of Catholic princes to defend church dogma, and stated emphatically that civil law was subordinate to church law. Before the assembled congregation, which included potential converts and Christian Pueblos accompanying the Spaniards, Governor Rosas interrupted the service, called the priest a liar, and left with most of his soldiers. "Many of the Christian Indians wondered how they will believe what the Fathers preached and taught if the governor said publicly that they lied," fretted fray Antonio.[46] The doctrinero's concerns were prophetic. Within two years, Taos rebels killed their friar and two other Spaniards, and tried to spread the uprising to neighboring Picuris. Violence prompted the missionaries to abandon Zuñi in 1639. The Jémez Pueblos rose against their resident guardian in 1644 and resisted Spanish retaliatory efforts until 1647. Two years later the Jémez, along with several Keres and Tiwa pueblos, rebelled again and did not surrender until 1653. Piros revolted between 1665 and 1668 and Salinas followed suit a few years later. Spanish punitive expeditions were not only tardy in most cases, but were an excuse to sack native towns rather than to reestablish Christian missions.[47]

Like the Indians, the doctrineros were up in arms. Fearing the volatility of mission Pueblos and the arbitrary leadership of the governor, the friars fled their posts. In April 1640, they convened at the custodian's church of Santo Domingo and agreed to send a two-man delegation to the capital to reason with Rosas. The governor was so enraged by the friars' actions that he bloodied the emissaries with a stick and threw their battered bodies in prison. Rosas eventually expelled them from Santa Fé and initiated a furious campaign against the power of the Franciscans. He seized mission herds kept in three Tewa pueblos and erected a garrison at San Ildefonso. Later, Rosas demolished church buildings at San Miguel, Sandia, and Cuarac, and allowed his men to rob sacristies and drive off the friars.[48] The governor's scandalous behavior nearly caused civil war.

Lengthy inquiries, Rosas' death, and the ascendancy of new governors and new custodians calmed the seething colony long enough for its friars and inhabitants to ready themselves for the next church-state crisis. Throughout the 1640s and 1650s ecclesiastical and secular authorities sent independent annual reports to Mexico City and secretly reported on the others' activities. Recriminations and counteraccusations marked the tenures of each new governor and custodian alike, and both sides were guilty of hyperbole. Governors continued to seek means of extracting wealth from the northern frontier, and Franciscans denied the sacraments to allies of the governors and excommunicated rivals with regularity.[49]

The combustible conflict met its spark in 1659 when Bernardo López de Mendizábal assumed the governorship of New Mexico. López wanted his appointment to be profitable, and knew that the missionaries, with their influence on Indians, stood in the way. He enlisted the *alcalde mayor*, his provincial administrator and justice of the peace, of the Salinas district, Captain Nicolás de Aguilar, to investigate natives' complaints about the friars' behavior. The governor wanted to drive a wedge between mission Pueblos and their guardians. Aguilar was the right man for the job. The captain traveled to several pueblos in his jurisdiction drumming up trade. In the process he announced to the Pueblos he met that "they might live just as they chose, and that they should be punished for no fault, either by the father, the fiscales, or the captains." To prove the veracity of his claims, Aguilar gently scolded two Indians caught in "illicit intercourse," and "set them at liberty without punishment." Word of the governor's leniency with natives' transgressions spread. Pueblos who had been punished by the friars for "concubinage" sought redress from López; the governor informed them that "they might leave their pueblos and go live wherever they wished." While departing their homes was little incentive, the license to do so emboldened the mission Indians. Fray Miguel de Sacristán suggested that the friars had lost the power "to correct, teach, or preach." "On the contrary the Indians have complete liberty of conscience," he lamented, and the governor assured both settlers and Pueblos that "the ministers have been deceiving them." Some friars claimed that when famine and disease hit the already unstable missions, they were forced to bribe their

congregations with an entire week's rations "to keep them from wandering away." The governor's campaign against the friars had made such
an impression on the natives that they no longer believed "what had
been preached and taught them, because it seemed false."[50] Intolerable
conditions were reason enough for native dissatisfaction, but New
Mexico's soldiers and friars did little to ease the Pueblos' distress.

At times it must have seemed that native adoption of Christianity
invited Spanish scorn rather than affection. The very Pueblos who
worked most closely with Spanish officials were marked for particular
torment. In June 1660, Humanas was a new and populous mission on
the eastern fringes of New Mexico. Its proximity to Apache and Plains
camps made it a potentially valuable trading post for the colonial economy as well. But recent skirmishes between Apaches and eastern Pueblos
threatened not only commercial interests but also the security of all
the missions. Governor López sent Captain Aguilar to wage war on the
Apaches of Los Siete Ríos (the Seven Rivers), and the situation was still
unstable when the feast day of Humanas' patron, San Buenaventura,
arrived. The Spaniards had only recently finished the Humanas church,
and the pueblo lacked Indian sacristans and acolytes to assist the
Catholic services. The guardian fray Diego de Santander invited fray
Nicolás de Freitas of nearby Cuarac to come with twenty cantors and
sacristans to liven up the celebrations. But when the Cuarac Pueblos
arrived, Captain Aguilar became irate. Several Apaches were at
Humanas, and the alcalde mayor worried that a mêlée might erupt.

What happened next was a source of some dispute. The friars
claimed that Aguilar ordered his men to give the Cuarac Christians "fifty
lashes" for coming to Humanas. Aguilar admitted that the Indians "had
been ordered not to go to the pueblos of Humanas and Tavira when
the Apaches are there because if they can avoid seeing each other they
will not go to war." But the captain denied beating the Cuaracs. Some
exchange occurred, however, for the festival was interrupted and the
Cuarac sacristans and cantors "have not dared to come [to Humanas]
to sing mass and the divine offices have been prevented."[51] In another
incident, fray Antonio Aguado from Abó accused Aguilar of scaring off
a talented interpreter "with whose aid he administered the sacraments
to the Indians, and supplied what he lacked of that language in administering to the Indians, and in preaching." Other Franciscans complained
that Aguilar turned out Indian fiscals who administered punishments

to native catechists, removed cantors and sacristans from their posts, and told the Pueblos that they should not be harmed by any Spaniards.[52]

Despite his own mistreatment of mission Pueblos, Captain Aguilar had legitimate complaints against the missionaries. His investigations uncovered numerous instances of the Franciscans' sexual impropriety and punitive excess. Some cases certainly were exaggerated, but enough misdeeds warranted censure by the custodian to suggest a pattern of misbehavior. Muza, a cantor from Tajique, accused fray Diego de Parraga of stealing his wife, fathering a child by her, and raping twenty other Indian women. Captain Aguilar contended that the guardian admitted his sins, but the custodian interceded on the wayward missionary's behalf. He was quietly removed from his post.[53] Governor López swore that fray Luís Martínez of Taos raped a Pueblo woman and, when she complained to the authorities, "cut the woman's throat" and hid the body in the church.[54]

Not all the accusations were so fantastic. Fray Nicolás de Freitas, also accused of rape, had a female penitent beaten and her hair cropped for some unrecorded offense. Captain Aguilar told Governor López that in the Hopi village of Shongopovi, fray Salvador Guerra discovered a cache of "feathers, or idols, and consequently seized them and ordered turpentine brought so as to set fire to them." The notary recording Aguilar's testimony was imprecise; it was not clear whether the captain meant that the friar burned the "idols" or the "idolaters," but a few Hopis were in fact scalded in the incident; one died.[55]

Less violent was the penance meted out in another Hopi mission. Missionaries imposed stiff punishments on the Pueblos who "walked about praying in penitence, carrying a cross and some large beads, and wearing haircloth shirts." Fray Benito de la Natividad of Socorro scandalously wrote down his congregation's confessions. Since he had poor command of the natives' language, he sent the Indians to confess to a neighboring missionary, who then reported the confessions to fray Benito. The doctrinero's violation of the sacrosanct confessional was ready fuel for the governor's attack on the missions.[56]

At the heart of the governor's assault was his desire to challenge the missionaries' economic clout. In this concern, López was not alone. The cabildo griped bitterly about the friars' stranglehold on native labor. "The inhabitants are few, poor, and have little knowledge of business affairs or of anything except arms, while the religious are many and enjoy rich profits, acquired from the labor of the natives and the poverty of the Spaniards," moaned the council of Santa Fé. "These profits were neither asked for nor given as alms but [acquired] from private dealings and contracts." The Franciscans' livestock holdings were opulent, according to the cabildo's reckoning. Each mission had "from one to two thousand sheep, while few inhabitants have as many as five hundred and most have no more than a hundred." As a remedy, the cabildo asked the viceroy to distribute the friars' cattle and sheep among the colony's poor. This solution would have residual benefits as well. "A great deal of trouble would be saved the Indians," claimed the council, "for they are now occupied in guarding the cattle and horses and the very large fields of wheat and corn that they plant as well as the vegetable gardens and orchards, and the stables." Native porters, cooks, woodchoppers, and millers would also win deserved relief from their missionary taskmasters.[57] Governor López could not have agreed more with the cabildo's assessment. "It cannot be to the interest of divine worship, nor does God desire, that [the friars] should keep the Indians in dungeons and workshops weaving frieze [coarse woolen fabric, like flannel] and sackcloth to be sold there and to be sent to other provinces, without paying the Indians for their labor," López reasoned. Moreover, the guardians corralled so many cattle and sheep around the convent that "one could not stand the stench in the church."[58]

The Franciscans detected quite a different odor, that of a rat. The governor revealed his true face as a heretic and duplicitous profiteer, the friars claimed, when he supported the Pueblos' right to dance the *kachinas*. Individual doctrineros had spoken out against the traditional Pueblo rites and most considered them a part of their congregations' "pagan" past. But López not only ordered visiting Pueblos to dance the kachinas for him, he dismissed the friars' concerns about their sinister inspiration. "This dance contains nothing more than this 'Hu-hu-hu,'" López said imitating the performers' chants, "and these thieving friars say that it is superstitious."[59] The governor was savvy enough to recognize that each pueblo practiced its own diverse customs, but he nevertheless believed that the kachinas were "simply an exhibition of agility," and had no more evil intentions than "the *zarambeque*" and other dances which the Spaniards dance."[60] Fray Francisco de Salazar, guardian of Senecú, warned that the license the governor gave to native dances left the Indians "totally lost, without faith, without law, and without devotion to the

Church or respect for their ministers." Fray Nicolás de Freitas wrote that the governor had destroyed "these tender children of the Church, who, even those who are only thirty years old, still recall the shadows of their heathenism."[61]

In an effort to counter the governor's assertion that the kachinas were harmless, New Mexican missionaries resorted to a technique familiar to their counterparts in Florida. They enlisted Indian help. Estéban Clemente, Tanoan governor of Las Salinas and valued interpreter of six Pueblo languages, penned a diatribe against "the catzinas which I know to be evil." Clemente described a variety of dances and rituals that included fasting, dancing in "very ugly painted masks," and supplicating the spirits with offerings on small public altars. The native governor's epistle validated the friars' concerns about the kachinas' demonic purposes. It suggested that the dancers "make the people think that they come from the other life to speak to them."[62] Maintaining that the Pueblos were impressionable and naïve, the friars worried that "the poor things" were so easily gulled by the apostate governor and the demonic native shamans.[63]

While some friars' analysis of Pueblo Christianity was rose-colored, there was no doubt that the mission Indians began dancing the kachinas openly and without blush. After the governor had permitted the traditional dances, Pueblo holy men returned from exile and announced that the people "might be happy now, for [they] had come to be with them."[64] The Pueblos "acted as if they had never been converted " and neglected all duties to their mission churches and their guardians. Predictably, the governor charged that the Indians "do not attend mass and the teaching of the doctrine . . . because they flee from the excessive work which the religious make them do under the guise of instruction." The friars blamed the governor's irresponsible orders and their enforcement by military dupes.[65] Ironically, it was the one thing on which the governor and the Franciscans agreed: the Pueblos no longer attended mission services. "They bring out to the plaza publicly little temples full of idols in order to worship them and make offerings to them," moaned fray Garcia de San Francisco; "this situation cannot be remedied."[66]

The Office of the Holy Inquisition settled the bureaucratic dispute between secular and ecclesiastical branches of New Mexico's colonial government. In 1662 they arrested Governor Bernardo López de Mendizábal, whose various trials lasted for four years. He died in an inquisition prison awaiting a resolution of his case. The end of the López affair reestablished the missionaries' rights to unpaid native labor and confirmed the governor's right to ensure the economic development of the colony. With it came the decision to revert to the status quo ante without resolving, once and for all, the jurisdictional squabbles that created such chaos.[67]

But the damage to the missionary effort had been done. The friars had lost not only authority with their native charges but any headway they had made in converting the Pueblo populations. New Mexico's governors had fought with the Franciscans over Indian labor and access to native trade, and in the process secular authorities repeatedly ordered Pueblos to ignore the friars and their commands. Each bilious controversy tainted the Spaniards' relations with the mission Indians. The Spanish conquest of New Mexico had established a mode of operation that the natives had begun to understand and use to their own satisfaction. But when clerics and governors traded caustic words and even came to blows, it was impossible for the Pueblos to know if the old rules still applied. They received conflicting messages from friars who instructed them to love their neighbors but not the soldiers; and from governors, who told them to obey Spanish hegemony but not its religious representatives. Instability led to widespread Pueblo defection and resumption of traditional forms of worship.

Spaniards in New Mexico had never effectively stamped out traditional Pueblo practices; suppression was sporadic. The kachina dances, as well as other Pueblo ceremonies, had continued throughout the Spaniards' seventeenth-century tenure. Under the circumstances of the sixteenth- and early seventeenth-century military conquest, the Pueblos wisely took their religious rites literally underground, into their kivas. Encouraged by Governor López' sanction and the intra-colonial combat among soldiers and missionaries, the Pueblos brought their secret practices into the light of day and threw off any pretense of adhering to the Spaniards' Christianity. The kachina wars of the 1660s revealed the friars' tenuous hold on the mission Pueblos and signaled the beginning of a dangerous new stage in Spanish-Indian relations in New Mexico. Governors expected prosperous economic and military colonies, while friars hoped for native cities of God. The Indians harbored suspicions about both.

By the 1670s, Indians in Florida and New Mexico had learned what colonization by Spanish missionaries and soldiers meant. Despite earlier impressions that friars could be flexible in their religious instruction and that native acceptance of foreign ideas was negotiable, natives discovered that the Spaniards were particular about native labor and faith. When cultural negotiations soured, Indians chose rebellion to make their cases. Prompted by and taking advantage of intra-colonial conflict between governors and missionaries, the Apalachee rebellion in 1647 and the Timucua revolt in 1656 demonstrated Indians' ability to threaten the operation of the Florida colony. By the 1670s, Spanish military suppression had made native uprisings ineffective. Friars and governors patched up their differences and briefly united to outlaw the natives' ballgame. Once the ecclesiastical and secular arms of Spain's colonial structure cooperated, Indians found it easier to return to the terms of cultural negotiation established in the 1630s. The Florida revolts failed to rid the peninsula of Spaniards, but succeeded in reintroducing the negotiation of culture in Spanish colonization.

For the Pueblos in New Mexico, revolts were not intended to achieve an understanding between conquered and conqueror. The Pueblos wanted to expel the Spanish invaders. Like their Florida counterparts, Indians found the virulent church-state conflict disturbing. But relations between governors and friars in New Mexico were far worse than those of Florida's colonizers. Farther removed from colonial supply sources and appellate overseers, New Mexico's secular and ecclesiastical authorities had more motive and opportunity to turn against each other than their counterparts in Florida. New Mexico's aridity and scant resources made competition for the Indians—the source of the colony's "wealth"—more intense. Labor and tribute burdens grew more demanding, and increased violence between Spaniards, Apaches, and Pueblos exacerbated already grim conditions. Increasingly caught in the middle of an escalating Spanish civil war, Pueblos opted to rid themselves of Spanish interlopers. By the 1670s, isolated uprisings and regional rebellions had failed to drive the Spaniards away. Pueblo rebellions were more numerous, too, because leaders did not have to establish a chiefdom-wide consensus. War-minded leaders convinced town councils, and at times neighbors, to implement quick attacks. The protracted negotiations among chiefs and councils required for Florida's native rebellions hurt the Indians' chances of success. Even if periodic revolts among the Pueblos did not permanently remove Spanish soldiers and missionaries from their towns, the Indians learned important lessons about unity in the face of a common enemy.

CHAPTER FIVE

Breaking Faith

If the jug goes too many times to the fountain, it finally is broken.
— fray antonio carbonel,
guardian of nambé pueblo,
march 31, 1696

The end of the Spanish missions in Florida and New Mexico was as prolonged as the conquest had been. Decisive moments—such as the Pueblos' successful revolt in 1680—punctuated protracted episodes of retreat, resettlement, and eventual abandonment. From the 1670s through the century's close, Indians and Spaniards moved to an increasingly discordant rhythm. Whether intended or not, decades of Spanish conquest and colonization brought Indians previously unknown pathogens, insatiable labor demands, adverse dietary changes, and increased tensions among testy native neighbors. All combined to disrupt and destabilize Indian-Spanish relations. Mission conditions became desperate as enemy attacks became more frequent and climatic changes exacerbated cycles of drought, crop failure, and famine. Facing annihilation, Indians had to assess the social, political, and religious repercussions of submitting to Spanish colonization.

Physical evidence was the most poignant indicator of the effects decades of conquest and missionization had. To be sure, native communities were not strangers to poor health or dire circumstances before the Spaniards arrived on the scene. Precontact peoples had altered their lives drastically around 1000 BCE (Before Common Era), when sedentary groups embraced an intensive agricultural regime. Committing valuable time to prepare soil, plant seeds, care for plants, harvest crops, and store produce restricted the days and weeks Indians had once dedicated to gathering, fishing, and hunting. Concern for their fields and homes limited native forays to less distant territories. Agricultural communities worked hard, but farming did not exact the same physical toll that the months of tracking game or reaping the fruits of frontier waters did. Supplementing native diets with gathered nuts and berries, animal protein, and seafood did not cease but declined, especially for the Apalachee and the land-locked Pueblo peoples. These complex agricultural communities relied more heavily on maize consumption. Corn's high sugar content contributed to greater tooth decay, and its lack of iron increased Indians' risk of anemia. Native nutrition became less balanced.[1]

Eating large amounts of maize was only one of several health concerns Indian communities faced before Spaniards arrived. Infant mortality was high, and it was common for children who survived birth to die before reaching their eighth birthday. The rasps of respiratory problems or the sharp stabs of gastrointestinal ailments were particularly ominous signs for young Indians. Those who reached maturity expected to live for a total of forty years, though native women were twice as likely to survive past forty-five. But surviving childhood did not mean that Indians were free from sickness. The most common afflictions came from parasites, particularly tapeworm, pinworm, nematodes, and fungi, which flourished in concentrated native communities that lived close to their dogs, food supply, and human waste. More deadly were the fevers, chills, fatigue and coughs of tuberculosis, and the lesions, ulcers, liver damage, and deterioration of the skeletal, cardiovascular, and nervous systems associated with venereal syphilis. Tuberculosis and syphilis scourged precontact peoples, but we know of no epidemic diseases that spread through Florida or New Mexico before Europeans landed on New World shores.[2]

The patterns precontact Indians had established for survival within their respective environments helped dictate how they reacted to Spanish colonists, animals, plants, and germs. Florida's natives congregated in towns, but their settlements were not permanent. Villages moved periodically to allow depleted areas to restore exhausted flora and soil. Yet southeastern Indians' mobility did not involve journeys far afield. Timucuas and Guales remained within relatively fixed boundaries, and so endured longer and more intensive contact with Spanish newcomers. Their contiguous settlements were more susceptible to disease than the Apalachees, who had less direct contact with Spanish missions. Pueblo communities did not seem to suffer the demographic collapse their Florida counterparts did because their traditional strategies for survival in the unforgiving Southwest better prepared them for the cultural collision with Spaniards. Pueblos were accustomed to cycles of drought, depletion of agricultural soils, and warfare, and had mitigated these conditions by migrating to newer, more fertile lands, by aggregating with other clans, and by creating smaller settlements to reduce the strain on local resources. By residing in small towns, separated by substantial distances, the Pueblos were better prepared for the effects immigrant diseases and Spanish colonial policies would have on their diets, physiological development, and death rate. Thus, not every mission village suffered similar rates of population decline, or experienced cultural contact with the same harshness.[3]

Once Spaniards established chains of doctrinas across the landscapes of the northern frontiers, the stress on mission Indians in each colony grew more intense. The process of reducing and congregating native communities for proselytizing created settlement crowd conditions like those in Europe. The Spaniards thought of native missions as New World versions of parishes and towns they remembered from home; unknowingly their strict regulation of native settlements allowed the ills of the Old World to run rampant in mission environments that were susceptible to disease. Concentrated populations living in poor or unsanitary sites encouraged the spread of pathogens, and drastically increased the incidence of diarrhea among mission Indians. The hacking cough of influenza and diphtheria's deadly wheeze were commonly heard in mission congregations; the pustules of smallpox and the red rash of typhus were more noticeable than the smear of holy oils. Diseased Indians, sweaty with fever, choked with phlegm, and clouded with delirium, must have been a terrible sight.[4]

The psychological trauma was as acute as the physical loss of kin and townspeople. Whether the demographic collapse was drastic and rapid, or limited and slow, the effect of mysterious microbes on Indians' minds, hearts, and spirits was cataclysmic. Even for Indians familiar with grim death and the fickleness of life, the symptoms of these new diseases were alarming and difficult to explain. The scars of smallpox and measles disfigured corpses and survivors alike. The sudden demise of ill family members and important political and religious leaders or the departure

of nervous townspeople for less infected villages disrupted social networks and community ties. Equally troubling was medicine men's inability to treat the sick. Traditional diagnoses and treatments rarely had the
desired effect, and the subsequent crisis in spiritual faith created greater
chaos in mission towns.

The changes that Spanish conquest imposed on native labor and diet
were radical as well. Spanish Franciscans, encomenderos, and public
officials required greater proportions of Indians' time than the native
elite had in precontact times. Demands for larger and more numerous
fields to support mendicant friars, military men, government officers,
land-holding colonists, and burgeoning export markets taxed Indian
workers. The Indians literally felt the work levies in their bones. The
lifting, pushing, carrying, and digging laborers did for Spaniards, cou-
pled with chronic dehydration and a greater consumption of carbohy-
drates, weakened Indians' skeletons. The detrimental effects that hard
labor and poor nutrition had on native growth and development were
visible in Indians' bent bodies, broken bones, and probable weight gain.
Mission Indians focused on planting corn to the exclusion of other foods;
missionization forced Indians to be more sedentary, and concentrated
their time on agriculture and herding. With corn readily available, natives
ate more of the sugar-packed starch and consumed less fish, meat, and
plants that had once given their blood much-needed iron, and their bodies the requisite vitamins. Indians of rank, like the Spanish colonists,
benefited from the nutritional variety afforded by European livestock,
but the majority of Indians did not eat beef, pork, chicken, or mutton.
Restrictions on native mobility curbed Indians' ability to supplement
their diets with a variety of foods, and the static work routine in the
missions and haciendas hindered their physical maturation.[5]

Demographically fractured, physically weakened, and nutritionally
limited, mission Indians received little respite. Seventeenth-century missionization in Florida and New Mexico also exacted social, political, and
spiritual tolls on the native inhabitants. When faced with the unenviable
choices of abandoning kith and kin or enduring the conditions in mission towns, Indians were understandably torn. But the social stress that
mission conditions created could not be solved easily. In both Florida
and New Mexico, warfare became a more insistent blight on mission villages. Each community had to decide whether to fight or flee, whether
to remain loyal to Spain or to cast its lot with another European or Indian

power, whether to embark on a future determined by, or devoid of, foreign influence. In missions throughout the Spanish frontiers, Indians chose their paths under vastly different circumstances.

In Florida, mission Indians seemed to remain subject to the machinations of outside forces. In the late seventeenth century, the Southeast became a crowded land. To the north, Chichimecos—called Westos by the English—pressed their way into eastern Georgia, and began raiding Guale territories. North of the Chichimecos settled something more ominous. English colonists, overflowing the entrepreneurial and territorial limits of Barbados and other Caribbean islands, relocated to coastal South Carolina and established Charles Town in 1670. The alliance forged between the Chichimecos and English Carolinians unleashed new and dangerous economic forces in the region. Both groups encroached on the trade that mission Indians conducted with non-Christian natives in the interior. Both groups claimed lands previously occupied by other Indians. But primarily both cooperated in a lucrative and increasingly voracious slave trade. Encouraged to provide labor for English plantations in Carolina and the Caribbean, the Chichimecos found the Spanish missions ideal sources of slaves. Helping raiders better execute their attacks, the English supplied them with plenty of ammunition and guns.[6]

Over the next four decades, mission Indians and Spanish settlers in Florida faced repeated attacks from English-allied Indians who relished the exotic trade goods offered in Carolina. Firearms, blankets, metal tools, and clothing came at a better price; the English did not require their native trade partners to accept their Protestant God, nor did they try to resettle them in missions or dictate rules for their "correct" behavior. Only later did the Chichimecos learn the hidden costs of dealing with Carolina.[7] Well supplied and ready for war, the Chichimecos raided Guale in 1661 and again in 1679 with new partners, the Chiluques and Yuchis. In 1680 the Chichimecos attacked the Atlantic coast a final time, but by then the ties that bound the Chichimecos to the English were frayed. The Chichimecos' strategic position and strength limited English attempts to reach the lucrative trade with the Apalachicolas in the interior, and the Carolinians resented having to deal through Indian allies. In 1682 the Westo War settled the matter; English Carolinians and Savannah warriors concentrated their wrath on the Chichimecos and nearly exterminated them. In their place migrated Shawnees and Yamasees, relative newcomers to the game of European alliances. They, like some of the mission Indians, were beginning to see which way the wind was blowing. Apalachicolas and some Yamasees grew more enmeshed with English traders and slavers.[8]

Increasingly, however, isolated attacks on individual Spanish-Indian settlements had wider, non-native appeal. The Florida frontier became embroiled in the imperial pretensions of European crowns. Wars pitting England, Holland, France, and Spain against one another reverberated on American fronts, and Florida's mission Indians and Spaniards began to feel the shock waves. At first, battles were decidedly unofficial. A series of pirate raids punctuated recurrent attacks from English-allied Indians on coastal and insular mission villages, and on St. Augustine. English corsair Robert Searles left Jamaica in 1668 to threaten Florida's capital, and the French pirates Michel, sieur de Grammont, and Nicolas Brigaut followed suit. Grammont raided in 1680 and joined Brigaut for another assault in 1683. Periodically, however, extralegal skirmishes matured into official declarations of war. That did not necessarily mean that England and Spain were always rivals. In fact, hostilities ceased in the Southeast between 1689 and 1697 during King William's War, which briefly united England and Spain in common cause against Louis XIV and France. But fighting a mutual foe in Europe did little to encourage cooperation in the colonies.[9] The wake created by Carolinians' designs on the Southeast threatened to become a tidal wave.

The agitated movement of native inhabitants in and out of vulnerable mission towns was a signal of the coming tempest. Spanish governors and friars preferred Indians to remain within the boundaries of mission villages unless called to labor or trade. Stable settlements were the first requirement of the Spaniards' religious and economic colonization. But frequent and costly invasions from northern territories and from Atlantic and Caribbean waters brought chaos to established towns, and uncertainty to mission Indians' councils. The stability of the mission chain—reckoned in terms of Indians' safety and Spaniards' effective administration of the colonies—was tenuous at best. Incessant raids robbed mission villages specifically and the colony in general of the people necessary to retain Spain's claim on the territory. The distance between St. Augustine and coastal missions grew perilously wide, as survivors from each attack fled to the capital for protection.

Convincing shell-shocked natives to return to their charred and violated homes or to move to new missions required some compromise.

Figure 9:
Friar's desk, at the reconstructed site of San Luis de
Talimali. Photograph courtesy
of Christopher R. Versen.

Some Indians wanted to build new homes, others were too afraid. In June 1680, Governor Pablo de Hita Salazar ordered Guale's provincial lieutenant, Francisco de Fuentes, to convoke native leaders to "impress upon them how important it is that they go to their houses and fields." Natives in Santa Cruz de Guadalquini had promised to move to San Juan Island, but had not done so. Their chief commanded them to relocate, and had supervised the construction of a new council house on the proposed site, but the Indians refused to go. Spanish soldiers sent to guard San Juan de Mocama were prepared to move to a new settlement with or without the local natives who dragged their feet. But the Mocamas claimed that they could not leave their planted fields.

Tupiqui Indians requested relocation, and even asked that the decimated community of San Felipe join with them for their mutual protection. But San Felipe's chief was not enthusiastic about the proposal. He feared that their numbers were so low that instead of joining, the Indians would flee into the woods. San Felipe's chief knew that moving would require his people to build a new council house and a new chieftain's home, and to plant new fields. The increased work load alone discouraged relocation. Eventually, the San Felipe Indians' fear of attack forced them to accept the plan, but they did so only on condition that the Spaniards construct a fort on the bar of San Pedro for their defense. The Indians refused to budge until the fort was completed.[10] Common Indians negotiated with their own chiefs and with the Spaniards for safer locations or better conditions before establishing new missions.

To help fill the distances created by outside invasions, Spanish authorities also encouraged Yamasee refugees fleeing the turmoil of English alliance to settle abandoned Guale towns. The Spaniards' new Yamasee allies provided a buffer between Indians armed with English guns and Spain's colonial capital. But the Spaniards went a step further. In some cases they moved Yamasee emigrants to established Christian Guale villages, and in others they settled them with Apalachees. Rebuilding after each assault made the coastal and northern settlement patterns into a political puzzle whose pieces did not quite fit. But the Spaniards were preoccupied with their tattered colonial organization and with the threat of outside attack. They were loathe to alienate Yamasees who might stabilize the colony. Their fear of defeat proved greater than their adherence to the requirements of colonization; Spaniards made only halfhearted attempts to convert Yamasee settlers. Without the pressure to accept the Spaniards' faith, Yamasees deflected Franciscan missionaries and promised to convert at some later time. When asked about their intentions, Yamasees replied that "they were not refusing to become so [Christians], but that there had not been anyone . . . who might teach them and tell them what the law of God contained." They only understood that "it is good," and that about twenty Christian Indians were buried in the church at Ivitachuco "after asking for baptism at death." But on the issue of labor, the Spaniards were more adamant. They required Yamasee repartimiento labor drafts.[11]

Tensions rose in Indian settlements where multiple native groups lived side-by-side. Authority was increasingly under dispute, and disgruntled Indians chose to leave camps and join other towns. Populations dropped so drastically that there were insufficient people to provide chieftains their privileges.[12] Fissures appeared not only in the missions' command chain but also in the governor's imperial authority. Natives avoided Spanish labor drafts with more regularity and success. With no religious connection to their European allies, the Yamasees were especially adept at evading repartimientos.[13]

To better defend distant missions and to enforce labor drafts, Governor Laureano de Torres y Ayala ordered fortifications built in Apalachee. As he explained to the king on April 15, 1696, the Apalachee Indians helped erect a wooden block house at San Luis "to assure the security of the people."[14] But the garrison proved troublesome for the Apalachees. Patricio Hinachuba, chief of Ivitachuco, and Andrés, cacique of San Luis, wrote to the king of Spain on February 12, 1699, to complain that the fort and the Spanish families that came with it were onerous. "The natives of San Luis are found withdrawn a league into the woods," the chiefs complained, "for their places have been seized for the Spaniards." The increased labor required to maintain an armed force and a respectable luxury for the commanding officer encouraged natives to quit their homes. Indian flight had religious implications as well. "For this reason, and because they flee from the continued labor of the deputy's house, they do not even go to Mass on feast days. And not only this, but there are many Apalachee Indians withdrawn to the province of Guale, where many die without confession, because they do not understand the language of the missionaries of that province." Discontent was also spreading in the Apalachee leadership. The chiefs warned the king that the chieftain of Tama, "who is new in the faith," and his people had been forced by the Spaniards to tan hides without pay. In his anger, the chief "went to the place of Saint George [Charles Town]," and the Apalachee leaders "fear others may follow him."[15]

Certainly the Spaniards' behavior worried the Apalachees. Patricio Hinachuba wrote to Governor Antonio Ponce de León in April 1699 that the provincial lieutenant, Francisco Florencia, had gone on a hunting trip with forty Chacato Indians. On the trail, they entered the territory of the Tuskegee Indians and met twenty-four of them who wished to trade buffalo skins, leather shirts, and madstones (*piedras besalas*—or kissing stones). Florencia refused to trade, but at midnight he sneaked to the Tuskegee camp, killed sixteen of the traders, scattered the rest, and plundered their trade goods. "It is certain that the deed is such that all of us will have to pay for these activities," lamented Hinachuba. The deputy's behavior caused "some to have fled to the woods, others to Saint George with the English."[16]

Conditions only grew worse. On February 22, 1701, Captain Don Juan de Ayala Escobar, appointed inspector general of the Apalachee and Timucua provinces by Governor Joseph de Zúñiga y Zerda, suspended trade between the mission Indians and their northwestern neighbors. He declared that "not for any motive or pretext [may] they continue to travel or go to the provinces of Apalachicolo to consult and trade with the said pagans" without the governor's explicit permission. But the ban was unilateral. Should the Apalachicolas come to the missions to trade, "receive them with all good will," Ayala Escobar instructed, and buy only the "customary goods." He specifically forbade the acquisition of anything "which may have been introduced by the English," or the trading of anything "marketable" to the English allies. He was particularly worried about Spanish horses and silver falling into enemy hands.[17] Trading with the enemy was permissible, but only to a point.

Yet executive orders failed to limit mission Indians' contact with English-influenced natives. When the tension became unbearable, mission Indians fought the native newcomers. For their part, Spanish officials thought that aberrant native customs inspired mission Indians to take up the hatchet and go to war. In an effort to quell heightened tensions between Florida's all-important mission province of Apalachee and its "heathen" rivals, Governor Zúñiga y Zerda ordered the abolition of "a custom so devilish as taking scalps, and the massacres they carried out in order to acquire them, without other motive or cause than to kill those they meet of different and distant tribes." Pressures created by English trade imperatives, the arrival of unfamiliar natives in an increasingly congested and contested Southeast, and the presence of Spanish soldiers made mission Indians restless and wary. The governor thought that by banning scalp dances and by trying to limit granting the honorific titles noroco and *tascaya* to "those who have taken [scalps] in legitimate war" would alleviate some of the tension.[18] But Indian definitions of "legitimate war" were different from Spanish views, and the Apalachees were defending their homes and peoples from those who had showed an interest in doing them harm. The governor's pleas fell on deaf ears.

And yet Spanish messages to mission Indians were inconsistent. Spaniards needed the mission Indians to be prepared for war, but wanted them to be peaceful so that trade, labor, and religious instruction could continue unimpeded. The Apalachees were having none of that. An attack on Santa Fé in Timucua by English-supported Apalachicolas on May 20, 1702, prompted a call for retribution from Apalachee war chiefs. They feared a similar raid from their less-than-friendly neighbors and requested permission to take eight hundred warriors and some allies among the Christian Chacatos "to avenge these slayings and hostilities." The governor was inclined to let them. Before asking for the assistance of one hundred guns, forty *arrobas* of powder, and one thousand gunflints from the Spanish outpost in Pensacola and French Mobile, Zúñiga y Zerda lamented that Florida had been unable to woo the "pagan" Indians to the Spanish side. He had to admit that non-Christian natives flocked to Carolina for "the aid that the English give them." But the governor decried the methods of the English, "to whose friendship they incline as barbarians because they do not impose on them the law that we do."[19]

Raids on missions were exacting a toll on Florida, and the Spaniards tried to stem the native flight to the English fold. The governor ordered that any native captured during an attack on Spanish holdings, whether "heathen" or apostate rebel, could be sold as a slave. He also invited all Catholics, especially English or Irish faithful, and any other peaceful Carolinians to come to Florida. In a calculated stroke, Zúñiga y Zerda declared that "all of the Negroes of Carolina, Christians or non-Christians, free or slave, who may wish to come, will be given the same treatment [as Europeans] and granted their complete freedom."[20]

Compounding Florida's defensive woes, friars continued to argue against establishing garrisons in Guale. Despite the violence and the pressing need for rapid military response, the missionaries were protective of their influence and suspicious of the governors' motives. The friars suggested that there was no immediate threat to the missions and fretted over "the paucity of the Indians and their misery." It sapped native laborers "to sow their fields and kill a deer from month to month for the fathers," warned the friars. Caring for an infantry on top of their normal duties would be oppressive. Friars also suggested that calls for a Spanish fort might be the desire of one mico (chief) and not the "common consent of all micos." Should one chief want the garrison, hinted the doctrineros, let his people support it. The Franciscans knew where to pinch native leaders.[21]

In their fight against Spanish fort construction, friars desperately clung to their regular modes of ministry and hoped that faith would be enough, but whose faith was the question. Under the tense circumstances of invasion, relocation, congregation, and confusion, many Indians chose to return to traditional ways of worship. Indians, provincial lieutenant Domingo de Leturiondo noted, still "heal with ancient usage" and took solace in "orations, superstitions, chants, and false rites." Spaniards permitted using "medicinal herbs," but failed to extirpate other traditional means of soothing Indians' spirits.[22] Some mission Indians overtly expressed disgust with Spanish policies. Visitador to Guale, Juan de Pueyo, was forced to declare that "no one be so bold as to smear paint on or to scribble on these orders that remain posted in the villages because they will be severely punished."[23] The worsening conditions in Florida tested native loyalty. Yet many mission Indians remained within the Spanish fold.

The storm gathering over Spanish frontier missions broke at the turn of the century. Once again, the clouds traveled from half a world away. Charles II, king of Spain, died in 1700 and the already potent Louis XIV of France sought to add Spain to his growing empire. Louis claimed the heirless Spanish crown for his grandson Philip, and in the process formed a Franco-Hispanic juggernaut that made other European kingdoms nervous. Contesting Louis' bid for Spain, England and Holland joined forces. The "War of Spanish Succession" was on. News of war in Europe reached the American colonies two years later. The war, known in British America as Queen Anne's War, opened the floodgates between Carolina and Florida. Charles Town's President of Council for South Carolina, Colonel James Moore, executed a preemptive strike on St. Augustine and on Spanish Florida for fear that French colonists along the Mississippi and in Mobile would fortify their allies and raid Carolina. He wished to cripple Florida's ability to raid English holdings. "We were more afraid of the Spaniards of Apalatchee and their Indians in conjunction [with] the French of Mississippi, and their Indians doing us harm by land," Moore reported to Carolina's Lords Proprietors, "than of any forces of the enemy by sea."[24] When Moore's initial raid of St. Augustine was repelled, he turned his wrath on the less protected missions. Governor Zúñiga y Zerda lamented that the English "seek to destroy the provinces and terrorize the Indians, pagan as well as Christian." Fifty Carolinians and one thousand Yamasee and Creek mercenaries stormed mission towns in Apalachee and Timucua, killing those who resisted, enslaving those captured, absorbing those who surrendered, and torturing those who held positions of status. Queen Anne's War lasted until 1713, but the missions were never the same after 1704.[25]

During his rampage, Moore led a devastating assault on La Concepción de Ayubale. The Apalachees and Spaniards knew that a large force was approaching the town. According to Juan Baptista de la Cruz, a soldier stationed at San Luis, fray Juan de Parga "preached a sermon in the Apalachian tongue which lasted more than an hour," in which he urged the Indians to fight those who "came to disturb the law of God and destroy the Christian provinces; that all those who may die in that conflict will go to enjoy God, having engaged in defense of his holy law." The Spaniards probably did not notice that the friar's speech was akin to traditional native war preparations, nor did they see the Indian reasons for native bravery in the face of torture. To the Spanish mind, torture for the faith was martyrdom. But for the forty Indian leaders and warriors who were tied to stakes and set afire, their defiance was an expression of Indian honor and testimony to the strength of their souls. One leader was tortured slowly, from dawn until his death as the sun began to set, with fire brands. But during his ordeal he told his tormenters that he was going to God "while they would go to hell." Feliciano, a principal man from San Luis, "taunted the pagans so that they would torture him, saying to them that the body would die but that his soul would go to God directly." Invading Indians slashed Luis Domingo's body with knives so that they could stick burning splinters into his wounds. He, too, preached until he died. Others had their ears and tongues cut off. The Catholic catechism and the Apalachees' death dance taught the same lesson: those with great will-power remain true until the end.[26]

Not every Apalachee, however, kept the faith. There were defectors in the invading army at Ayubale, and others used their intimacy with the Spaniards to lure some into traps. Friars opened convent doors to familiar faces only to be met with mortal blows. Spanish soldiers marched into the field with allies who turned on them when the fighting became too fierce and the tide seemed to turn. As rumors of the torture inflicted on Christian Indians spread, fewer Apalachees chose to fight. Fear caused some mission Indians to switch sides to save their lives, and the Spanish Council of War recognized that many "have voluntarily gone over to the enemy." Others were "weary of waiting for aid from the Spaniards: that they did not wish merely to die." Indians felt betrayed and pointed out that "for a long time [the Spaniards] had misled them with words, [saying] that reinforcements were to come." Some fled to the woods, others to the sea islands.[27]

Governor Francisco Corcoles y Martínez reported to the king in January 1708 that all the Christian Indians of Apalachee, Timucua, Guale and Mayaca and Jororo were gone. He estimated that between ten and twelve thousand had been enslaved during decades of English-inspired or English-led raids, and that approximately three hundred men, women, and children were gathered at the Castillo de San Marcos in St. Augustine. Modern estimates suggest that in Moore's 1704 attack alone, thirteen hundred Apalachees voluntarily went with the invaders to Carolina and a thousand more were taken as slaves. The Florida missions and the native peoples who lived there were gone.[28]

Florida's mission Indians paid dearly for their affiliation with Spain. Immigrant viruses and microbes, harsh colonial labor systems, and imperial warfare among European rivals hindered the Indians' capacity to defend their homes and their lives. Florida natives were pinched between English and Indian newcomers to the Southeast who encroached on mission lands and imposed on mission inhabitants. Depleted by disease, weakened by unrelenting work duties, and divided by a century of revolt and suppression that sometimes pitted Timucuas against Apalachees, Florida Indians failed to unite across provincial lines. Faced with wave after wave of English, French, and "pagan" Indian assaults, individual mission settlements broke apart, and survivors allied with whomever could best provide protection from the tides of war.

⟡

Where outside forces brought violent changes to Florida and forced Indians to make difficult choices, internal colonial corrosion threatened New Mexico and encouraged natives to challenge the colonial system. Mission Pueblos did suffer from more frequent conflicts with nomadic Athabaskan peoples, but unlike the Chichimecos and Yamasees in Florida, neighboring Navajos and Apaches were not regional newcomers. The Athabaskans had a centuries-long love/hate relationship with their sedentary neighbors. At times they exchanged goods peacefully or joined them to combat common enemies. At others they plundered Pueblo homes, fought Pueblo warriors, and seized Pueblo captives. Athabaskans traveled in small groups and never remained in one location for long. Their migratory existence hindered close relations with the Spaniards, who preferred to deal with settled, "civilized" people. The mobility and independent organization of Navajo and Apache bands frustrated Spanish attempts to missionize them, but small bands based in defenseless camps attracted Spaniards with ulterior motives. New Mexico's soldiers and settlers seemed to have more in common with the

English and French corsairs in Florida; they participated openly in the traffic of human lives, sending captured Indians to the mining provinces of northern New Spain. Intermittent and ill-advised slaving sorties on nomadic peoples near the borders of Pueblo villages prompted violent and costly reprisals on missions. Vengeful Navajos and Apaches quickly capitalized on the missions' vulnerability. Jurisdictional wars between governors and friars exacerbated conditions by sapping the resources of the Spanish colonists and by distracting them from their obligation to defend the Pueblos. While revenge was the primary cause for Navajo and Apache attacks, Spanish livestock and technological novelties also enticed Indian raiders. Athabaskans enviously watched Pueblos herding sheep and cattle, and especially admired their growing skill on horseback. In the coming decades, Navajos and Apaches would vigorously adopt Spanish animals into their traditional life.[29]

Even more daunting than episodes of Indian warfare in New Mexico were drastic climatic changes. The environment itself seemed to conspire against mission Indians. Successive droughts from 1666 to 1671 shriveled livestock and mission crops. Famine, in turn, created a ripe environment for disease.[30] Spanish officials, more concerned with abolishing native traditional religious rites, squabbling over Indian labor, and raiding "pagans," were oblivious to Pueblo suffering and dismissive of their growing discontent. Colonial New Mexico was different from Florida. The chaotic feel of Florida's repeated invasions, migratory Indians, and fluid loyalties was absent in the Southwest. Instead, the Pueblos seethed; a slow, steady burn of discontent lay at the root of all Spanish-Indian relations. Heavy-handed Spanish administration, bickering friars and governors, harsh treatment from lieutenants, and overzealous doctrineros fomented Pueblo fear and suspicion. The combination of disease, drought, and famine, and increased Apache warfare created new pressures and intensified old tensions on mission Indians. Epidemics swept through starving and impoverished communities, weakening their capacity to combat attack or even to sustain their families. Drought conditions drove hungry Apache and Navajo raiders into Pueblos and Spanish haciendas alike. If they had not already done so, mission Indians openly returned to native religion, and shamans audaciously practiced their ceremonies. In some instances, dissatisfaction festered into rebellion.

As early as 1644, restless Pueblos had begun to challenge Spanish authority and were willing to risk annihilation to free themselves of

Spanish domination. Spaniards' harsh punishments of rebelling Indians did not quell dissension; it only built resentment. In 1647, Governor Fernando de Argüello Carvajal "hanged, lashed, and imprisoned more than forty Indians" from Jémez who had dared to challenge Spanish hege-mony. In 1650, Governor Hernando de Ugarte y la Concha learned of a plan by shamans and chiefs in Alameda and Sandia to attack the Spaniards on Holy Thursday night when they assembled for mass. At the outset of the attack, Pueblos drove off herds of horses to hinder the Spaniards' abil-ity to fight. But some soldiers followed the retreating rebels, captured them, and uncovered the plot. They reported to the authorities that the uprising had widespread support in several missions. Soldiers rounded up conspirators from several towns, hanged nine leaders, and sold the others into slavery or jailed them.[31]

Other natives tried to spark a colony-wide rebellion. But while they might have elicited sympathy outside their home towns, Pueblo upris-ings remained local. Surprisingly, Spanish authorities never recognized the warning signs. When Estéban Clemente—a Hispanicized governor of the Tano pueblos of Las Salinas, interpreter of six languages, and Spanish ally in the kachina wars—rebelled, Spanish officials should have been at least unsettled. Clemente ordered Christian Indians to drive the horses of all the Pueblo jurisdictions "to the sierras, in order to leave the Spaniards on foot." Then on the night of Maundy Thursday, just as the Alameda and Sandia rebels had planned a decade earlier, the mis-sion Indians "must destroy the whole body of Christians, not leaving a single religious or Spaniard." His plan was betrayed before it had a chance to spread, and Clemente was hanged for conspiracy against the colo-nial government. When investigating soldiers sequestered the rebel's property, they "found in his house a large number of idols and entire kettles full of idolatrous powdered herbs, feathers, and other trifles."[32] Spaniards abhorred the supposed religious "idolatry" and shook their heads at the attempted rebellion, but they did not change their treatment of mission Indians nor address any of the natives' concerns. Spaniards quashed violent Pueblos but were helpless to stem drought and famine. Even when Spanish colonists pleaded with governors to help them fend off starvation, colonial authorities were slow to respond. Indians and Spaniards alike were malnourished and both took extreme measures to sate their hunger. People soaked and washed leather straps and animal hides and toasted them with corn or boiled them with gathered herbs and roots.[33] Only the determined survived. When conditions became intolerable, the Spaniards abandoned the natives to their fate. The Manzano Tiwa and the Tompiro missions closed in the face of famine and continued Apache raids.[34] The Spaniards proved more adept at punishing recalcitrant Pueblos than defending their missions from Apache attack. Adverse conditions in the Southwest fostered intra-Pueblo empathy where it had engendered provincial jealousies in Florida. With each defiant act, Pueblos across New Mexico moved closer to political and military cooperation.

Spanish relations with the Pueblos were noticeably frayed by 1675. Governor Juan Francisco de Treviño faced growing unrest among many village war chiefs and medicine men. But the Tewas in and around San Ildefonso acted on their convictions. They bewitched the pueblo's friar and Spanish settlers living in a nearby estancia. When an Indian interpreter denounced the holy men as idolaters and sorcerers, the shamans tried to kill him. Soldiers arrested forty-seven Tewas; they found four guilty of witchcraft and sentenced them to death. Instead of submitting to Spanish punishment, one shaman hanged himself. One of the three remaining leaders was executed at Jémez as a warning to those who might still rebel. As was customary, Spanish officials seized the rebels' property and, as expected, they found "idols, powders, and other things" in the shamans' houses. Some of the others were released with a reprimand, but the majority suffered the humiliation and pain of public lashing and imprisonment. But the Spaniards' suppression of the Tewa leaders did not have the desired effect. More than seventy Tewa warriors, armed with *macañas* and leather shields, entered Treviño's house. They brought with them "eggs, chickens, tobacco, beans, and some small deerskins" in exchange for their imprisoned leaders. Though they offered the Spaniards compensation, their weapons and their refusal to leave without satisfaction suggested that the relationship between conquerors and conquered had subtly changed. They had also left an armed band in the mountains should reinforcements be needed. The Tewas directly challenged the governor's authority; Treviño wisely forfeited the prisoners.[35]

Pueblo tolerance of the Spanish regime was at the breaking point. It was in this atmosphere that word of a new prophesy spread throughout the mission pueblos. A Tewa holy man called Popay had been visited by the Pueblo spirit Poheyemo and three lesser spirits in a Taos kiva. The lesser spirits—Caidi, Tilim, and Thewme—related Poheyemo's strategy to Popay and inspired awe by emitting fire from their extrem-ities. Popay himself, Poheyemo's representative, was transformed into a tall black figure with giant yellow eyes. The spirits told Popay that they were returning to the underground lake of Copala, and wanted him to carry out Poheyemo's wishes. The great spirit wanted the Pueblos to rise as one, to expel the Spaniards from their homes, and to rid them-selves of Christianity. The Pueblo spirits urged the natives to return to the spiritual traditions of their ancestors. Popay explained that the spir-its' revolution was just because it allowed Indians to return to their lives "as they had when they came out of the lake of Copala." As a final warn-ing, the Tewa shaman said that any one who opposed the orders "would be known from his unclean face and clothes and would be punished." Popay had been one of the holy men whipped, imprisoned, and begrudgingly released by Treviño.[36]

The realization of Popay's prophesy was violent but amazingly suc-cessful. On August 8 and 9, 1680, messages from Tesuque pueblo alerted the Spaniards that "all the natives of this kingdom" were "forming a con-federation with the heathen Apaches," and that they planned a coordi-nated rebellion on August 13. The orders to rise up had been passed from pueblo to pueblo on deerskins and with knotted maguey ropes that indi-cated the number of days until the revolt's start. Afraid that the element of surprise had been lost, the numerous Pueblo leaders—Popay, Taqu of San Juan, Saca from Taos, Francisco of San Ildefonso, and Pedro Naranjo among others—accelerated their plans. On August 10 warriors "wearing war paint, with bows, arrows, shields, and lances" attacked mis-sions and estancias throughout the colony. Embattled Spaniards wrote desperately for help, revealing that rebel leaders had ordered warriors to start "killing the priests and the Spaniards, so that only the women and children would be left. They say that the remaining men must be killed, even to male children at the breast." Ironically, the Pueblo mil-lenarian uprising took a page from the Spaniards' own war book.[37] With surprising speed, rebel fighters killed friars, encomenderos, settlers, and soldiers; they drove off herds of livestock, seized horses and Spanish weapons. The rebellion sent New Mexico into a tailspin and forced Governor Antonio de Otermin to order the parish priest at the villa of Santa Fé "to consume the holy sacrament, and take the images, sacred vessels, and the things appertaining to divine worship, close the church and convent, and bring everything to the palace."[38]

Figure 10:
Campo santo of the original San Gerónimo, Taos. The church was destroyed in the tumult between 1680 and 1696. It was rebuilt and then destroyed a second time by the U.S. army during the Mexican-American War. Photograph by the author.

Reports from two Indian messengers sent from the capital to the countryside relayed what the rebels were saying. They declared that "God and Santa María were dead, that they were the ones whom the Spanish worshipped, and that their own God whom they obeyed never died." Others declared that "now the God of the Spaniards, who was their father, is dead, and Santa María, who was their mother, and the saints, who were pieces of rotten wood" had no power. Juan, one of the native messengers, returned to the villa as a rebel captain. He brought with him two crosses, one red and one white, and told the governor to choose one. The red meant war, the white meant that the Spaniards would abandon New Mexico. The governor told Juan that he would forgive the rebels and that they should consider their Christian faith, but the rebels "derided and ridiculed this reply," and welcomed Juan back into the rebel camp with shouts, celebrations, and peals of confiscated mission bells. "Now we shall live as we like and settle in this villa and wherever we see fit," the rebels reportedly exulted.[39]

Native leaders immediately urged Pueblos to reclaim traditional practices. A Tesuque Indian named Juan later told Spanish investigators that rebel leaders commanded that all natives "should discard the names given them in holy baptism and call themselves whatever they liked," and that they could "take any one whom they might wish," as a wife, disregarding marriages blessed by the Franciscans. Juan explained further that "they were not to mention in any manner the name of God, of the most holy Virgin, or of the Saints, on pain of severe punishment." As the rebellion spread, Pueblos removed Christian images, crosses, and rosaries from their homes and burned them in the plazas, as the friars had once done to kachina masks and traditional sacra. Many former Christians bathed in rivers and symbolically washed the effects of baptism away with *amole* (root soap). Anti-Spanish sentiments ran so high that rebels ordered natives "not to teach the Castilian language in any pueblo and to burn the seeds which the Spaniards sowed and to plant only maize and beans." Leaders promised warriors the pleasures of one woman for every Spaniard they killed and ordered that all Spanish servants should not be spared. The rebels drew a firm line between what was Spanish and what was not. During the siege of the Villa of Santa Fé, rebels even demanded that "all classes of Indians who were in our [Spanish] power be given up to them," including servants, Apache prisoners, and Mexican Indians who had no cultural connection to the Pueblos. In this revolution, natives were natives and Spaniards were not.[40]

The rebels proved remarkably brave once they had gone down the path of war. During the siege of the villa, when the outcome was not yet decided and when Spanish arms could still do some damage, Taos, Picurís, Jémez, Keres, and Tewa warriors "were so dexterous and so bold that they came to set fire to the doors of the fortified tower," the heart of the palace's defenses.[41] The Pueblo peoples, pushed too far and finally free to vent eighty years of pent frustrations, assaulted the symbols of Spanish religion as violently as they did the Spaniards themselves. The townspeople of Sandia ripped the doors from the convent cells and sacked the church and its contents. "Images had been taken from the church," observed one Spanish soldier, "and on the main altar there was a carved full-length figure of Saint Francis with the arms hacked off by an axe." The Indians filled the nave and choir loft with straw and then lit it. The sacristy and its store of religious objects had been ransacked, and individual rebels took vessels, silver implements, vestments, and images as trophies.[42] New Mexico's cabildo recorded further reports from Sandia that "images of saints were found among excrement, two chalices were found concealed in a basket of manure, and there was a carved crucifix with the paint and varnish taken off by lashes." As the Spaniards marched south out of New Mexico, they witnessed the remains of similar destruction in thirty-four pueblos, estancias, and houses. More disturbing for the survivors, however, was recalling the eighteen friars and 380 Spanish men, women, and children who would never leave the colony.[43]

Pueblos took up arms against their Spanish conquerors for many reasons. Bartolomé, the cantor for Galisteo pueblo, reported that many thought that the climatic conditions and consequent famine should have prompted changes in the colonial work detail. The Pueblos were "tired of working for the Spaniards and friars because they did not allow them to plant or do other things for their own needs," the native explained. Josephe, a Spanish-speaking native, concurred. The Spaniards, who "beat them, took away what they had, and made them work with out pay," suffered for their greed.[44] Some rose up so they could enjoy the plenty that Poheyemo promised them. Rebels would "harvest a great deal of maize, many beans, a great abundance of cotton, calabashes, and very large watermelons and cantaloupes." These hopeful rebels wished to "erect their houses and enjoy abundant health and leisure."[45]

Other Pueblo rebels cited ideological reasons for the revolt. Pedro Nanboa from Alameda, captured by retreating Spaniards, claimed that decades of Spanish suppression of Pueblo shamans made people rise up. The Spanish notary put his own spin on Nanboa's testimony that "because the Spaniards punished sorcerers and idolaters, the natives of the Teguas, Taos, Pecuries, Pecos, and Jemez had been plotting to rebel and kill the Spaniards and the religious, and that they had been planning constantly to carry it out, down to the present occasion." Indignation over the persecution of native spiritual leaders and the destruction of traditional religious images and sacra was strong. But Nanboa pointed out to his Spanish questioners that "they have inherited successfully from their old men the things pertaining to their ancient customs," despite Spanish efforts to eradicate them. Pueblo parents had passed on deep resentment toward the Spanish invaders since their children were old enough to understand.[46] Not every Pueblo joined the revolt at the outset. Antonio, a Tewa rebel, had been captured by the Spaniards but escaped because he thought that if the Spaniards survived they would take him with them on their retreat. He had no desire to leave his home, so he fled. Some Christian Pueblos came to the villa to be with the Spaniards, ignoring the call to rebel despite the risk. Whole towns, too, chose not to join the rebel cause. Sevilleta, Socorro, Alamillo, and Seneca sided with the Spaniards and 317 warriors from the four villages passed muster. But peer pressure and the threat of retribution were significant motivators for those who might have joined the colonists. Isleta pueblo initially refused to rebel. When their neighbors at Alameda and Sandia rose up, many felt compelled to join. And yet more than half of the town joined the Spaniards on their retreat. They knew that sympathy for the conquerors meant the rebels' wrath.[47] There was little doubt that the Spaniards felt betrayed. In their minds, Spanish conquest had brought economic benefits, technological advances, and religious salvation to the natives. What stunned the Franciscans the most was the list of rebel leaders. "The Indians who have done the greatest harm," bemoaned fray Antonio de Sierra, "are those who have been most favored by the religious and who are most intelligent."[48] It was true that many of the war captains and strategists during the uprising were sacristans, cantors, interpreters, and governors, those Pueblos who had the most contact with doctrineros and who, ostensibly, were the most Christian. Alonso Catiti, leader of the rebels at Santo Domingo and one of the top war chiefs of the rebel coalition, was a Spanish-speaking interpreter. Governor Otermín was astounded that one of his own messengers returned to the villa as a rebel captain during the siege of Santa Fé.[49] The friars could not fathom that Spanish "favor" would not be appreciated.

The Spaniards were surprised at the Pueblos' violence and at the depth of their revulsion at anything to do with Christianity. Their shock, and their fear, evoked bitter comments about the Pueblos once the smoke began to clear. Bartolomé de Estrada, governor of El Parral, called for retribution in an angry missive to the viceroy. "The destruction of all the temples, sacred vessels, and vestments, shows the iniquity of those barbarians and the hatred which they feel for our holy faith," he raged. "There are sufficient reasons for war being waged against them without mercy, and for declaring all those who may be captured slaves for a period of ten years."[50] Governor Otermín was blind with rage and identified a different source for the Pueblos' unrest. He vowed to recapture New Mexico, so that "Christianity may not perish and so that, through failure to take such steps as are possible, the discord of the devil may not gain control among the natives, with idolatries and superstitions, which is that to which their stupid ignorance predisposes them."[51] But exacting retribution was easier to threaten than to achieve.

In planning the reconquest over a year later, the Spaniards were careful not to make the same mistakes twice. They followed specific orders not to arm or give horses to Indians, mestizos, or mulattos who accompanied their army.[52] The Spaniards marched into Cebolleta facing an armed populace, but rather than firing missiles at the invaders, the Pueblos surrendered. When questioned, the Pueblos informed Otermín that they were prepared for an Apache attack, but not for the return of the Spaniards. Just as Juan de Oñate had done, Otermín presided over an elaborate ceremony designed to reclaim the people of Cebolleta for the Spanish crown and the Christian God. Franciscans accompanying the punitive force ordered a local shaman arrested amid shouts of "Ave María" from the Pueblos. Never short on ceremony, the Spaniards spent four days performing services, baptizing children, and blessing apostates.[53]

But the army's progression did not pass unnoticed. Pueblo scouts spotted them and warned the inhabitants of the Spaniards' return with smoke signals. Most towns were abandoned when soldiers reached them, and they found only the remains of what the rebellion had achieved. Pueblos had reclaimed their homes and commandeered the spaces once dedicated to disseminating foreign religious concepts and imposing belief systems of a conquering people for their own ends. Otermín's second in command, Juan Domínguez de Mendoza, discovered that the Indians in Sandía had turned the convent into a ritual house. Inside the friars' former cells, shamans stored kachina masks, altars, and traditional sacra alongside whatever Christian implements remained. It also seemed that members of the community lived in the cloister, private oratory, and refectory. In an effort to taint the rebels as pawns of the Devil, Domínguez described a wooden panel, once the centerpiece for the main altar of Sandía's church, on which had been painted the Immaculate Conception of Mary with a dragon at her feet. "The eyes and mouth of the figure were ruined and there were signs that the rest of the body had been stoned," wrote Domínguez, "while the accursed figure at her feet was whole and unspoiled."[54]

Other towns revealed a slightly different picture. At Alameda, Spaniards discovered a chalice with its paten in the house belonging to a former sacristan. The Indian had carefully placed the communion pieces in a box with a figure of Christ. Despite the revolt's wrath, these Christian items held spiritual power and were handled with reverence. In other mission villages and at each estancia and hacienda, Spaniards found evidence that the Pueblos had made use of the ruins. Lands once worked by natives for encomenderos and friars now yielded crops for Pueblos. Church grounds that had once been the exclusive domain of Franciscan doctrineros served rebel Indians as storage rooms for personal items and harvests and livestock corrals.[55]

Otermín intended to recover the colony lost on his watch. But lack of organization, poor funding, and a lack of conviction among his own people doomed the reconquest effort from the start. Sargento Mayor Luis de Quintana observed that the Pueblos appeared "well content with the life they are living for they have always desired it." Quintana swore that "most of them have never forsaken idolatry, and they appear to be Christians more by force than to be Indians who are reduced to the holy faith." Fray Francisco de Ayeta, the top-ranking Franciscan among Otermín's *reconquistadores*, agreed. "The hope of their reduction was based upon these apostates being a settled people of long experience in organized living, and with a natural inclination toward all kinds of agriculture, brought up in comfort, clothed after their fashion, neat and careful of their houses, and accustomed for a hundred years to this life," the friar explained. His fellow friars once believed that it was "almost impossible that they should change and be willing to live without these conveniences." The rebellion, however, "unloosed the undying hatred for Christianity which was concealed in their hearts."[56] There could be little hope of reconciliation.

In 1683, Otermín left the colony ignominiously, never to return. But others vowed to bring the Pueblos back into the Spanish sphere of influence. In 1694, Diego de Vargas took an army into New Mexico and found the Pueblos at war with each other and ill-prepared to repel another Spanish invasion. His first entrada won promises to submit; his second secured it "by force of arms." Again, Franciscans established missions among the Pueblos. Again in 1696 many of the mission Indians rebelled. This time, however, not all the Pueblos joined. Pecos, Santa Ana, Zia, and San Felipe helped suppress the rebels. Despite its failure, the uprising finally established the natives' right to practice their own traditions free from forced conversion. The Franciscans, embittered toward the Pueblo "Judases," failed to proselytize with the zeal that their predecessors had. They had good reason: no one was listening. Converting the Indians was no longer a necessary part of Spanish colonization in New Mexico. The Pueblos had made their point. As fray Francisco de Vargas explained to the viceroy on November 28, 1696, after the last Pueblo revolt had been quelled, the natives "want peace with the Spaniards only for their trade and commerce and not to observe our holy law." [57]

It took the Spaniards more than a hundred years to learn what the Pueblos wanted. They learned the lesson the hard way, at the price of Spanish and Indian blood. Both Florida and New Mexico suffered debilitating episodes of warfare at the end of the seventeenth century. In fact, the century closed in much the same way it opened: with great violence. But in both cases, the bloodshed that destroyed the Spanish missions was strangely European in scope, execution, and results. European technologies played pivotal roles in the demise of Spain's two colonies. English-supplied guns, powder, and cannons allowed invading natives to run rampant in Florida's mission villages. Horses, steel swords, and carefully coordinated, highly organized military strategy made the Pueblo Revolt a success in New Mexico.[58] The loss of life was incredibly high by the standards of traditional Indian warfare, and the defeat of Spanish hegemony was an unexpected result in both cases.

Florida and New Mexico would again be in Spanish hands and would again witness the construction of Christian missions among its native inhabitants, but never again with the same intensity. The world was certainly new.

CHAPTER SIX

Reckoning

CONQUERED BY YOU, THE NEW WORLD
HAS CONQUERED YOU IN TURN.
— FLEMISH SCHOLAR JUSTUS LIPSIUS
to a SPANISH FRIEND, 1603

The seventeenth-century Spanish missions in Florida and New Mexico were contested ground. Despite imposing colonial governance over the Guales, Timucuas, Apalachees, and Pueblos through military conquest, the Spaniards could not compel mission Indians to adopt Christianity. While some natives did become practicing Catholics for their own motives, many others either rejected their conquerors' faith or incorporated its tenets into Indian theologies. As long as Spaniards negotiated the conditions of mission life and the terms of religious adherence with natives, relations in mission towns were civil if not amicable. But when forced to choose between native and Spanish beliefs, most Indians opted for tradition and only returned to the missions at sword point.

From the outset, Indian contact with Spanish settlers followed somewhat different paths in Florida and New Mexico. Florida's Guales and Timucuas witnessed Spanish brutality against French Huguenots in 1565, and wisely chose to ally themselves with the newcomers from *España*. They avoided provoking the Spaniards by siding with them. When the cloak of Spanish alliance proved heavy, Guales threw it off. Spain's violent suppression of the rebels proved the seriousness of the newcomers' intentions. Pueblos in New Mexico lacked an immediate example of Spanish military ruthlessness, but the memory of former Spanish expeditions into Pueblo territory gave them pause. Like the Guales, some

Pueblos challenged Spanish soldiers directly when colonial demands grew burdensome. The rebels were summarily defeated in 1599. Where Florida's Timucua Indians assumed that they were partners with the powerful Spaniards, the Guales and Pueblos understood that they were subject peoples. Southeastern natives, familiar with the responsibilities inherent in chiefdoms, cooperated with Spanish settlers and accepted demands for labor; independent Pueblos resented colonization and acquiesced to Spanish commands only because they were forced. From the beginning, the Indian-Spanish relationship seemed more adversarial in the Southwest.

Yet the central component of early Spanish colonization of Florida and New Mexico was not martial or even economic, but religious. During the first decades of colonization, the royal government in Spain retained the two settlements on the extreme frontiers of their vast New World empire for evangelical reasons alone. The two colonies were not profitable; in fact, the operations of Florida and New Mexico were financial drains on the king's coffers. But exaggerated reports indicating thousands of Indian conversions mitigated the economic disaster and secured the colonies' survival with crown money. Evangelical Spanish Catholicism provided the backbone for the colonies' organization. Franciscan missionaries moved to existing native towns and attempted to convert native peoples. Once they were faithful Christians, the mission Indians could become loyal subjects of the Spanish empire. Of course, Spanish colonists could not realistically wait for the friars to complete their task; fields needed planting, municipal structures needed building, sheep and cattle herds needed tending. Mission Indians found themselves in a missionary co-op of sorts. Natives worked while they learned Christian doctrine. For the Spaniards assumed that Christian supremacy and the prize of Christian heaven justified the colonial process, and evangelical missions became the primary mechanism by which they subdued the frontier. This is not to say that economic imperatives for Florida and New Mexico were unimportant, or that the goal of economic solvency was secondary. But it did mean that the economic aspirations Spanish authorities had were entirely dependent upon Franciscan missions.[1]

Colonial survival was contingent upon the missions' success, and Spanish officials readily believed the early friars' heady sanguinity. Missionaries described miraculous events, cited heavenly intercession in the conversion of the "heathens," and described native populations devoid

Figure 11:
Reconstructed bedroom of
a Spanish colonial house,
San Luis de Talimali.
Photograph courtesy of
Christopher R. Versen.

of religion and eager for Christian guidance. The Franciscans' loaded
reports were intoxicating to Spanish audiences, who felt that the poor
economic fortunes of Florida and New Mexico would reverse under God's
divine sanction. But the "salvation" of a multitude of Indians cultivated
more optimism than success. The friars' superficial descriptions and mis-
shapen expectations left the Spaniards ill equipped to handle the ensuing native discontent in the frontier missions.

In the first decades of frontier colonization, the doctrinas and visitas that the Franciscans administered reflected Spanish hopes more than
reality. For the native inhabitants of Florida and New Mexico, mission
villages were hometowns, not religious training grounds under the stew-
ardship of foreigners. Changes in the Indians' lives during the late sixteenth-century conquests were significant, but not drastic enough to
utterly alter native perceptions of their lands. Mission Indians started
to view the dangers of their world differently only after imported disease and Spanish labor drafts disrupted and dispersed native populations.
In the face of greater demographic instability, some Indians questioned

native religious leaders and traditional sacred practices. From the natives' perspective, religion was not only spiritual but also medicinal. "Health" referred to one's harmony with the universe; faith was therefore a cure and a spiritual salve. As larger numbers of mission Indians fell ill, grew weak from colonial labor, or became disoriented by the myriad changes in their world, many natives reevaluated their spiritual loyalty. The invaders' faith grew more attractive and seemed more able to protect its adherents from the ravages of colonization.

The spiritual combat that ensued between Indians and Spaniards was ferocious though the battle lines were unclearly drawn. There was no template to guide mission Indians through the turmoil of colonization and indoctrination. They had to choose their paths according to the particular circumstances they faced. Some Indians incorporated aspects of Christianity into traditional practices, some compartmentalized the two religions, some embraced the newcomers' faith wholesale, and some entirely rejected Spanish beliefs. Similarly, Franciscan doctrineros negotiated the terms of conversion and adjusted their approach depending on the people they tried to convert. Initially, friars were willing to bend on church construction and decoration, even on native behavior, to achieve stability in newly conquered and demographically strapped mission settlements. Solitary Franciscans living among conquered Indians without the benefit of immediate Spanish guard were wise to compromise. Despite the Spaniards' dogmatic approach to others' faiths, a rigidity formed during the Catholic Reformation, missionaries' flexibility eased the beginning of Spanish cultural negotiations with Indians.

Natives initially welcomed Christian missionaries for non-religious reasons. Chiefs maintained political power and in some cases enhanced their local and regional influence by allying with Spaniards. Access to European trade goods also strengthened leaders' statuses and revolutionized native material culture. For centuries, Indians had traded similar objects with one another. Technology rarely changed and technological leaps were rarer still. When European goods reached Indian hands, their impact could hardly be overestimated. Metal bells, iron tools, glass beads, mirrors, and numerous domesticated animals were unprecedented treasures. The technological explosion attracted Indians to the Spanish fold. For the political and economic benefits, accepting seemingly innocuous friars in native villages appeared a favorable exchange. But the impact of military conquest, disease, and voracious labor drafts dispelled any native illusions about Spanish occupation. While conversion may have afforded neophytes personal tranquility, the decision to abandon native tradition had a ripple effect on mission villages. Native communities emphasized community over the individual. There certainly were Indian mechanisms that allowed for individual expression and merit—prowess in war or the hunt, skill at weaving or ceramics, eloquence in council, special favor with the spirits—but individuals generally used their talents for the good of the group. The first thought of each tribal member was of his or her family, clan, and town. Choosing to darken the Christian church door was a disruptive, individual act in itself.

Despite the unsettling influence Christian missionaries had on Indian populations, natives either tolerated or embraced the ministers' proselytizing as long as the Spaniards honored established political and economic agreements. But once conquest settled into colonization, ecclesiastical and secular Spaniards were less inclined to observe recognized codes of cultural negotiation. After the colonial routine became accepted convention, governors and friars expected natives to obey economic, political, and religious directives without discussion. By discarding gift giving ceremonies, gentle religious instruction, patient communication, and co-operative decision making, Spaniards antagonized Indians. Indian acceptance of the newcomers' religion was always subject to other colonial issues, no matter what the invaders believed. Native leaders were especially sensitive to the terms of their political alliance, the operation of their economic agreements, and recognition of their traditional status. When chiefs felt that the demands from soldiers and friars had become intolerable, they reacted. For many mission Indians, the combination of disease, famine, warfare, drought, labor demands, intra-colonial squabbling, forced conversion, and the loss of some political autonomy was too much.

Yet Indians in Florida were not easily provoked. The Guales rebelled in 1597, the Apalachees rose up in 1647, and the Timucucas revolted in 1656, but none resorted to violence more than once. Florida's native peoples did not choose rebellion as quickly or as often as Pueblos did. Guales, Timucuas, and Apalachees took up arms only when the established conditions of Spanish colonization were compromised. The Timucua revolt of 1656 was specifically designed to redress native leaders' grievances against Spanish political and diplomatic neglect. The Guale and Apalachee rebels were less patient than their Timucua neighbors. They acted in the early stages of Spanish colonization and hoped to sever their ties with the Spanish interlopers. But each remained an isolated, intra-provincial uprising. Only the 1597 Guale Revolt, by virtue of its timing early in the Spanish settlement of Florida, threatened Spain's hold on the colony.

Like the uprisings in Florida, most seventeenth-century Pueblo revolts were local. But Pueblos rebelled with more frequency, and occasionally succeeded in eliminating Spanish influence in their towns. Pueblo rebellions were more common in distant communities to the north, west, and south of the colonial capitol, and revealed New Mexican officials' inability to keep the extensive territory under control. Taos (1639), Jémez (1623, 1640s, early 1650s), Zuñi (1632), Piros (1665–1668), Salinas (1669), Southern Tiwas and Keres (early 1650s), and San Ildefonso (1675) each independently rebelled against Spanish domination. The Spaniards abandoned

Figure 12:
North House, Taos. Photograph by
the author.

their missions in Taos and Zuñi for several years as a result of Pueblo resistance. While Pueblos did not entirely eschew less drastic forms of cultural
negotiation, they were more likely to fight Spanish dominance than Florida's
mission Indians were.

The different landscape and settlement pattern accounted for some
of the disparity between uprisings on the two frontiers. Florida was a
closely knit colony with mission villages rarely more than a days' journey from one another; New Mexico's pueblos were separated by several
day's travel over treacherous terrain. Florida's woods and swamps provided temporary sanctuary for rebellious natives but were not impene-
trable to Spanish soldiers bent on retaliation. New Mexico's mountains,
on the other hand, were ready havens, and while conditions in these
regions were far from ideal, the labyrinth-like mesas and canyons allowed
Pueblos to better evade Spanish sorties. The openness of New Mexico's

landscape also permitted Pueblo scouts to quickly identify Spanish forces and afforded rebels the necessary time to retreat further into the hills and ravines.

The colonies' distinctive structures also made for differing Spanish responses to Indian unrest. Spanish punitive forces in the Southeast reacted more quickly and more consistently to incidents of violence than their southwestern counterparts. Florida was a military colony where municipal offices were military posts and all ranking colonists were soldiers. New Mexico adopted a more conventional Spanish colonial system, with a local council, appointed officers, and civil servants. Nevertheless, the perpetual squabbling and occasional violence between secular and ecclesiastical Spaniards in both Florida and New Mexico was a fundamental feature in the missions' declining conditions.

Perhaps the differences between Spaniards' backgrounds played a role in the disparate perceptions of colonial governance. Sixteenth- and seventeenth-century Spaniards were fond of ethnic categories and put great stock in biological and social labels. *Peninsulares*, those born in Spain, were more sophisticated, better educated, and had more sympathy with the royal colonial strategy, according to Spanish settlers. *Criollos*, on the other hand, were American-born Spaniards who had the reputation for being socially inferior, intellectually limited, and less trustworthy. Even the friars who worked in frontier missions fell into categories. *Gachupines* were peninsular priests who entered the Franciscan Order in Spain. *Hijos de provincial* ("sons of the province") were peninsular Spaniards who donned the habit in American provinces, and criollos, like their secular counterparts, were friars born and trained in the New World. Perhaps church-state fights in New Mexico were much more volatile because most of their friars were criollos from Mexico, while Florida's friars were predominantly peninsulares.[2]

But there were other factors with greater impact on the deterioration of the colonial regimes of Florida and New Mexico. Local conditions, specific personal rivalries, and the ability of colonial leaders to take advantage of loosely supervised frontiers were more significant issues than the geographic backgrounds of the colonists. Intra-colonial fights were bitter and hateful at times because governors and friars lived among a conquered majority, had conflicting goals for native peoples, and were far removed from authorities who could oversee their handiwork. In unstable colonial conditions and with little economic promise, ecclesiastical and secular colonists fought ferociously over what they could eke from the native inhabitants. In the process, the Spaniards compromised their observance of diplomatic rituals and recognition of native sovereignty.

New Mexico's intra-colonial warfare was more violent and fierce because the colony had fewer commodities to exploit and less arable land. With scarce opportunities, settlers and friars fought viciously over the one "resource" that made New Mexico potentially valuable: the Indians. Keenly aware of their precarious command of local resources, Pueblos felt the colonial demand for tribute and labor more deeply than their Florida counterparts. Pueblo political structures were free of elaborate chiefdoms, and their independence allowed local leaders to organize and exact rebellions with more speed and frequency. Recurrent rebellions further destabilized New Mexico's colonial system. That the southwestern colony was further isolated from Spain's other New World settlements exacerbated Spaniards' squabbling. Contact with the outside world came in the form of intermittent supply caravans and irregular commercial ventures. Trains of wagons and horses made the sixteen-hundred-mile trek from Mexico City to Santa Fé occasionally, and often stopped to "rest" for several months en route. New Mexico's extreme isolation led to delayed communications, glacial investigation and punishment of wrongdoing, and tardy resolution of disputes. Comparatively, travel to Florida was supersonic. The arrival of ships from Cuba and other Caribbean ports was more regular and the journey was less expensive to undertake. It was not that sailing to Florida was risk free; dangerous weather, unpredictable seas, and treacherous coastlines could wreck any vessel bound for the peninsula. But the geographic proximity of supervisory officials and the more frequent shipments to Florida shores made for less extreme attitudes among the peninsula's governors and friars.[3]

Contributing to the greater conflict in New Mexico was the availability of religious leverage in the church-state conflict. Mexican clerics established a branch of the Holy Office in Santo Domingo, and the Inquisition provided the friars a powerful weapon that they occasionally abused. New Mexico's Franciscans could sanction, excommunicate, arrest, and imprison governors, soldiers, and settlers for the slightest provocations. Southwestern governors resented the friars' power and often misused gubernatorial authority to check their ecclesiastical rivals. Florida had its share of civil unrest, but there was little doubt that the highest colonial authority resided in the governor's palace, not in the friars' convents.

The contest between friars and governors was, at the very least, out in the open. But the missionaries were stunned when they discovered an underground spiritual resistance operating in their own mission villages. The Franciscans learned too slowly that Indian acceptance of Christian teachings was predominantly on native terms. Underground ceremonial spaces, tight-knit clan control, isolated native settlements, and suspicious religious leaders allowed Pueblos to compartmentalize Spanish practices while retaining the core of traditional system. In Florida, Spaniards failed to appreciate the depth of traditional native spirituality and misunderstood its significance in their every endeavor, even their sport. When Franciscans realized that traditional rites continued even among baptized mission Indians, they felt betrayed. The friars struck out at "heathen" rites with zealous ferocity. The friars' crackdown not only expressed their realization that there was more Indian spirituality than innocuous theater involved in native dances and games. The missionaries were also attempting to reassert their control over Indians' lives. Secular Spanish authorities were gaining influence in mission villages and, according to the friars, were hindering the Franciscans' holy work. The friars' assault on "pagan" traditions was a two-pronged attempt to conquer Indians' spirits and to weaken the secular Spanish authorities' power.

Native responses to intensified religious suppression by the Franciscan missionaries differed. In Florida, the governor, the settlers, and a few Apalachee chiefs and leaders aided fray Juan de Paiva's attack on the natives' ball game. The Apalachees ostensibly accepted the extirpation of the sport while the Timucuas held firm. Neither openly rebelled. In New Mexico, on the other hand, governors sided with Pueblo chiefs when friars tried to regulate native ceremonial dances. As friars destroyed kachina masks and kivas, the Pueblos grew less obedient and more violent. By the 1670s, the Indians in both frontier colonies were increasingly discontented with Spanish heavy-handedness.

The missions in Florida and New Mexico both ended in violence, but the bloodshed came from different sources. External pressures forced Florida's Indians to choose to remain within the Spanish fold, to join English newcomers, to flee with other native groups, or to retreat to French colonies. There was no general Indian revolt against Spanish settlers. The Guales, Timucuas, and Apalachees lacked a pan-Indian prophecy that could have united mission Indians against Spaniards. They never formed a supra-village confederacy against the colonists because they strove so hard to achieve a more balanced alliance with them. When English-led forays ravaged mission towns, survivors had difficulty determining where best to invest their loyalty.

If Florida was bombarded by pressures from outside the region, New Mexico imploded from internal strife. Extensive church-state conflict, drought, famine, intensified Apache assaults, and colonial abuse encouraged Pueblos to set aside long-standing enmities. Their mutual loathing of the Spanish invaders led to a coordinated and successful rebellion. Pueblo leaders formed a coalition by articulating a millenarian movement that resonated with natives throughout the mission pueblos. The degree of cooperation was an indication of how desperate the situation had become, and how atrocious Spanish colonization was for Pueblos. The Spaniards had created an atmosphere of mistrust over a century of recrimination, warfare, and cruelty. Disparate Pueblos from hundreds of miles away joined to force every Spanish settler from the entire region.

Spain's colonial imperatives—to extract economic wealth for the enrichment of both settlers and crown while securing native "heathen" for providence—conflicted at times. Despite an honest wish to "civilize" and "save" native peoples, Spaniards' colonial ambitions exceeded their grasp on the northern frontiers. Indians, initially acquiescent or cautious, were emboldened by Spaniards' mistreatment, neglect, inability to defend the missions, and political infighting. Indians acted to save their lives by remaining loyal to Spain, fleeing doctrinas, or rebelling against their invaders.

For nearly a century in the occupied lands of Florida and New Mexico, Indians and Spaniards were locked in an intimate if awkward embrace. Military force kept Indian-Spanish relations closer than perhaps natives wanted. Once Spanish settlers proved their intentions to remain among the native peoples of the Southeast and Southwest, Indians faced their changed world with resignation, with resolve, and sometimes with the determination to reject the newcomers. Whether they cast their lot with Spaniards, merged with other natives or Europeans, or renewed their commitment to their own people, Indians attempted to preserve their cultural identity by endlessly recreating it.

NOTES

Introduction

1.   David J. Weber, *The Spanish Frontier in North America* (New Haven: Yale University Press, 1992), 90. Florida's fourteen hundred "Spanish" settlers included some African slaves and Hispanicized Indians.

2.   For discussions of the meaning and significance of the Spanish frontiers and borderlands, see Jeremy Adelman and Stephen Aron, "From Borderlands to Borders: Empires, Nation-States, and the Peoples in Between in North American History," *American Historical Review* 104 (June 1999): 814–41. Adelman and Aron have written the clearest distinction, defining *frontier* as "a meeting place of peoples in which geographic and cultural borders were not clearly defined," and *borderlands* as "the contested boundaries between colonial domains." Weber, *Spanish Frontier in North America*, esp. 11–13, sees frontiers as "zones of interaction between two different cultures;" Amy Turner Bushnell and Jack P. Greene, "Peripheries, Centers, and the Construction of Early Modern American Empires: An Introduction," in *Negotiated Empires: Centers and Peripheries in the Americas, 1500–1820*, ed. Christine Daniels and Michael V. Kennedy, 1–14 (New York and London: Routledge, 2002) surveys various definitions and applications of the core-periphery model throughout the Americas.

3.   For the best discussions of ethnohistory and its meaning, see James Axtell, *Natives and Newcomers: The Cultural Origins of North America* (New York: Oxford University Press, 2001), 1–14; Bruce G. Trigger, "Ethnohistory: Problems and Prospects," *Ethnohistory* 29 (1982): 1–19; Trigger, "Ethnohistory: The Unfinished Edifice," *Ethnohistory* 33 (1986): 253–67. For studies that apply ethnohistorical methods to analyze European conversion of natives, see James Axtell, *The Invasion Within: The Contest of Cultures in Colonial North America* (New York: Oxford University Press, 1985); Axtell, "Some Thoughts on the Ethnohistory of Missions," *Ethnohistory* 29 (1982): 35–41; Robert Conkling, "Legitimacy and Conversion in Social Change: The Case of French Missionaries and the Northeastern Algonkian," *Ethnohistory* 21 (1974): 1–24; Kenneth Mills, "The Limits of Religious Coercion in Mid-Colonial Peru," *Past and Present* 145 (1996): 84–121; Kenneth M. Morrison, "Baptism and Alliance: The Symbolic Mediation of Religious Syncretism," *Ethnohistory* 37 (1990): 416–37; Vicente L. Rafael, "Confession, Conversion, and Reciprocity in

Early Tagalog Colonial Society," *Comparative Studies in Society and History* 29 (1987): 320–39.

4. The best recent studies of Spanish relations with Indians in Florida and New Mexico include: Jerald T. Milanich, *Laboring in the Fields of the Lord: Spanish Missions and Southeastern Indians* (Washington and London: Smithsonian Institution press, 1999); Amy Turner Bushnell, *Situado and Sabana: Spain's Support System for the Presidio and Mission Provinces of Florida*, American Museum of Natural History, Anthropological Papers, No. 74 (Washington, D.C.: Smithsonian Institution Press, 1994); John E. Worth, *Timucuan Chiefdoms of Spanish Florida*, 2 vols. (Gainesville: University of Florida Press, 1998); Ramón A. Gutiérrez, *When Jesus Came, the Corn Mothers Went Away: Marriage, Sexuality, and Power in New Mexico, 1500–1846* (Stanford: Stanford University Press, 1991); Carroll L. Riley, *The Kachina and the Cross: Indians and Spaniards in the Early Southwest* (Salt Lake City: University of Utah Press, 1999).

5. See David Hurst Thomas Jr., ed., *Columbian Consequences: Archaeological and Historical Perspectives on the Spanish Borderlands*, 3 vols. (Washington, D.C.: Smithsonian Institution Press, 1989–91); Erick Langer and Robert H. Jackson, eds., *The New Latin American Mission History* (Lincoln: University of Nebraska Press, 1995); Donna J. Guy and Thomas E. Sheridan, eds., *Contested Ground: Comparative Frontiers on the Northern and Southern Edges of the Spanish Empire* (Tucson: University of Arizona Press, 1998).

6. See Nicholas Griffiths and Fernando Cervantes, eds., *Spiritual Encounters: Interactions between Christianity and Native Religions in Colonial America* (Lincoln: University of Nebraska Press, 1999); Daniels and Kennedy, eds., *Negotiated Empires*.

7. José Rabasa, *Writing Violence on the Northern Frontier: The Historiography of Sixteenth-Century New Mexico and Florida and the Legacy of Conquest* (Durham and London: Duke University Press, 2000); Weber, *The Spanish Frontier in North America*, 9.

8. Analyses of the role missions and missionaries played in New World colonization are voluminous. I have been especially influenced by Axtell, *The Invasion Within*; Griffiths and Cervantes, *Spiritual Encounters*; and Weber, *The Spanish Frontier in North America*.

9. For analyses of Spanish friars and their flexible approach to New World natives, see Griffiths and Cervantes, *Spiritual Encounters*, 1–25; Samuel Y. Edgerton, *Theaters of Conversion: Religious Architecture and Indian Artisans in Colonial Mexico* (Albuquerque: University of New Mexico Press, 2001), 78–105, 274–97.

10. My understanding of Indians' responses to contact, conquest, and conversion comes from John and Jean Comaroff, *Ethnography and the Historical Imagination* (Boulder: Westview Press, 1992); James Axtell, *Natives and Newcomers*; Inga Clendinnen, *Ambivalent Conquests: Maya*

and *Spaniard in Yucatan, 1517–1570* (Cambridge: Cambridge University Press, 1987); Alfonso Ortiz, ed., *New Perspectives on the Pueblos* (Albuquerque: University of New Mexico Press, 1972).

Chapter One

1. René de Laudonnière, "L'histoire notable de la Floride," in *New American World: A Documentary History of North America to 1612*, 5 vols., ed. David B. Quinn, 2:283, 322, 343–44 (New York: Arno Press and Hector Bye, Inc., 1979); John Sparke, "Report on Florida," in *New American World*, Quinn, 2:363; John H. Hann, ed. and trans., "1630 Memorial of Fray Francisco Alonso de Jesús on Spanish Florida's Missions and Natives," *The Americas* 50 (July 1993): 93–94; Francisco Vázquez de Coronado, "Report given by Francisco Vázquez de Coronado," in *Narratives of the Coronado Expedition, 1540–1542*, ed. George P. Hammond and Agapito Rey, 130 (Albuquerque: University of New Mexico Press, 1940); Pedro de Castañeda, "Narrative of the Expedition to Cíbola," in *Narratives of the Coronado Expedition*, Hammond and Rey, 256–57; Hernán Gallegos, "Relation and Report of the Expedition made by Francisco Sánchez Chamuscado," in *The Rediscovery of New Mexico, 1580–1594: The Expeditions of Chamuscado, Espejo, Castaño de Sosa, Morlete, and Leyva de Bonilla and Humaña*, ed. George P. Hammond and Agapito Rey, 84–85 (Albuquerque: University of New Mexico Press, 1966).
2. John E. Worth, *The Struggle for the Georgia Coast: An Eighteenth-Century Spanish Retrospective on Guale and Mocama*, Anthropological Papers no. 75 (New York: American Museum of Natural History, 1995), 9; Felix Zubillaga, *Monumenta Antique Florida, 1566–1572*, in *Ethnology of the Indians of Spanish Florida*, ed. David Hurst Thomas, Jr., 5 (New York and London: Garland Publishing, Inc., 1991); John E. Worth, *Timucuan Chiefdoms of Spanish Florida*, 1:1–4; John H. Hann, *Apalachee: The Land Between the Rivers* (Gainesville: University Press of Florida, 1988), 5–23, 96–101. See Lewis H. Larson, *Aboriginal Subsistence Technology on the Southeastern Coastal Plain During the late Prehistoric Period* (Gainesville: University Press of Florida, 1980) for a thorough description of Florida's environment, plant life, and animal population.
3. Linda S. Cordell, *Prehistory of the Southwest* (San Diego: Academic Press, 1984), 2–4, 20–38; Barton Wright, *Pueblo Cultures*, Institute of Religious Iconography, State University of Groningen, sec. 10, fasc. 4 (Leiden: E. J. Brill, 1986), 2–3, 6–22; Frances Levine, *Our Prayers Are in This Place: Pecos Pueblo Identity over the Centuries* (Albuquerque: University of New Mexico Press, 1999), 3–8.
4. Jerald T. Milanich and William C. Sturtevant, eds., *Francisco Pareja's 1613*

Confessionario: A Documentary Source for Timucuan Ethnography (Tallahassee: Division of Archives, History, and Records Management, Florida Department of State, 1972), 28, 30–31.

5. John R. Swanton, Early History of the Creek Indians and Their Neighbors (Gainesville: University Press of Florida, [1922] 1998), 80–128; Charles Hudson, The Southeastern Indians (Knoxville: University of Tennessee Press, 1976), 120–83, 336–51; Elsie Clews Parsons, Pueblo Indian Religion, 2 vols. (Lincoln: University of Nebraska Press, [1939] 1996), 1:170–209; Alfonso Ortiz, The Tewa World: Space, Time, Being, and Becoming in a Pueblo Society (Chicago and London: University of Chicago Press, 1969), 13–28; Wright, Pueblo Cultures, 6–22.

6. Hann, Apalachee, 160–73; David R. Wilcox and W. Bruce Masse, eds., The Protohistoric Period in the North American Southwest, AD 1450–1700, Anthropological Research Papers, no. 24 (Tempe: Arizona State University, 1981), 354–409.

7. Pareja, Confessionario, 23–27, 31; Jacques le Moyne, Brevis Narratio, in Settlement of Florida, ed. and trans. Charles E. Bennett, 44–48, 52–58, 68, 72 (Gainesville: University of Florida Press, 1968); Laudonnière, in New American World, Quinn, 2:282–83; Alonso de Jesús, "Memorial," 91; Parsons, Pueblo Religion, 1:478–85, 493–549, 2:554–89, 686–707, 790–801, 827–46.

8. Pareja, Confessionario, 23–24, 26–27.

9. Parsons, Pueblo Religion, 1:76, 84–97, 275, 285, 443–53, 462; Coronado, in Narratives of the Coronado Expedition, Hammond and Rey, 175–76; Castañeda, in Narratives of the Coronado Expedition, Hammond and Rey, 214, 218, 286; Joe Sando, Pueblo Nations: Eight Centuries of Pueblo Indian History (Santa Fe, New Mexico: Clear Light, 1992), 30–33; William L. Merrill, Edmund J. Ladd, and T. J. Ferguson, "The Return of the Ahayu:da: Lessons for Repatriation from Zuni Pueblo and the Smithsonian Institution," Current Anthropology 34 (December 1993): 525.

10. Pareja, Confessionario, 24, 32, 35; Parsons, Pueblo Indian Religion, 1:270–91, 413–16, 443–53; Antonio Espejo, "Report of the expedition," in The Rediscovery of New Mexico, 1580–1594, Hammond and Rey, 220; Francisco de Valverde y Mercado, "Investigation of the conditions in New Mexico, 1601," in Don Juan de Oñate, Colonizer of New Mexico, 1595–1628, 3 vols., ed. George P. Hammond and Agapito Rey, 2:650 (Albuquerque: University of New Mexico Press, 1953); Gutiérrez, When Jesus Came, the Corn Mothers Went Away, 7–10, 14, 20–23.

11. Pareja, Confessionario, 28–29, 31–32; Parsons, Pueblo Religion, 1:484–85.

12. William A. Christian, Jr., Local Religion in Sixteenth-Century Spain (Princeton: Princeton University Press, 1981), 15–28, 37–55, 78–96; William A. Christian, Jr., Apparitions in Late Medieval and Renaissance Spain (Princeton: Princeton University Press, 1981), 2–3, 13–15.

13. Christian, Local Religion, 179; Christian, Apparitions, 19–20. See also John

Alexander MacKay, *The Other Spanish Christ: A Study in the Spiritual History of Spain and South America* (New York: The Macmillan Co., 1993) and Timothy Mitchell, *Passional Culture: Emotion, Religion, and Society in Southern Spain* (Philadelphia: University of Pennsylvania Press, 1990).

14. A. D. Wright, *Catholicism and Spanish Society Under the Reign of Philip II, 1555–1598, and Philip III, 1598–1621* (Lewiston, Queenston, and Lampeter: The Edwin Mellen Press, 1991), 4–8, 99–119, 195–237; Jean Pierre Dedieu, "'Christianization' in New Castile: Catechism, Communion, Mass, and Confirmation in the Toledo Archbishopric, 1540–1650," in *Culture and Control in Counter-Reformation Spain*, ed. Anne J. Cruz and Mary Elizabeth Perry, 3–24 (Minneapolis and Oxford: University of Minnesota Press, 1992); Sara T. Nalle, *God in La Mancha: Religious Reform and the People of Cuenca, 1500–1650* (Baltimore and London: The Johns Hopkins University Press, 1992), 30–49, 84–86, 103–7, 154–70, 209; Henry Kamen, *Spain, 1469–1714: A Society of Conflict*, 2nd ed. (London and New York: Longman Group UK Ltd., 1991), 48–56, 181–84.

15. Nalle, *God in La Mancha*, 135; Wright, *Catholicism and Spanish Society*, 135–36, 195–203.

16. St. Francis, "The Rule of 1221," in *St. Francis of Assisi, Writings and Early Biographies: English Omnibus of the Sources for the Life of St. Francis*, trans. Benen Fahy O.F.M., ed. Marion Habig, 31–53 (Chicago: Franciscan Herald Press, 1973); St. Francis, "The Rule of 1223," ibid., 57–64; St. Francis, "The Admonitions," ibid., 77–87; John Moorman, *A History of the Franciscan Order From Its Origins to the Year 1517* (Oxford: Clarendon Press, 1968), 3–5; *New Catholic Encyclopedia*, 10 vols. (New York: McGraw-Hill, 1967), 6:36–40.

17. Richard C. Trexler, *Naked Before the Father: The Renunciation of Francis of Assisi*, Humana Civilitas: Studies and Sources Relating to the Middle Ages and the Renaissance, vol. 9. (New York: Peter Lang, 1989), 105–9. See also Michael Robson, *St. Francis of Assisi: The Legend and the Life* (London: Geoffrey Chapman, 1997).

18. Mt. 19:21.

19. St. Francis, "Rule of 1221," 31–34; Moorman, *History of the Franciscan Order*, 15–18, 51–58, 152; Jill R. Webster, *Els Menorets: The Franciscans in the Realms of Aragon from St. Francis to the Black Death*, Studies and Texts 114 (Toronto: Pontifical Institute of Mediaeval Studies, 1993), 175–90; Jim Norris, "The Franciscans in New Mexico, 1692–1754: Toward a New Assessment," *The Americas* 51 (October 1994): 152–59; Gutiérrez, *When Jesus Came*, 66–71.

20. Mt. 10:16; St. Francis, "Rule of 1221," 43.

21. 1 Pet. 2:13; St. Francis, "Rule of 1221," 43.

22. St. Francis, "Rule of 1221," 43; E. Randolph Daniel, *The Franciscan Concept of Mission in the High Middle Ages* (Lexington: University Press of Kentucky, 1975), 22–46, 51–76; Gutiérrez, *When Jesus Came*, 71–76.

23. St. Francis, "Rule of 1221," 44.

24. Moorman, *History of the Franciscan Order*, 10–31.

25. Ibid., 53.

26. Ibid., 20–31, 83–95, 105–22, 307–19; *New Catholic Encyclopedia*, 6:41–42.

27. Pareja, *Confessionario*, 23–26, 28, 30–31; René de Laudonnière, *Three Voyages: René de Laudonnière*, ed. and trans. Charles E. Bennett (Gainesville: University Press of Florida, 1975), 8, 13, 40–41, 120; Laudonnière, in *New American World*, Quinn, 2:282; Parsons, *Pueblo Religion*, 1:413–33; Swanton, *Early History of the Creek Indians*, 374, 381–87; Geoffrey Kimball, "A Grammatical Sketch of Apalachee," *International Journal of American Linguistics* 53 (April 1987): 141; Gutiérrez, *When Jesus Came*, 20–30.

28. Pareja, *Confessionario*, 23, 26, 29, 30–31; Parsons, *Pueblo Religion*, 1:77–84; Hernán Gallegos, "Relation and Report of the expedition made by Francisco Sánchez Chamuscado," in *The Rediscovery of New Mexico, 1580–1594*, Hammond and Rey, 82; Espejo, in *Rediscovery of New Mexico*, Hammond and Rey, 220; Valverde y Mercado, in Hammond and Rey, *Colonizer of New Mexico*, 2:628, 637, 643, 648; Wright, *Pueblo Cultures*, 21; Gutiérrez, *When Jesus Came*, 32.

29. Pareja, *Confessionario*, 28, 30, 31.

30. Parsons, *Pueblo Religion*, 1:270–348, 352–65.

31. Pareja, *Confessionario*, 28, 30–31; Parsons, *Pueblo Religion*, 1:95–6, 413–33, 450–67; 2:708–28.

32. Laudonnière, in *New American World*, Quinn, 2:282, 302–3, 327–31, 343; Le Moyne, in *Settlement of Florida*, 24–34, 64, 72; Dominique de Gourgues, "The Recapture of Florida," in *Settlement of Florida*, Bennett, 213, 216–23.

33. John H. Hann, ed. and trans., "Translation of Alonso de Leturiondo's Memorial to the King," *Florida Archaeology* 2 (1986): 202; John R. Swanton, *The Indians of the Southeastern United States* (Washington: Smithsonian Institution Press, 1979), 791–92; Alonso de Jesús, "Memorial," 93. See also Charles M. Hudson, ed., *Black Drink: A Native American Tea* (Athens: The University of Georgia Press, 1979).

34. Laudonnière, in *New American World*, Quinn, 2:283; René de Laudonnière, "L'histoire de la Floridé", in *Three Voyages: René de Laudonnière*, Charles E. Bennett, 14. The two most recent translations of Laudonnière's *L'histoire* are Sarah Lawson's *A Foothold in Florida: The Eye-Witness Account of Four Voyages made by the French to that Region and Their Attempt at Colonisation, 1562–1568* (Somerset, England: Castle Cary Press, 1992) and Charles E. Bennett, *Laudonnière and Fort Caroline: History and Documents* (Tuscaloosa: University of Alabama Press, 2001).

35. Swanton, *Indians of the Southeastern US*, 791–92.

36. Sparke, in *New American World*, Quinn, 2:367.

37.   Parsons, *Pueblo Religion*, 1:385–90, 402–13; Gallegos, in *Rediscovery of New Mexico*, Hammond and Rey, 100–101; George P. Hammond and Agapio Rey, eds., and trans. *Obregón's History of 16th Century Explorations in Western America: Chronicle, Commentary, or Relation of the Ancient and Modern Discoveries in New Spain and New Mexico, Mexico, 1584*, (Los Angeles: Wetzel Publishing Co., Inc., 1928), 177, 284, 296, 325; Valverde y Mercado, in *Colonizer of New Mexico*, Hammond and Rey, 2:636; Gutiérrez, *When Jesus Came*, 22–33. Ethnographies of various Pueblo peoples enumerate the complexity of Pueblo religion, social organization, and ceremony. Among the best are Fred Eggan, *Social Organization of the Western Pueblos* (Chicago: University of Chicago Press, 1950); Leslie A. White, *The Pueblo of San Felipe*, Memoirs of the American Anthropological Association, no. 38 (Menasha, Wisconsin: American Anthropological Association, 1932); and Edward P. Dozier, *The Pueblo Indians of North America* (Prospect Heights, Il.: Waveland Press, 1983); For a village's study of itself, see Laura Bayer with Floyd Montoya and the Pueblo of Santa Ana, *Santa Ana: The People, the Pueblo, and the History of Tamaya* (Albuquerque: University of New Mexico Press, 1994).

38.   Laudonnière, in *Foothold in Florida*, Lawson, 13; Laudonnière, in *New American World*, Quinn, 2:283.

39.   Pareja, *Confessionario*, 23, 27–28, 31, 32; Le Moyne, in *Settlement of Florida*, Bennett, 42.

40.   Parsons, *Pueblo Religion*, 1:413–76.

41.   Pareja, *Confessionario*, 28, 35; Laudonnière, in *Foothold in Florida*, Lawson, 8.

42.   Parsons, *Pueblo Religion*, 1:91; Gutiérrez, *When Jesus Came*, 17–20, 33–36. Some natives vigorously refuted Gutiérrez' analysis of Pueblo society; see "Commentaries," complied by the Native American Studies Center, University of New Mexico, *American Indian Culture and Research Journal* 17 (1993): 141–77.

43.   Richard Fletcher, *Moorish Spain* (Berkeley and Los Angeles: University of California Press, 1992), 1, 10, 19, 27; Joseph F. O'Callaghan, *A History of Medieval Spain* (Ithaca: Cornell University Press, 1975), 91–162.

44.   Stanley G. Payne, *Spanish Catholicism: An Historical Overview* (Madison: The University of Wisconsin Press, 1984), 7–8; O'Callaghan, *Medieval Spain*, 98–108, 163–90, 250–81, 333–55.

45.   Payne, *Spanish Catholicism*, 9–10; O'Callaghan, *Medieval Spain*, 32; Fletcher, *Moorish Spain*, 22.

46.   Payne, *Spanish Catholicism*, 19–22; O'Callaghan, *Medieval Spain*, 150–52, 283–99; Fletcher, *Moorish Spain*, 35–36, 95.

47.   O'Callaghan, *Medieval Spain*, 494–97; Webster, *Els Menorets*, 4–19, 28, 72–79.

48.   Webster, *Els Menorets*, 4, 38, 72, 74.

49.   Ibid., 72–105.

50.   Ibid., 74, 78; Payne, *Spanish Catholicism*, 27.

51. Ibid., 79–80; Payne, *Spanish Catholicism*, 30–31.
52. Ibid., 75, 148.
53. O'Callaghan, *Medieval Spain*, 574–81; Lyle N. McAlister, *Spain and Portugal in the New World, 1492–1700* (Minneapolis: University of Minnesota Press, 1984), 56–57.
54. O'Callaghan, *Medieval Spain*, 657–76; McAlister, *Spain and Portugal*, 56–68; Kamen, *Spain*, 9–61.
55. John Leddy Phelan, *The Millennial Kingdom of the Franciscans in the New World: A Study of the Writings of Gerónimo de Mendieta, 1525–1604* (Berkeley and Los Angeles: University of California Press, 1956), 5–11, 42–50, 83–85.

Chapter Two

1. See Anthony M. Stevens-Arroyo, "The Inter-Atlantic Paradigm: The Failure of Spanish Medieval Colonization of the Canary and Caribbean Islands," *Comparative Studies in Sociology and History* 35 (July 1993): 515–43; John E. Kicza, "Patterns in Early Spanish Overseas Expansion," 229–53; Stuart B. Schwartz, *The Iberian Mediterranean and Atlantic Traditions on the Formation of Columbus As a Colonizer* (Minneapolis: University of Minnesota Press, 1986).

2. For mission theory in Spanish America, see Erick Langer and Robert H. Jackson, eds., *The New Latin American Mission History* (Lincoln: University of Nebraska Press, 1995); Nicholas Griffiths and Fernando Cervantes, eds., *Spiritual Encounters*; John Leddy Phelan, *The Millennial Kingdom of the Franciscans in the New World*.

3. Bartolomé de las Casas, *A Short Account of the Destruction of the Indies*, ed. and trans. Nigel Griffen (London: Penguin, 1992); Lewis Hanke, *All Mankind is One: A Study of the Disputation between Bartolomé de las Casas and Juan Ginés de Sepúlveda in 1550 on the Intellectual and Religious Capacity of the American Indians* (DeKalb: Northern Illinois University Press, 1974); Bartolomé de las Casas, *In Defense of the Indians: The Defense of the most Reverend Lord, Don Fray Bartolomé de las Casas, of the Order of Preachers, Late Bishop of Chiapa, Against the Persecutors and Slanderers of the Peoples of the New World Discovered Across the Seas*, ed. and trans. Stafford Poole (DeKalb: Northern Illinois University Press, 1974).

4. See Lyle N. McAlister, *Spain and Portugal in the New World, 1492–1700*, 77–82, 89–107; Alfred W. Crosby, *Ecological Imperialism: The Biological Expansion of Europe, 900–1900* (Cambridge: Cambridge University Press, 1986), 71–103; Kicza, "Patterns in Early Spanish Overseas Expansion," 229–53; Stevens-Arroyo, "The Inter-Atlantic Paradigm," 515–43.

5. David J. Weber, *The Spanish Frontier in North America*, 23–25, 50.

6. There are many translated and printed accounts of Spaniards' explorations

in the northern borderlands. See Alvaro Núñez Cabeza de Vaca, *His Account, His Life, and the Expedition of Pánfilo de Narváez*, ed. and trans. Rolena Adorno and Patrick C. Pautz (Lincoln: University of Nebraska Press, 1999); Alvaro Núñez Cabeza de Vaca, *The Narrative of Cabeza de Vaca*, ed. and trans. Rolena Adorno and Patrick C. Pautz (Lincoln: University of Nebraska Press, 2003); Lawrence A. Clayton, Vernon James Knight, Jr., and Edward C. Moore, eds., *The De Soto Chronicles: The Expedition of Hernando de Soto to North America in 1539–1543*, 2 vols. (Tuscaloosa: University of Alabama Press, 1993); James Alexander Robertson, ed. and trans., *True Relation of the Hardships Suffered by Governor Fernando de Soto & Certain Portuguese Gentlemen During the Discovery of the Province of Florida. Now Newly Set Forth by a Gentleman of Elvas*, 2 vols. (Deland: The Florida State Historical Society, 1933); Jeanette Thurber Connor, ed. and trans., *Colonial Records of Spanish Florida*, 2 vols. (Deland: The Florida State Historical Society, 1925, 1930); David K. Snow, ed., *The Native American and Spanish Colonial Experience in the Greater Southwest: Introduction to the Documentary Records* (New York and London: Garland Publishing, 1992); George P. Hammond and Agapito Rey, eds., *Narratives of the Coronado Expedition, 1540–1542* (Albuquerque: University of New Mexico Press, 1940); George P. Hammond and Agapito Rey, *The Rediscovery of New Mexico, 1580–1594*.

7. "Records of the marches by the army and Acts of Obedience and Vassalage," in *Don Juan de Oñate, Colonizer of New Mexico, 1595–1628*, George P. Hammond and 1:317–60; "Alónso Sánchez to Rodrigo del Río, February 28, 1599," in ibid., 1:426; "Trial of Indians at Acoma," in ibid., 1:427–78; "Captain Velasco to the Viceroy," in ibid., 2:614–19; Marc Simmons, *The Last Conquistador: Juan de Oñate and the Settling of the Far Southwest* (Norman: University of Oklahoma Press, 1991), 112–14, 119–20, 132–35; Weber, *The Spanish Frontier in North America*, 84–87.

8. Francisco de Valverde y Mercado, "Investigation of the Conditions in New Mexico, 1601," in *Don Juan de Oñate, Colonizer of New Mexico*, Hammond and Rey, 2:675.

9. Gonzalo Solís de Merás, "Memorial," in *New American World: A Documentary History of North America to 1612*, 5 vols. ed. David Beers Quinn, 2: 492–526 (New York: Arno Press and Hector Bye, Inc., 1979); Bartolomé Barrientos, "Vida y hechos de Pero Menéndez de Avilés," in ibid., 2:526–29; "Laudonnière-Gourgues account of the French revenge attack on San Mateo," in ibid., 2:568; Hernando de Escalante, "Memorial," in ibid., 5:7–16; Eugene Lyon, *The Enterprise of Florida: Pedro Menéndez de Avilés and the Spanish Conquest of 1565–1568* (Gainesville: University Presses of Florida, 1976).

10. "Gonzálo Méndez de Canzo to Philip II," in *New American World*, Quinn, 5:86–87; "The Franciscans of Florida to Philip III," in ibid., 5:138–40; Weber, *Spanish Frontier*, 69–82.

11. Luis Gerónimo de Oré, *The Martyrs of Florida, 1513–1616*, trans. Maynard Geiger (New York: Joseph F. Wagner, 1936), 100–103; "Report of the Indian uprising which led to the loss of Santa Elena," in *New American World*, Quinn, 5:17–19; "Pedro Menéndez Marqués reports on the situation in Florida at his arrival," in ibid., 5:20–24, 25–28; "The Uprising of the Guale Indians and Its Suppression, 1597–1598," in ibid., 5:69–92.

12. Oré, *Martyrs of Florida*, 33–41; John E. Worth, *Timucuan Chiefdoms of Spanish Florida*, 1:36–54.

13. Archivo General de Indias, 54—5—9, bundle 80, St. Augustine, Fray Francisco de Pareja and Fray Alonso de Peñaranda to the King, November 20, 1607, Stetson Collection, University of Florida Library.

14. "Don Luis de Velasco to the King," in *Colonizer of New Mexico*, Hammond and Rey, 2:1067.

15. "The Viceroy to the King," in ibid., 2:957.

16. "New Mexico to be Maintained, Decree regarding what fathers Fray Lázaro Ximénez and Fray Ysidro Ordóñez have been ordered to take to New Mexico," in ibid., 2:1076–77; Robert Matter, *Pre-Seminole Florida: Spanish Soldiers, Friars, and Indian Missions, 1513–1763* (New York and London: Garland Pubs., 1990), 52–54.

17. E. Randolph Daniel, *The Franciscan Concept of Mission in the High Middle Ages*, 37–41, 107–8, 117, 122–126. See Luke 9:24; Matthew 5:10; John 15:20; Matthew 5:11–12; Matthew 10:28; Fray Francisco Morales, *Ethnic and Social Background of the Franciscan Friars in Seventeenth Century Mexico* (Washington, D.C.: Academy of American Franciscan History, 1973), 54–55, 73; Jim Norris, "The Franciscans in New Mexico, 1692–1754: Toward a New Assessment," 152–65; Michael V. Gannon, *The Cross in the Sand: The Early Catholic Church in Florida, 1513–1870* (Gainesville: University Presses of Florida, 1965), 36–48.

18. Lewis Hanke, *The Spanish Struggle for Justice in the Conquest of America* (Philadelphia: University of Pennsylvania Press, 1949), 33–34; Stephen Greenblatt, *Marvelous Possessions: The Wonder of the New World* (Chicago: University of Chicago Press, 1991), 12–14, 97–98.

19. "Act of Taking Possession of New Mexico," in *Colonizer of New Mexico*, Hammond 1:333. For reference to similar ceremonies in Florida, see "Fray Francisco de Marrón to Philip II, July 6, 1594," in *New American World*, Quinn, 5:53–54; "Fray Francisco de Marrón to Philip II, January 23, 1596," in ibid., 54–55.

20. "Appointment of Don Juan de Oñate as Governor and Captain General of New Mexico," in *Colonizer of New Mexico*, Hammond and Rey, 1:62–63.

21. "Instructions to the Sargento Mayor for the Punishment of Acoma," in *Colonizer of New Mexico*, Hammond and Rey, 1:458–59.

22. See France V. Scholes, "Church and State in New Mexico, 1610–1650," *New Mexico Historical Review* (January 1937), 78–106; France V. Scholes, "Troublous Times in New Mexico, 1659–1670," *New Mexico Historical*

Review (July 1941), 313–27; Hann, *Apalachee*, 16–19, 21–23, 197, 255–58; Amy Turner Bushnell, *Situado and Sabana*, 148–61.

23.   Oré, *Martyrs of Florida*, 129.

24.   John H. Hann, "1630 Memorial of Fray Francisco Alonso de Jesús on Spanish Florida's Missions and Natives," 100–101; Fray Alonso de Benavides, *Memorial of 1630*, trans. Peter P. Forrestal (Washington, D.C.: Academy of American Franciscan History, 1954), 36. The *Oxford English Dictionary* notes that catechesis comes, via Latin, from the Greek roots meaning "instruction by word of mouth" and originally "to resound."

25.   Samuel Y. Edgerton, *Theaters of Conversion: Religious Architecture and Indian Artisans in Colonial Mexico*, 275–80; Kurt E. Dongoske and Cindy K. Dongoske, "History in Stone: Evaluating Spanish Conversion Efforts Through Hopi Rock Art," in Robert W. Preucel, ed., *Archaeologies of the Pueblo Revolt: Identity, Meaning, and Renewal in the Pueblo World* (Albuquerque: University of New Mexico Press, 2002), 114–15. The only evidence of superimposition of a church over an extant kiva in New Mexico was at the Hopi village Awatovi.

26.   Published archaeological records of Florida missions are extensive. A few of the best follow. Calvin B. Jones and Gary Shapiro, "Nine Mission Sites in Apalachee," in David Hurst Thomas, ed., *Columbian Consequences*, 3 vols. (Washington, D.C.: Smithsonian Institution Press, 1990), 2:491–509, describes a model of Florida mission construction across the province of Apalachee. Rebecca Saunders, "Mission-Period Settlement Structure: A Test of the Model at San Martín de Timucua," *Historical Archaeology* 30, no. 4 (1996), 24–35, demonstrates that Florida mission structures were complex and more flexible than the "mission model" suggested. David Hurst Thomas, "The Archaeology of Mission Santa Catalina de Guale: Our First 15 Years," in *The Spanish Missions of La Florida*, ed. Bonnie G. McEwan, 8–21 (Gainesville: University Press of Florida, 1993), outlines the basic components of Spanish mission construction. Kenneth W. Johnson, "Mission Santa Fé de Toloca," in ibid., 145–58, shows the difficulties of excavating a Timucua village that was inhabited over long periods of time. Rochelle A. Marrinan, "Archaeological Investigations at Mission Patale, 1984–1992," in ibid., 255–68, 274–82, updates Jones and Shapiro in light of recent excavations and research, and briefly compares Florida's missions to what he calls the "southwestern mission model." However, the "model" theory in the Southwest is just as suspect as its southeastern counterpart. See Edgerton, *Theaters of Conversion*, 247–97. Gary Shapiro and Richard Vernon, "Archaeology at San Luis: The Church Complex," *Florida Archaeology* 6 (1992), 179–81, 199–205, 217–21, describes the excavations of an Apalachee capital and mission in great detail; Brent Richards Weisman, *Excavations on the Franciscan Frontier: Archeology at the Fig Springs Mission* (Gainesville: University Press of Florida, 1992), 54–74, 100–103, is a thorough report of investigations at a Timucua mission. For a glimpse of a reconstructed Florida mission, see the San Luis

website at http://dhr.dos.state.fl.us/bar/san_luis/whatsnew.html.

27. Excavations of Pueblo missions and villages also abound. Gordon Vivian, *Gran Quivira: Excavations in a 17th-Century Jumano Pueblo*, Archaeological Research Series, no. 8 (Washington, D.C.: National Park Service, 1979), 62–93, describes San Isidro and briefly compares its features to other nearby missions. Joseph H. Toulouse, Jr., *The Mission of San Gregorio de Abó: A Report on the Excavation and Repair of a Seventeenth-Century New Mexico Mission*, Monographs of the School of American Research, no. 13 (Albuquerque: University of New Mexico Press, 1949), 7–13, 23–25, shows how extensive New Mexican mission structures could be. Florence Hawley Ellis, *San Gabriel del Yungue: As Seen by an Archaeologist* (Santa Fe: Sunstone Press, 1989), 65–76, describes the first church the Spaniards built in New Mexico. James E. Ivey, "The Baroque in New Mexico, 1620–1630," *Catholic Southwest* 9 (1998): 9–23, describes the design changes in mission complexes in the early years of New Mexican missionization.

28. For detailed descriptions of Pueblo mission architecture, see Edgerton, *Theaters of Conversion*, 275–92; Ross Gordon Montgomery, Watson Smith, and John Otis Brew, *Franciscan Awatovi*, in *The Spanish Missions of New Mexico I: Before 1680*, ed. John L. Kessell and Rick Hendricks, 373–88 (New York and London: Garland Publishing, 1991); James E. Ivey, "Abo," Construction of San Gregorio," in ibid., 393–421; Ivey, "The Patio and Kivas of Abo and Quarai," in ibid., 449–54; Suzanne G. Kenagy, "Stepped Cloud and Cross: The Intersection of Pueblo and European Visual Symbolic Systems," *New Mexico Historical Review* 64 (July 1989): 325–40.

29. Edgerton, *Theaters of Conversion*, 279–97; France V. Scholes, "The Supply Service of the New Mexican Missions in the Seventeenth Century," *New Mexico Historical Review* 5 (January 1930): 96–113; John H. Hann, "Church Furnishings, Sacred Vessels and Vestments Held by the Missions of Florida: Translation of Two Inventories," *Florida Archaeology* 2 (1986): 148–50.

30. Edgerton, *Theaters of Conversion*, 280–83, 293–97; France V. Scholes, "The Supply Service of the New Mexican Missions in the Seventeenth Century," *New Mexico Historical Review* (April 1930 and October 1930): 186–210, 386–404; Hann "Church Furnishings," 155–56.

31. "Record of the marches by the army," in *Colonizer of New Mexico*, Hammond and Rey, 1:327.

32. Benavides, *Memorial*, 12, 21, 29–30, 32–35; Oré, *Martyrs of Florida* 102, 106, 113.

33. Benavides, *Memorial*, 21–22.

34. Ibid., 21–22, 28, 59; Oré, *Martyrs of Florida* 106.

35. Benavides, *Memorial*, 59.

36. Worth, *Timucuan Chiefdoms*, 1:103–15; Benavides, *Memorial*, 28; Oré, *Martyrs of Florida*, 100; "Petition of Father Juan de Prada," in *Historical Documents Relating to New Mexico, Nueva Vizcaya, and Approaches Thereto, to 1773*, 3 vols., ed. and trans. Charles Wilson Hackett, 3:110, 112.

(Washington, D.C.: The Carnegie Institution of Washington, 1923); "Petition of Don Francisco de la Mora," in ibid., 3:117–18; "Declaration of Captain Andrés Hurtado," in ibid., 3:188, 191.

37. France V. Scholes, "Church and State in New Mexico, 1610–1650," 164–66; France V. Scholes, "Troublous Times in New Mexico, 1659–1670," *New Mexico Historical Review* (October 1937), 398–409; John H. Hann, ed. and trans., "Translation of Governor Rebolledo's 1657 Visitation of Three Florida Provinces and Related Documents," *Florida Archaeology* 2 (1986): 81–86; Bushnell, *Situado and Sabana*, 148–61.

38. Worth, *Timucuan Chiefdoms*, 1:36–43; "Act of Obedience and Vassalage by the Indians," in *Colonizer of New Mexico*, Hammond and Rey, 1:337–46; "Doña María, chief of Nombre de Dios, to Philip III," in *New American World*, Quinn, 5:102–3.

39. Oré, *Martyrs of Florida*, 106; Benavides, *Memorial*, 36–37,65–67; Gutièrrez, *When Jesus Came the Corn Mothers Went Away*, 75–84. For similar tactics in Central Mexico and Canada, see Olive Patricia Dickson, "Campaigns to Capture Young Minds: A Look at Early Attempts in Colonial Mexico and New France to Remold Amerindians," *Historical Papers* (1987): 44–66.

40. Fray Francisco Pareja, *Catechismo y breve exposicion de la doctrina christiana; muy util y necessaria, asi para los Españoles como para los naturales, en lengua Castellana, y Timuequana, en modo de preguntas, y respuestas* (Mexico: en casa de la viuda de Pedro Balli, por C. A. Cesar, 1612), 83–84.

41. Pareja, *Catechismo*.

42. "Doctrina Christiana; y explicación de sus Misterios, en nuestro idioma Español, y en lengua Arda," in *Le Royaume d'Arda et son Èvangèlisation au XVII siècle*, ed. Henri Labouret et Paul Rivet, (Paris: Institut D'ethnologie, Université de Paris, 1929); Bushnell, *Situado and Sabana*, 95–103.

43. Hann, "Rebolledo's 1657 Visitation," 91–95; "Hearing of Nicolás de Aguilar," in *Historical Documents*, Hackett, 3:141. It is uncertain how common "excessive" punishments were in Florida and New Mexico. The records reveal few instances, and friars themselves claimed that incidents of over-zealousness were aberrant. For a discussion of the issues involved, see Inga Clendinnen, "Disciplining the Indians: Franciscan Ideology and Missionary Violence in Sixteenth-Century Yucatán," *Past and Present* 94 (February 1982): 27–48. For other discussions of whipping, see France V. Scholes, "Troublous Times in New Mexico, 1659–1670," 144–48; Bushnell, *Situado and Sabana*, 74, 96–98; Hann, *Apalachee*, 256–59.

44. Benavides, *Memorial*, 50; Lincoln Bruce Spiess, "Church Music in Seventeenth-Century New Mexico," *New Mexico Historical Review* 11 (1965): 5–21. There is no mention of musical instruments in John H. Hann, "Church Furnishings, Sacred Vessels and Vestments Held by the Missions of Florida: Translation of Two Inventories," 147–52.

45. Theodor Klauser, *A Short History of the Western Liturgy: An Account and*

Some Reflections, trans. John Halliburton (London: Oxford University Press, 1969), 119–120; Archdale A. King, *Liturgy of the Roman Church* (Milwaukee, Wisconsin: The Bruce Publishing Co., 1957), 42–54, 209–394; Edgerton, *Theaters of Conversion*, 279–97.

46. Benavides, *Memorial*, 28.
47. Oré, *Martyrs of Florida*, 113–14.
48. Benavides, *Memorial*, 29–30.
49. Oré, *Martyrs of Florida*, 101–2.
50. Ibid., 104–111, at 107.
51. Testimony of Lope Izquierdo, guardian of San Miguel, in *Colonizer of New Mexico*, 2:677.
52. Oré, *Martyrs of Florida*, 105.
53. Benavides, *Memorial*, 35–36.
54. Alonso de Jesús, "Memorial," 100; Benavides, *Memorial*, 3–6
55. Oré, *Martyrs of Florida*, 106.

Chapter Three

1. "Petition of Juan de Prada," in *Historical Documents Relating to New Mexico, Nueva Vizcaya, and Approaches Thereto, to 1773*, 3:108; Elinore M. Barrett, *Conquest and Catastrophe: Changing Rio Grande Pueblo Settlement Patterns in the Sixteenth and Seventeenth Centuries* (Albuquerque: University of New Mexico Press, 2002), 1–16, 53, 66–79; John H. Hann, "Demographic Patterns and Changes in Mid-Seventeenth Century Timucua and Apalachee," *Florida Historical Quarterly* (April 1986): 380–81. The extent, rate, and timing of native population declines are among the most hotly contested debates among scholars of New World contact. Henry F. Dobyns, *Their Number Become Thinned: Native American Population Dynamics in Eastern America* (Knoxville: The University of Tennessee Press, 1983), supports large precontact population numbers, high percentages of population decline from disease, and precipitous population decline ahead of Europeans' arrival in some locales; Ann F. Ramenofsky, *Vectors of Death: The Archaeology of European Contact* (Albuquerque: University of New Mexico Press, 1987), largely corroborates Dobyns' findings, but suggests that population decline from disease varied in timing and extent. Shepard Krech III, *The Ecological Indian: Myth and History* (New York: W.W. Norton, 1999), challenges Dobyns' high numbers and conclusions and suggests that there were fewer natives in the Americas before contact, and that disease had a variety of effects on native populations. Regardless of precontact numbers or percentages of population decline, disease had a catastrophic effect on native peoples.

2. James Axtell, "Some Thoughts on the Ethnohistory of Missions," *Ethnohistory* 29 (1982): 35–41; Nicolas Griffiths and Fernando Cervantes, "Introduction," in *Spiritual Encounters: Interactions between Christianity and Native Religions in*

Colonial America, 1–42; John and Jean Comaroff, *Ethnography and the Historical Imagination*, 3–48.

3. In New Mexico, Franciscans adopted blue cloaks sometime during the seventeenth century to memorialize martyred brothers and to symbolize their special status in the colony. See the exhibit at the Museum of New Mexico, Palace of the Governors, Segesser Hides Exhibit, Santa Fe, New Mexico.

4. Ramón A. Gutiérrez, *When Jesus Came, the Corn Mothers Went Away*, 46–94, suggests that Pueblos viewed Spanish friars and soldiers as foreign versions of their inside and outside chiefs, and explains Franciscan semiotics, training, and evangelism; Susan Schroeder, "Chimalpahin's View of Spanish Ecclesiastics in Colonial Mexico," in *Indian-Religious Relations in Colonial Spanish America*, ed. Susan Ramírez, 21–38, Foreign and Comparative Studies/Latin American Series 9, Maxwell School of Citizenship and Public Affairs (Syracuse University, 1989), examines Spanish strategies of missionization; John E. Worth, *Timucuan Chiefdoms of Spanish Florida*, 1:35–102, explains the methods friars used in conversion efforts in Florida, but emphasizes how Timucuas were able to influence the friars and retain power in the missions.

5. James Axtell, "Native Reactions to the Invasion of America," in *Natives and Newcomers*, 296. Others have examined some natives' responses to missions in Florida and New Mexico before. See David J. Weber, *The Spanish Frontier in North America*, 122–46; Jerald Milanich, *Laboring in the Fields of the Lord: Spanish Missions and Southeastern Indians*, 130–74.

6. Oré, *The Martyrs of Florida*, 76–78, 87–93; "The Joint Report of Cabeza de Vaca and His Companions," in *New American World* ed. David Beers Quinn, 2:69–71. For the definitive edition of Cabeza de Vaca's account, see Álvar Núñez Cabeza de Vaca, *The Narrative of Cabeza de Vaca*.

7. "Record of the marches of the army," in *Don Juan de Oñate, Colonizer of New Mexico, 1595–1628*, Hammond and Rey, 1:322; Axtell, *Natives and Newcomers*, 79–141; Christopher L. Miller and George R. Hamell, "A New Perspective on Indian-White Contact: Cultural Symbols and Colonial Trade," *The Journal of American History* 73 (September 1986): 311–28.

8. Axtell, *Natives and Newcomers*, 79–141; Worth, *Timucuan Chiefdoms*, 1:38–40; David J. Weber, "Blood of Martyrs, Blood of Indians: Toward a More Balanced View of Spanish Missions in Seventeenth-Century North America," in *Columbian Consequences*, David Hurst Thomas, 2:433–38.

9. Worth, *Timucuan Chiefdoms*, 1:12–14, 176–214; Amy Turner Bushnell, *Situado and Sabana*, 104–124; France V. Scholes, "Civil Government and Society in New Mexico in the Seventeenth Century," *New Mexico Historical Review* 10 (April 1935): 71–111; Elizabeth A. H. John, *Storms Brewed in Other Men's Worlds: The Confrontation of Indians, Spanish, and French in the Southwest, 1540–1795*, 2nd ed. (Norman: University of Oklahoma Press, 1996), 58–97.

10.   "Don Luís de Velasco to the King," in *Don Juan Oñate, Colonizer of New Mexico*, Hammond and Rey, 2:1068; "Memorial of Fray Francisco de Velasco," in ibid., 2:1093–95; "Fray Francisco de Marrón to Philip II," in *New American World*, Quinn, 5:54; "Francisco Pareja and Alonso Serrano to Philip III on the need of the missionaries," in ibid., 2:135; "The Franciscans of Florida to Philip III," in ibid., 2:139–40.

11.   John H. Hann, trans., "1630 Memorial of Fray Francisco Alonso de Jesús on Spanish Florida's Missions and Natives," 99–100; Oré, *Martyrs of Florida*, 115; "Testimony of Fray Lópe Izquierdo," in *Don Juan Oñate, Colonizer of New Mexico*, Hammond and Rey, 2:679–80; "Don Luís de Velasco to the King," in ibid., 2:1067–68; "Licentiate, Don Francisco de Leóz, king's fiscal, to the King," in ibid., 2:1071–73; "New Mexico to be Maintained, Decree regarding what fathers Fray Lázaro Ximénez and Fray Ysidro Ordóñez have been ordered to take to New Mexico," in ibid., 2:1076–77; "The King to the Viceroy," in ibid., 2:1078; "Viceroy Velasco to the King," in ibid., 2:1080; "Governor Don Pedro de Peralta's instructions," in ibid., 2:1088–90; "Memorial of Fray Francisco de Velasco," in ibid., 2:1093–94.

12.   "The triumphal visitation of the Bishop of Cuba," in *New American World*, Quinn, 5:130–33.

13.   "Testimony of Fray Nicolás Freitas," in *Historical Documents*, Hackett, 3:158; "Letter of Esteban Clemente, Pueblo of Humanas," in ibid., 3:165; "Hearing of June 16, 1663, Requested by Don Bernardo López de Mendizabal," in ibid., 3:207; "Reply of López de Mendizabal," in ibid., 3:223–24; Louis A. Hieb, "Meaning and Mismeaning: Toward an Understanding of the Ritual Clown," in *New Perspectives on the Pueblos*, Alfonso Ortiz, 163–95; Alfonso Ortiz, "Ritual Drama and the Pueblo World View," in ibid., 135–61.

14.   Oré, *Martyrs of Florida*, 107, 110n14. Julian Granberry's *A Grammar and Dictionary of the Timucua Language*, 3rd ed. (Tuscaloosa and London: University of Alabama Press, 1993), does not directly define this word but indicates that the root *utina* meant "region or province," and by extension "power" or "powerful," and that the suffix *-ma* meant "the."

15.   Granberry, *A Grammar and Dictionary of the Timucua Language*, 157.

16.   "Pedro de Castañeda's Narrative of the Expedition to Cíbola," in *Narratives of the Coronado Expedition, 1540–1542*, Hammond and Rey, 214, 218; "Diego Pérez de Luxán's Account of the Antonio de Espejo Expedition into New Mexico, 1582," in *The Rediscovery of New Mexico, 1580–1594*, Hammond and Rey, 190–91.

17.   Elsie Clews Parsons, *Pueblo Indian Religion*, 2:604, 1:360–65.

18.   Alonso de Benavides, *Benavides' Memorial of 1630*, 21–22, 26–30, 32–34; Frederick Webb Hodge, George P. Hammond, and Agapito Rey, eds., *Fray Benavides' Revised Memorial of 1634* (Albuquerque: University of New Mexico Press, 1945), 97–98; Oré, *Martyrs of Florida*, 100, 112; "The

Franciscans of Florida to Philip III," in *New American World*, Quinn,
5:138–40; "Memorial of Fray Francisco de Velasco," in *Juan de Oñate,
Colonizer of New Mexico*, Quinn, 2:1094–95; John L. Kessell, *Kiva, Cross,
and Crown: The Pecos Indians and New Mexico, 1540–1840* (Tucson:
Southwest Parks and Monuments Association, 1987), 107, 111. Humanas
was a Tompiro settlement; Jumanos were nomadic peoples in northern
Mexico south of El Paso. See Carroll L. Riley, *Kachina and the Cross*, 53, 97;
Gary Clayton Anderson, *The Indian Southwest, 1580–1830: Ethnogenesis and
Reinvention* (Norman: University of Oklahoma Press, 1999), 15–66 for dis-
tinctions between these names and people.

19. "The Franciscans of Florida to Philip III," in *New American World*, Quinn,
5:139.

20. "Declaration of Miguel de Noriega," in *Historical Documents*, Hackett,
3:184; "Hearing of June 16, 1663, Requested by Don Bernardo López de
Mendizabal," in ibid., 3:207; Kessell, *Kiva, Cross, and Crown*, 112, 150, 168.

21. Oré, *Martyrs of Florida*, 73–74; "The joint report of Cabeza de Vaca and his
companions," in *New American World*, Quinn, 2:69–70; Bushnell, *Situado
and Sabana*, 65–66.

22. Oré, *Martyrs of Florida*, 73–75; "The joint report of Cabeza de Vaca and his
companions," in *New American World*, Quinn, 2:70–71.

23. Oré, *Martyrs of Florida*, 74–76; "The joint report of Cabeza de Vaca and
his companions," in *New American World*, Quinn, 2:70–71.

24. Oré, *Martyrs of Florida*, 94–99; *Testimonyo de la obediencia de los caciques
de guale en que piden mysericordia del delito q ancome tido de ma tarlos
religiosos, 18 Mayo de [1]600*. St. Augustine. Archivo General de Indias
[AGI], 54-5-9, bnd. 802, Stetson Collection, reel 7, p. 112–18, University of
Florida Library [UFL].

25. Oré, *Martyrs of Florida*, 94–100; Royal Officials. St. Augustine, November
27, 1601, AGI 54-5-9, bnd. 833, Stetson Collection, reel 8, p.103–10, UFL.

26. Spanish missionaries' definitions of "conversion," and friars' approaches
to Indians in missions were not uniform. Sabine MacCormack, "'The
Heart Has Its Reasons:' Predicaments of Missionary Christianity in Early
Colonial Peru," *Hispanic American Historical Review* 65 (1985): 443–66,
argues that early efforts to persuade Andean peoples to adopt Christianity
gave way to a Spanish insistence that natives recognize Spanish authority,
both religious and cultural. Inga Clendinnen, "Ways to the Sacred:
Reconstructing 'Religion' in Sixteenth Century Mexico," *History and
Anthropology* 5 (1990): 105–41, focuses on "religion as performed," and
finds numerous and complex ways that Indians and Spaniards approached
spirituality, the practice of religion, and sacred behavior. Cynthia
Radding, "Cultural Boundaries between Adaptation and Defiance:
The Mission Communities of Northwestern New Spain," in *Spiritual
Encounters: Interactions between Christianity and Native Religions in
Colonial America*, Griffiths and Cervantes, 116–35 (Lincoln: University of

Nebraska Press, 1999), looks at ways natives appropriated and redefined
Spanish religious symbols. Lance Grahn, "Chicha in the Chalice?
Spiritual Conflict in Spanish American Mission Culture," in ibid., 255–75,
examines ways Indians resisted what Spaniards taught through ritual acts,
defiance, and revolt.

27. Worth, *Timucuan Chiefdoms*, 1:35–40; Milanich, *Fields of the Lord*, 104–9,
118, 121, 124, 131–37; Edgerton, *Theaters of Conversion*, 2–16.

28. James Axtell, *The Indians' New South: Cultural Change in the Colonial
Southeast* (Baton Rouge: Louisiana State University Press, 1997), 25–44;
Gary Shapiro and Richard Vernon, "Archaeology at San Luis, Part Two,"
177–278.

29. Edgerton, *Theaters of Conversion*, 247–97.

30. James E. Ivey, "The Patio Kivas of Abo and Quarai," in *"In the Midst of
Loneliness": The Architectural History of the Salinas Missions* (Santa Fe:
National Park Service, 1988), 415–21.

31. Edgerton, *Theaters of Conversion*, 79–84, 155, 183–86, 247–50, 271–97.

32. See Christian, *Local Religion in Sixteenth-Century Spain.*

33. Alonso de Jesús, "Memorial," 101; "Hearing of May 11, 1663," in *Historical
Documents*, Hackett, 3:141–42; "Copy of a letter from Fray Miguel de
Sacristán," in ibid., 3:148–50; "Letter from Fray Francisco de Salazar,
Minister of Senecú," in ibid., 3:150; "Letter from Fray Nicolás de Freitas,"
in ibid., 3:150–51; "Hearing of June 16, 1663, Requested by Don Bernardo
López de Mendizabal," in ibid., 3:209; Kessell, *Kiva, Cross, and Crown*, 111.

34. Alonso de Jesús, "Memorial," 99; René de Laudonnière, "L'histoire notable
de la Floride," in *New American World*, Quinn, 2:283, 302–3, 327–29;
"Customs of the Indians of Florida," in ibid., 2:539; Jacques le Moyne,
"Brevis Narratio," in *Settlement of Florida*, Bennett, 38–40, 70, 82; Hudson,
The Southeastern Indians, 317–36. Scholars have studied the various burial
practices of Florida's natives in depth. For Apalachees, see Hann,
Apalachee: *The Land between the Rivers*, 97, 263; John F. Scarry, "The
Apalachee Chiefdom: A Mississippian Society on the Fringe of the
Mississippian World," in *The Forgotten Centuries: Indians and Europeans in
the American South, 1521–1704*, ed. Charles Hudson and Carmen Chaves
Tesser, 162–63, 169–70 (Athens: University of Georgia Press, 1994). For
Guales and Timucuas, see William N. Morgan, *Precolumbian Architecture
in Eastern North America* (Gainesville: University Press of Florida, 1999),
206–9; Jerald T. Milanich, *Archaeology of Precolumbian Florida*
(Gainesville: University Press of Florida, 1994), 134–37, 148–50, 173–94,
267–74, 343–48, 368–80.

35. "Pedro de Castañeda's Narrative of the Expedition to Cibola," in *Coronado
Expedition*, Hammond and Rey, 253; Hernán Gallegos, "Relation and
Report of the Expedition made by Francisco Sánchez Chamuscado and
eight soldier companions in the exploration of New Mexico and new
lands, and its outcome," in *Rediscovery of New Mexico*, Hammond and

Rey, 99; Francisco de Valverde y Mercado, "Investigation of Conditions in New Mexico," in Don Juan de Oñate, *Colonizer of New Mexico*, Hammond and Rey, 2:628, 637; Hammond and Rey, *Obregón's History of 16th Century Explorations in Western America*, 297, 337; Parsons, *Pueblo Indian Religion*, 1:68–74; Wright, *Pueblo Cultures*, 9–10; Ortiz, *The Tewa World*, 15–16, 50–57, 96–97, 102–3, 123–24; E. Charles Adams, *The Origin and Development of the Pueblo Katsina Cult* (Tucson: University of Arizona Press, 1991), 9–12, 35, 60–62, 120, 155.

36. Oré, *Martyrs of Florida*, 105; Nalle, *God in La Mancha*, 179–205; Carlos Eire, *From Madrid to Purgatory: The Art and Craft of Dying in Sixteenth-Century Spain* (Cambridge: Cambridge University Press, 1995). For excavations of mission cemeteries in Florida, see McEwan, *The Spanish Missions of La Florida*, 13–21, 145–56, 176–77, 188, 193–227, 263–74, 276–86, 404–10.

37. Clark Spencer Larsen, "On the Frontier of Contact: Mission Bioarchaeology in *La Florida*," in *The Spanish Missions of La Florida*, McEwan, 322–56; Vincent Scully, *Pueblo: Mountain, Village, Dance*, 2nd ed. (Chicago: University of Chicago Press, 1989), 227–87, esp. 246–63; Kenagy, "Stepped Cloud and Cross," 325–40; Mary K. Sedgwick, *Acoma, the Sky City: A Study in Pueblo-Indian History and Civilization* (Cambridge, Mass.: Harvard University Press, 1927), 34–39.

38. Oré, *Martyrs of Florida*, 104; Benavides, *Memorial*, 35–37.

39. Oré, *Martyrs of Florida*, 127–29; Benavides, *Memorial*, 54–56; Benavides, *Revised Memorial*, 91–92; Lucy Wenhold, "A Seventeenth Century Letter of Gabriel Diaz Vara Calderón, Bishop of Cuba, Describing the Indian Missions of Florida," *Smithsonian Miscellaneous Collections*, vol. 95, no. 16 (Washington, D.C.: Smithsonian Institution, 1936), 2–14.

40. Chieftainess of Nombre de Dios, María, Letter to the King, Feb. 20, 1600. AGI, SD 231 Jeannette Thurber Connor Papers, reel 4, UFL.

41. "Testimony of Fray Nicolás de Freitas," in *Historical Documents*, Hackett, 3:163.

42. Alonso de Jesús, "Memorial," 101.

43. Francisco Pareja, *Catechismo*, 83–84.

44. "Denunciation by María de Albisu, Santa Fe," in *Historical Documents*, Hackett, 3:183; "Declaration of Joseph Nieto," in ibid., 3:273; Kessell, *Kiva, Cross, and Crown*, 153; France V. Scholes, "The First Decade of the Inquisition in New Mexico," *New Mexico Historical Review* 10 (July 1935): 195–241.

45. John H. Hann, "The Chacato Revolt Inquiry," *Florida Archaeology* 7 (1993): 32, 36–53.

46. Hann, "Chacato Revolt," 44–49, 52–75.

47. Hann, "Visitations and Revolts in Florida, 1656–1695," *Florida Archaeology* 7 (1993): 89–93, 107.

48. Parsons, *Pueblo Indian Religion*, 1:15, 108; 2:1094–97; Kessell, *Kiva, Cross,*

and Crown, 110, 132; William N. Fenton, Factionalism at Taos Pueblo, New Mexico, Bureau of American Ethnology, Bulletin 164, Anthropological Papers, no. 56 (Washington, D.C.: United States Government Printing Office, 1957), 297–344; David H. French, Factionalism in Isleta Pueblo, American Ethnological Society, Monograph 14 (New York, 1948), 1–47.

49. "Declaration of the lieutenant general of cavalry," in Revolt of the Pueblo Indians of New Mexico and Otermín's Attempted Reconquest, 1680–1682, 2 vols., ed. and trans. Charles W. Hackett and Charmion C. Shelby, 2:266 (Albuquerque: University of New Mexico Press, 1942); "Declaration of Diego López Sambrano," in ibid., 2:299–300; David M. Brugge, "Pueblo Factionalism and External Relations," Ethnohistory 16 (Spring 1969): 191–200; Hann, "Visitations and Revolts in Florida, 1656–1695," 34–93.

50. Oré, Martyrs of Florida, 106, 43.

51. "Declaration of Fray Nicolás de Chávez," in Historical Documents, Hackett, 3:153.

52. "Declaration of Captain Andrés Hurtado," in Historical Documents, Hackett, 3:188–89; Scholes, "Civil Government," 105–111; Milanich, Laboring in the Fields of the Lord, 149–74.

53. "True Report Based on Oñate's Letters," in Don Juan de Oñate, Colonizer of New Mexico, 2: 620.

54. "Petition of Father Juan de Prada," in Historical Documents, Hackett, 3:113; "Hearing of February 26, 1661," in ibid., 3:136; "Hearing of June 16, 1663, Requested by Don Bernardo López de Mendizabal," in ibid., 3:201. For the best studies of native middlemen and translators, see Eugene Lyon, "Cultural Brokers in Sixteenth-Century Spanish Florida," in Pedro Menéndez de Avilés, ed. Eugene Lyon, (New York: Garland Press, 1995), 329–36; Axtell, Natives and Newcomers, 46–75; Frances Karttunen, "Interpreters Snatched from the Shore: The Successful and the Others," in The Language Encounter in the Americas, 1492–1800, ed. Edward G. Gray and Norman Fiering, 215–29 (New York and Oxford: Berghahn Books, 2000); Isaías Lerner, "Spanish Colonization and the Indigenous Languages of America," ibid., 281–92.

55. Edward H. Spicer's, "Spanish-Indian Acculturation in the Southwest," American Anthropologist 56 (August 1954): 665–70, specifies that "compartmentalization" denotes instances when cultures were able to accept "traits and trait complexes which remained peripheral to their major cultural interests and to resist traits which would have altered the main orientations of their culture." Amy Turner Bushnell contends that Florida's natives did not compartmentalize but allowed Spanish traits to exist along with Indian ones. I concur with David Weber, who suggested that the destruction of Florida's native missions renders a definitive answer impossible. See Bushnell, "Missions and Moral Judgment," OAH Magazine of History 14 (Summer 2000): 21–22; and Weber, The Spanish Frontier in North America, 118. For definitions of "syncretism," see Spiritual

Encounters, ed. Griffith and Cervantes, 3, 26 n.4. Religion scholars distinguish between "conversion" and "adhesion" instead. Conversion is "a turning which implies... that the old was wrong and the new is right," while adhesion "led to an acceptance of new worships as useful supplements and not as substitutes." See Arthur Darby Nock, *Conversion: The Old and the New in Religion from Alexander the Great to Augustine of Hippo* (Oxford: Oxford University Press, 1933, reprint 1961), 7.

56. "Hearing of May 11, 1663," in *Historical Documents*, Hackett, 3:141; Oré, *Martyrs of Florida*, 115.

57. Worth, *Timucuan Chiefdoms of Spanish Florida*, 1:4–5, 13, 18, 81. Worth acknowledges that there are variations on the "chiefdom" theme, but admirably demonstrates how Apalachees and Timucuas fit the definition. For Guales, see John E. Worth, *The Struggle for the Georgia Coast: An Eighteenth-Century Spanish Retrospective on Guale and Mocama*, American Museum of Natural History, Anthropological Papers, no. 75 (Athens: University of Georgia Press, 1995), 9–15. For Apalachees, see Scarry, "The Apalachee Chiefdom: A Mississippian Society on the Fringe of the Mississippian World," in *The Forgotten Centuries*, Hudson and Tesser, 156–78; Randolph J. Widmer, "The Structure of Southeastern Chiefdoms," in ibid., 125–55.

58. The literature on Pueblo political and social structure is extensive. Though there was great variety among Pueblo peoples, I relied most heavily on Ortiz, *The Tewa World*, and Sando, *Pueblo Nations*.

59. Brenda J. Baker and Lisa Kealhofer, eds., *Bioarchaeology of Native American Adaptation in the Spanish Borderlands* (Gainesville: University Press of Florida, 1996), esp. ch. 5.

60. Petition of Father Juan de Prada," in *Historical Documents*, Hackett, 3:111; "Testimony of Fray Nicolás de Freitas," in ibid., 3:162; "Hearing of June 16, 1663, Requested by Don Bernardo López de Mendizabal," in ibid., 3:204; "Report of the People Who Remained in New Mexico, October 2, 1601," in *Don Juan de Oñate, Colonizer of New Mexico*, Hammond and Rey, 2:705; "Testimony of Captain Alonso Gómez Montesinos," in ibid., 2:716; John H. Hann, "Demographic Patterns," 371–92.

Chapter Four

1. Amy Turner Bushnell, *Situado and Sabana: Spain's Support System for the Presidio and Mission Provinces of Florida*, American Museum of Natural History, Anthropological Papers, no. 74 (Athens: University of Georgia Press, 1994), 30–44; John E. Worth, *Timucuan Chiefdoms of Spanish Florida*, 2 vols. (Gainesville: University Press of Florida, 1998) 1: 78; France V. Scholes, "Civil Government and Society in New Mexico in the Seventeenth Century," *New Mexico Historical Review* 10 (April 1935): 74–90; David J. Weber, *The Spanish Frontier in North America* (New Haven: Yale University Press, 1992), 128–29.

2. Scholes, "Civil Government," 81, 93–95, 105–111; Thomas D. Hall, *Social Change in the Southwest, 1350–1880* (Lawrence, Kansas: University Press of Kansas, 1989), 50–86.

3. Bushnell, *Situado and Sabana*, 43–48; Worth, *Timucuan Chiefdoms*, 1: 116–18; Weber, *The Spanish Frontier in North America*, 183.

4. France V. Scholes, "The First Decade of the Inquisition in New Mexico," *New Mexico Historical Review* 10 (July 1935): 195–241; France V. Scholes, "Problems in the Early Ecclesiastical History of New Mexico," *New Mexico Historical Review* 7 (January 1932): 32–74.

5. Bushnell, *Situado and Sabana*, 30–31; Worth, *Timucuan Chiefdoms*, 1:116–25; Scholes, "Civil Government," 91–111.

6. Charles R. Cutter, *The Legal Culture of Northern New Spain, 1700–1810* (Albuquerque: University of New Mexico Press, 1995), 32.

7. John H. Hann, *Apalachee: The Land between the Rivers* (Gainesville: University Presses of Florida, 1988), 10–18.

8. Hann, *Apalachee*, 19; Robert Allen Matter, *Pre-Seminole Florida: Spanish Soldiers, Friars, and Indian Missions, 1513–1763* (New York and London: Garland Publishing, 1990), 58–59; Bushnell, *Situado and Sabana*, 212.

9. "Captain Martín Alcayde de Cordoba, Testimony, May 2, 1660," in John E. Worth, "The Timucuan Missions of Spanish Florida and the Rebellion of 1656" (Ph.D. diss., University of Florida, 1992), 404.

10. Jerald T. Milanich, *Laboring in the Fields of the Lord: Spanish Missions and Southeastern Indians* (Washington, D.C.: Smithsonian Institution Press, 1999), 161–64; Worth, *Timucuan Chiefdoms*, 2:1–37.

11. John H. Hann, ed. and trans., "Visitations and Revolts in Florida, 1656–1695," *Florida Archaeology* 7 (1993): 7–11; John H. Hann, ed. and trans., "Translation of Governor Rebolledo's 1657 Visitation of Three Florida Provinces and Related Documents," *Florida Archaeology* 2 (1986): 83–84, 89; Worth, *Timucuan Chiefdoms*, 2:38–60.

12. Worth, *Timucuan Chiefdoms*, 2: 38–65; Fred Lamar Pearson, Jr., "Timucuan Rebellion of 1656: The Rebolledo Investigation and the Civil-Religious Controversy," *Florida Historical Quarterly* 61 (January 1983): 260–62.

13. Hann, "Visitations and Revolts," 13.

14. See John Leddy Phelan, *The People and the King: The Comunero Revolution in Colombia, 1781* (Madison: University of Wisconsin Press, 1978).

15. Worth, *Timucuan Chiefdoms*, 2: 59–64.

16. Hann, "Rebolledo's 1657 Visitation," 103–6; Worth, *Timucuan Chiefdoms*, 2: 66–116.

17. Hann, "Rebolledo's 1657 Visitation," 87–89; John H. Hann, "Governor Rebolledo's Reply to the Friars," *Florida Archaeology* 2 (1986): 111–13.

18. Hann, "Visitations and Revolts," 15–16.

19. Hann, "Rebolledo's 1657 Visitation," 87, 92, 96–97.

20. Ibid., 90, 92, 93, 97, 101.

21. Ibid., 87; see also 97.

22. John H. Hann, "Letter of Provincial and his Council," *Florida Archaeology* 7 (1993): 8; John H. Hann, "Petition of Friars to Governor Rebolledo," *Florida Archaeology* 2 (1986): 108.

23. John H. Hann, "Apalachee Friars' Counterreply," *Florida Archaeology* 7, (1993): 23.

24. John H. Hann, "Fray Juan Gómez de Enguada to Fray Francisco Martínez, Commissary of Florida," *Florida Archaeology* 2 (1986): 127.

25. Gabriel Díaz Vara Calderón, "A 17th Century Letter of Gabriel Díaz Vara Calderón, Bishop of Cuba, Describing the Indians and Indian Missions of Florida," trans. Lucy L. Wenhold, *Smithsonian Miscellaneous Collections*, vol. 95, no.16 (Washington, D.C.: Smithsonian Institution, 1936), 13–14.

26. John H. Hann, "The Ballgame Manuscript," in *Apalachee: The Land between the Rivers* (Gainesville: University Presses of Florida, 1988), 75, 333–34, 344–46; Amy Turner Bushnell, "'That Demonic Game': The Campaign to Stop Indian *Pelota* Playing in Spanish Florida, 1675–1684," *The Americas* 35 (July 1978): 6–8.

27. Hann, "Ball Game Manuscript," 331–32.

28. Ibid., 345–48.

29. Ibid., 348–49.

30. Ibid., 352; Bushnell, "That Demonic Game," 14–19.

31. John H, Hann, "Visitation Records of 1677–1678," *Florida Archaeology* 7 (1993): 78, 103.

32. Hann, "Visitation Records of 1677," 103, 110, 120.

33. Ibid., 127–28, 139.

34. John H. Hann, "Visitation Records of 1694–1695 and Related Documents," *Florida Archaeology* 7 (1993), 156.

35. "Visitation Records of 1694," 191; see also 205, 211.

36. Ibid., 162–64, 171–75, 178–79, 190–91, 201–2, 205–6, 208, 227–30.

37. Hann, "Visitation Records 1694–95," 162–64, 175, 178–79, 181–82, 190–91, 197–202, 208–11.

38. France V. Scholes, "Church and State in New Mexico, 1610–1650," *New Mexico Historical Review* 11 (January 1936): 30–38, 40–50; Scholes, "Inquisition in New Mexico," 195–98.

39. France V. Scholes, "Church and State in New Mexico, 1610–1650, Chapter III," *New Mexico Historical Review* 11 (April 1936): 167 n.5, 8, 168 n. 10–13, 169 n. 14–16. Scholes transcribed portions of Spanish documents in his footnotes.

40. Ibid., 169 n. 17, 170 n. 18–21, 171 n. 22–25.

41. Lansing B. Bloom, "The Royal Order of 1620 to Custodian Fray Estéban de Perea," *New Mexico Historical Review* 5 (July 1930), 292, 294–95; Lansing B. Bloom, "A Glimpse of New Mexico in 1620," *New Mexico Historical Review* 3 (October 1928): 364–67. Bloom transcribes and translates Viceroy Diego Fernandez de Cordova's response to the complaints of both the governor

and the friars. Eulate's original letter has not been discovered, but its contents can be gleaned from the viceroy's orders to the governor.

42. Bloom, "Glimpse of New Mexico," 364; Bloom, "Royal Order of 1620," 296.

43. Scholes, "Church and State, Ch. III," 157–65; Scholes, "First Decade of the Inquisition," 198–200.

44. France V. Scholes, "Church and State in New Mexico, 1610–1650, Chapter IV," *New Mexico Historical Review* 11 (July 1936): 287, 291 n. 9–10, 288–89, 292 n. 12.

45. France V. Scholes, "Church and State in New Mexico, 1610–1650, Chapter V," *New Mexico Historical Review* 11 (October 1936): 300, 326 n. 6–7, 327 n. 8-9.

46. Ibid., 301–4, 328–29 n. 17. Translation mine.

47. Ibid., 319–20, 323–24.

48. Ibid., 322–324; John L. Kessell, *Kiva, Cross, and Crown: The Pecos Indians and New Mexico, 1540–1840* (Tucson: Southwest Parks and Monuments Association, 1987), 156–65; Scholes tends to believe the friars' testimony more than the claims of secular authorities.

49. "Case brought by Fray Estévan de Perea against Juan López," in Charles Wilson Hackett, ed. and trans., *Historical Documents Relating to New Mexico, Nueva Vizcaya, and Approaches Thereto, to 1773*, 3 vols. (Washington, D.C.: The Carnegie Institution of Washington, 1937), 3: 130–131.

50. "Fray Nicolás de Freitas' testimony, Hearing of February 21, 1661," in Hackett, ed. and trans., *Historical Documents*, 3: 135; "Copy of a letter from Fray Miguel de Sacristán," in ibid., 3:148–50; "Excommunication Fulminated against Nicolás de Aguilar on May 29, 1660," in ibid., 3:167–68; "Deposition of Nicolás de Aguilar," in ibid., 3:170; "Hearing of June 16, 1663, Requested by Don Bernardo López de Mendizabal," in ibid., 3:200–201, 204. See France V. Scholes, "Troublous Times in New Mexico," *New Mexico Historical Review* (April 1937), 134–74; (October 1937), 380–452; (January 1938), 63–84; (July 1940), 249–68; (October 1940), 369–467; (January 1941), 15–40; (July 1941), 313–27, for a detailed history of Governor López's tenure. For a more even-handed analysis of the governor's motives and the actions of his *alcalde mayor*, see Joseph P. Sánchez, "Nicolás de Aguilar and the Jurisdiction of Salinas in the Province of New Mexico, 1659–1662," *Revista Complutense de Historia de América*, Servicio de Publicaciones, UCM, Madrid 22 (1998), 139–59.

51. "Fray Nicolás de Freitas' testimony, Hearing of February 21, 1661," in Hackett, ed. and trans., *Historical Documents*, 3:135–36; "Hearing of Nicolás de Aguilar, May 11, 1663," in ibid., 3:143–44; "Letter from Villar, Galisteo, June 14, 1660," in ibid., 3:151; "Testimony of Fray Nicolás de Freitas," in ibid., 3:160.

52. "Fray Nicolás de Freitas' testimony, Hearing of February 21, 1661," in Hackett, ed. and trans., *Historical Documents*, 3: 136–39; "Testimony of

Fray Nicolás de Freitas," in ibid., 3:159, 160; "Deposition of Nicolás de
Aguilar, May 8, 1663," in ibid., 3:172. For Aguilar's responses to the friar's
specific charges see Hackett, ed. and trans., *Historical Documents*, 3:144–46.

53. "Declaration of Fray Nicolás de Freitas, Mexico, January, 1661," in Hackett, ed.
and trans., *Historical Documents*, 3:134–35; "Copy of a letter from Fray Miguel
de Sacristán," in ibid., 3:148; "Excommunication Fulminated against Nicolás
de Aguilar on May 29, 1660," in ibid., 3:167–68, 170, 174; "Hearing of June 16,
1663, Requested by Don Bernardo López de Mendizabal," in ibid., 3:202–5.

54. "Reply of Don Bernardo López de Mendizabal," in Hackett, ed. and trans.,
Historical Documents, 3:215–17.

55. "Hearing of May 11, 1663," in Hackett, ed. and trans., *Historical Documents*,
3:141; "Reply of Don Bernardo López de Mendizabal," in ibid., 3:218;
"Declaration of Juan Domínguez de Mendoza, June 20, 1663," in ibid., 3:234.

56. "Hearing of May 11, 1663," in Hackett, ed. and trans., *Historical
Documents*, 3:141; "Hearing of Don Bernardo López de Mendazabal," in
ibid., 3:196–97.

57. "Report to the viceroy by the cabildo of Santa Fe, New Mexico, February
21, 1639," in Hackett, ed. and trans., *Historical Documents*, 3:66–72.

58. "Reply of Don Bernardo López de Mendazabal," in Hackett, ed. and trans.,
Historical Documents, 3:213–14; see also 3: "Hearing of May 11, 1663," in
ibid., 3:144; "Declaration of Captain Andrés Hurtado," ibid., 3:190–93.

59. "Deposition of Thomé Domínguez, Retired Sargento Mayor," in Hackett,
ed. and trans., *Historical Documents*, 3: 178.

60. "Deposition of Thomé Domínguez, Retired Sargento mayor," in Hackett, ed.
and trans., *Historical Documents*, 3:177; "Reply of Don Bernardo López de
Mendizabal," in ibid., 3:223. A *zarambaque* is a kind of merry and noisy dance.

61. "Letter from Fray Francisco de Salazar," in Hackett, ed. and trans.,
Historical Documents, 3:150–51.

62. "Letter of Esteban Clemente, Pueblo of Humanas, November 30, 1660," in
Hackett, ed. and trans., *Historical Documents*, 3:165.

63. "Testimony of Fray Nicolás de Freitas," in Hackett, ed. and trans.,
Historical Documents, 3:160. For Spanish conceptions of native
"demonology" see Fernando Cervantes, *The Devil in the New World: The
Impact of Diabolism in New Spain* (New Haven and London: Yale
University Press, 1994).

64. "Letters of religious in Salinas, 1660," in Hackett, ed. and trans., *Historical
Documents*, 3:137; "Declaration of Francisco Valencia, Isleta, May 24, 1661,"
in ibid., 3:180.

65. "Declaration of Captain Diego de Truxillo," in Hackett, ed. and trans.,
Historical Documents, 3:181; "Testimony of Nicolás de Freitas,"in ibid.,
3:162; "Letter from Fray García de San Francisco to the Inquisitor,
December 10, 1660," in ibid. 3:164.

66. "Letter from Fray García de San Francisco to the Inquisitor, December 10,
1660," in Hackett, ed. and trans., *Historical Documents*, 3:164; see also

"Letter of Fray Alónso de Posadas, to the Holy Office, May 23, 1661," in ibid., 3:166; "Deposition of Thomé Domínguez, Retired Sargento Mayor," in ibid., 3:179–80; "Declaration of Francisco Valencia, Isleta, May 24, 1661," in ibid., 3:180; "Declaration of Captain Diego de Truxillo," in ibid. 3:181; "Letter of Fray Alónso de Posadas, December 5, 1661," in ibid. 3:231.

67.   Lauren Benton, "Making Order Out of Trouble: Jurisdictional Politics in the Spanish Colonial Borderlands," *Law and Social Inquiry: Journal of the American Bar Foundation* 26 (Spring 2001), 373–40. Benton summarizes various scholars' interpretations of the jurisdictional dispute between Spanish religious and secular authorities on 388–89. She focuses on the legal issues at stake in the Spanish world, much as France V. Scholes did. Ramón Gutiérrez contended that the conflict was a struggle between the sacred and the secular components of the colonial authority and that the Indians only rejected them both when the friars were unable to protect the Indians from the ravages of disease and increased labor demands. I tend to agree more with Charles Cutter, who suggested that control over Indians, their goods, and labor, was the primary problem between the Spanish friars and governors in New Mexico. While legal conflicts certainly were important factors, the fact that the religious–civil struggle in New Mexico was more intense than in Florida suggests that other factors created a more combustible atmosphere in the Southwest. See also, Sánchez, "Jurisdiction of Salinas," 157–59.

Chapter Five

1.   Charles F. Merbes, "Patterns of Health and Sickness in the Precontact Southwest," in *Columbian Consequences*, Thomas, 1:47–50; C. Margaret Scarry and Elizabeth J. Reitz, "Herbs, Fish, Scum, and Vermin: Subsistence Strategies in Sixteenth-Century Spanish Florida," in ibid., 2:343–54; Philip L. Walker, "A Spanish Borderlands Perspective on La Florida Bioarchaeology," in *Bioarchaeology of Spanish Florida: The Impact of Colonialism*, ed. Clark Spencer Larsen, 276–81 (Gainesville: University Press of Florida, 2001). See Milanich, *Archaeology of Precolumbian Florida*, for a detailed description of precontact peoples in Florida.

2.   Merbes, "Patterns of Health," 44–50; Walker, "Spanish Borderlands Perspective," 281–84; Clark Spencer Larsen, Margaret J. Schoeninger, Dale L. Hutchinson, Katherine F. Russell, and Christopher B. Ruff, "Beyond Demographic Collapse" Biological Adaptation and Change in Native Populations of La Florida," in *Columbian Consequences*, 2:409–28; Clark Spencer Larsen, "Bioarchaeology of Spanish Florida," in *Bioarchaeology of Spanish Florida*, Larsen, 25–43; Thomas E. Andreoli, et al, *Cecil Essentials of Medicine*, 3rd ed. (Philadelphia: W.B. Saunders Company, 1993), 256, 353, 604–8, 650, 662–63, 696–98.

3.   Clark Spencer Larsen, Christopher B. Ruff, and Mark C. Griffen,
       "Implications of Changing Biomechanical and Nutritional Environments
       for Activity and Lifeway in the Eastern Spanish Borderlands," in
       Bioarchaeology of Native American Adaptation in the Spanish Borderlands,
       Baker and Kealhofer, 95–125; Ann L. W. Stodder, "Paleoepidemiology of
       Eastern and Western Pueblo Communities in Protohistoric and Early
       Historic New Mexico," in ibid., 148–51, 166–67; Ann M. Palkovich,
       "Historic Depopulation in the American Southwest: Issues of
       Interpretation and Context-Embedded Analyses," in ibid., 180, 184–85, 191;
       Lisa Kealhofer and Brenda J. Baker, "Counterpoint to Collapse:
       Depopulation and Adaptation," in ibid., 210–11, 214; Ann F. Ramenofsky,
       "The Problem of Introduced Infectious Diseases in New Mexico: AD
       1540–1680," *Journal of Anthropological Research* 52 (1996), 161–84. These
       scholars have demonstrated that disease did not affect native populations
       in uniform ways and depended on a variety of factors including settle-
       ment patterns, diet, climate, duration of European contact, timing of
       European contact, native medicine, and native economies.

4.   Merbes, "Patterns of Health," 48–50; Steadman Upham and Lori Stephens
       Reed, "Regional Systems in the Central and Northern Southwest:
       Demography, Economy, and Sociopolitics Preceding Contact," in
       Columbian Consequences, Thomas, 1:57–76; Mark C. Griffin, Patricia M.
       Lambert, and Elizabeth Monahan Driscoll, "Biological Relationships and
       Population History of Native Peoples in Spanish Florida and the
       American Southeast," in *Bioarchaeology of Spanish Florida,* Larsen, 226–73.

5.   Larsen, *Bioarchaeology of Spanish Florida,* 113–41, 146–75, 181–200, 207–25;
       Elisabeth J. Reitz, "Evidence for Animal Use at the Missions of Spanish
       Florida," in *The Spanish Missions of La Florida,* McEwan, 376–98;
       Katherine A. Spielmann, Margaret J. Schoeninger, and Katherine Moore,
       "Plains-Pueblo Interdependence and Human Diet at Pecos Pueblo, New
       Mexico," *American Antiquity* 55 (1990), 745–65; Stodder,
       "Paleoepidemiology," 148–76; Merbes, "Patterns of Health," 47, 50–55.

6.   Worth, *The Struggle for the Georgia Coast,* 22–27, 46, 104–6, 169; Milanich,
       Laboring in the Fields of the Lord, 166–72.

7.   James Axtell, *The Indians' New South: Cultural Change in the Colonial
       Southeast* (Baton Rouge: Louisiana State University Press, 1997), 40–44, 61,
       63; Alan Gallay, *The Indian Slave Trade: The Rise of the English Empire in
       the American South, 1670–1717* (New Haven: Yale University Press, 2002),
       40–69, 127–54, 199–222.

8.   Milanich, *Laboring in the Fields of the Lord,* 172, 177, 183; Worth, *Struggle
       for the Georgia Coast,* 20–25, 35, 45–61, 90–101; Worth, *The Timucuan
       Chiefdoms of Spanish Florida,* 2: 140, 144.

9.   Worth, *Struggle for the Georgia Coast,* 15–24, 35–39, 45–50, 76–86, 146,
       173–74; Bushnell, *Situado and Sabana,* 134–47, 161–71, 190–94.

10.   Worth, *Struggle for the Georgia Coast,* 84, 85–87; John H. Hann, "Visitation

Records of 1694–1695 and Related Documents," *Florida Archaeology* 7 (1993), 187–88, 202, 205–6, 208–9, 226, 236, 242–44; John H. Hann, "Visitation Records of 1677–1678," *Florida Archaeology* 7 (1993), 130–31.

11. Hann, "Visitation of 1677–1678," 118; Worth, *Struggle for the Georgia Coast,* 20–22, 75–82, 89, 186–87.

12. Worth, *Struggle for the Georgia Coast,* 71–73; Hann, "Visitation of 1677–1678," 108, 135; Hann, "Visitation of 1694–1695," 163, 178–79, 187–88, 190, 197, 201–3, 205–6, 208.

13. Worth, *Struggle for the Georgia Coast,* 77–78; Hann, "Visitation of 1694–1695," 190, 208, 211, 242–45.

14. Mark F. Boyd, "Fort San Luis: Documents Describing the Tragic End of the Mission Era," in *Here They Once Stood: The Tragic End of the Apalachee Missions,* ed. Mark F. Boyd, Hale G. Smith, and John W. Griffin, 21 (Gainesville: University Press of Florida, [1951] 1999).

15. Ibid.; Amy Turner Bushnell, "Patricio de Hinachuba: Defender of the Word of God, The Crown of the King, and the Little Children of Ivitachuco," *American Indian Culture and Research Journal* 3:3 (1979): 1–21.

16. Boyd, "Fort San Luis," 26.

17. Ibid., 34.

18. Ibid., 35; Hann, "Visitation of 1677–1678," 104; Hann, Visitation of 1694–1695," 150.

19. Boyd, et. al., *Here They Once Stood,* 37–38; Worth, *Timucuan Chieftains,* 2: 144.

20. Boyd, "Fort San Luis," 45–46.

21. Worth, *Struggle for the Georgia Coast,* 93.

22. Ibid., 110.

23. Hann, "Visitation of 1694–1695," 245.

24. Boyd, "Fort San Luis," 94; Worth, *Struggle for the Georgia Coast,* 146–64.

25. Bushnell, *Situado and Sabana,* 190–194; Milanich, *Laboring in the Fields of the Lord,* 173–74.

26. Boyd, "Fort San Luis," 49, 53, 74–75; Hann, *Apalachee,* 264–317.

27. Boyd, "Fort San Luis," 54, 57–58, 61, 78; Worth, *Timucuan Chiefdoms,* 2:145–46; Hann, *Apalachee,* 284–317.

28. Boyd, "Fort San Luis," 90, 93; Milanich, *Laboring in the Fields of the Lord,* 184–85; Hann, *Apalachee,* 265–83, disputes Moore's calculations of his attack and questions Boyd's transcription and translation of various documents.

29. James F. Brooks, *Captives and Cousins: Slavery, Kinship, and Community in the Southwest Borderlands* (Chapel Hill: University of North Carolina Press for the Omohundro Institute of Early American History and Culture, 2002), 48–55. Brooks shows how slaving created intercultural networks of exchange and provided a means for men to acquire honor in the century following the Pueblo Revolt. Slaving and honor were issues in

New Mexico before the revolt, but Brooks is less interested in the seventeenth century. John, *Storms Brewed in Other Men's Worlds*, 59–64, 71–77; Jonathan Haas and Winifred Creamer, "Warfare Among the Pueblos: Myth, History, and Ethnography," *Ethnohistory* 44 (Spring 1997): 235–61; Curtis F. Schaafsma, "Pueblo and Apachean Alliance Formation in the Seventeenth Century," in *Archaeologies of the Pueblo Revolt*, Preucel, 199–210.

30. See James E. Ivey, "'The Greatest Misfortune of All': Famine in the Province of New Mexico, 1667–1672," *Journal of the Southwest* 36 (1994): 76–100.

31. "Declaration of Diego López Sambrano," in *Revolt of the Pueblo Indians of New Mexico and Otermín's Attempted Reconquest, 1680–1682*, Hackett and Shelby, 2:299.

32. Ibid., 2:299–300; John L. Kessell, "Esteban Clemente: Precursor of the Pueblo Revolt," *El Palacio* 86:4 (Winter 1980–81), 16–17.

33. John, *Storms Brewed*, 92–94.

34. J. Manuel Espinosa, *The Pueblo Indian Revolt of 1696 and the Franciscan Missions in New Mexico: Letters of the Missionaries and Related Documents* (Norman: University of Oklahoma Press, 1988), 30–31.

35. "Declaration of Diego López Sambrano," in *Revolt of the Pueblo Indians*, Hackett and Shelby, 2:292–302; Espinosa, *Pueblo Indian Revolt of 1696*, 31–32.

36. "Declaration of the Indian Juan," in *Revolt of the Pueblo Indians*, Hackett and Shelby, 2:233; "Declaration of Josephe, Spanish-Speaking Indian," in ibid., 2:239; "Declaration of Pedro Naranjo of the Queres Nation," in ibid., 2:245–48; Alfonso Ortiz, "Popay's Leadership: A Pueblo Perspective," *El Palacio* 86:4 (Winter 1980–1981), 18–22, examines the message, the man, and the Pueblo context of the revolt's leader; Stefanie Beninato, "Popé, Pose-yemu, and Naranjo: A New Look at Leadership in the Pueblo Revolt of 1680," *New Mexico Historical Review* 65 (October 1990): 417–35, suggests that others had leadership roles and that the social structure of Pueblos' cultures suggests that several natives led the revolt.

37. "Auto and judicial process, Santa Fe, August 13–20, 1680," in *Revolt of the Pueblo Indians*, Hackett and Shelby, 1:16; "Declaration of Josephe, Spanish-Speaking Indian," in ibid., 2:239.

38. "Autos drawn up as a result of the rebellion of the Christian Indians, Santa Fe, August 9, 1680," in ibid., 1:3, 4; "Declaration of Pedro Hidalgo, soldier," in ibid., 1:6; "Auto of Antonio de Otermín," in ibid., 1:8; "Auto, Santa Fe, August 13, 1680," in ibid., 1:11. Scholars offer different perspectives on the Pueblo Revolt of 1680. Marc Simmons, "The Pueblo Revolt: Why Did It Happen?" *El Palacio* 86:4 (Winter 1980–81), 11–15, suggests that unrest in the decade preceding the revolt led to violence; Thomas E. Chavez, "But Were They All Natives?" *El Palacio* 86:4 (Winter 1980–81): 32, recognizes Apache influences on the rebels; Gutiérrez, *When Jesus Came*,

the *Corn Mothers Went Away*, 95–140, emphasizes the role strict Franciscan missionaries played in antagonizing their charges; Henry Warner Bowden, *American Indians and Christian Missions: Studies in Cultural Conflict* (Chicago: Chicago University Press, 1981), 53–58, cites 1670s drought conditions, but suggests that Pueblo religion played an important role; Andrew L. Knaut, *The Pueblo Revolt of 1680: Conquest and Resistance in Seventeenth-Century New Mexico* (Norman: University of Oklahoma Press, 1995), cites unrest in the Pueblos throughout the seventeenth century and addresses the significance of native leadership, drought, Spanish and native factionalism, and colonization.

39. "Auto and judicial process, Santa Fe, August 13–20, 1680," in *Revolt of the Pueblo Indians*, Hackett and Shelby, 1:13; "Declaration of Josephe Spanish-Speaking Indian," in ibid., 2:239–40.

40. "Declaration of an Indian rebel," in *Revolt of the Pueblo Indians*, Hackett and Shelby, 1:20; "Declaration of Pedro Garcia, an Indian of the Tagno [Tano] nation, a native of Las Salinas," in ibid., 1:24; "Letter of the governor and captain-general, Don Antonio de Otermin, from New Mexico," in ibid., 1:98–99; "Declaration of the Indian Juan," in ibid., 2:235; "Declaration of Josephe, Spanish-Speaking Indian," in ibid., 2:239–40; "Declaration of Lucas, Piro Indian," in ibid., 2:244; "Declaration of Pedro Naranjo of the Queres Nation," in ibid., 2:247; "Declaration of Juan Lorenzo and Francisco Lorenzo, brothers," in ibid., 2:251; "Declaration of Sargento Mayor Luis de Quintana," in ibid., 2:286.

41. "Letter of the governor and captain-general, Don Antonio de Otermin, from New Mexico," in *Revolt of the Pueblo Indians*, Hackett and Shelby, 1:100–103.

42. "Otermin's march, August 26, 1680," in ibid., 1: 26.

43. "Opinion of the Cabildo of Santa Fe, La Salineta, October 3, 1680," in ibid., 1:177–78.

44. "Declaration of Pedro Garcia, an Indian of the Tagno nation, a native of Las Salinas," in ibid., 1:25; "Declaration of Josephe, Spanish-Speaking Indian," in ibid., 2:239; "Declaration of Juan Lorenzo and Francisco Lorenzo, brothers," in ibid., 2:250; "Declaration of the lieutenant of cavalry," in ibid., 2:262. See also Barbara De Marco, "Voices from the Archives, Part 1: Testimony of the Pueblo Indians in the 1680 Pueblo Revolt," *Romance Philology* 53, pt. 2 (Spring 2000): 375–448. Some Apaches joined the rebellion but did so to capture slaves, redeem kidnapped kin, to reestablish trade ties with eastern Pueblos, and to secure honor and prestige. See Brooks, *Captives and Cousins*, 48–59. Their goals were contrary to Pueblo millenarian thinking that necessitated the expulsion of Spaniards from the Southwest. Apache allies played a supporting rather than a lead role in the revolt.

45. "Declaration of Pedro Naranjo of the Queres Nation," in *Revolt of the Pueblo Indians*, Hackett and Shelby, 2:248.

46. "Declaration of one of the rebellious Christian Indians who was captured on the road," in *Revolt of the Pueblo Indians*, Hackett and Shelby, 1:60; "Statement of Pedro García," in ibid., 1:62.

47. "Declaration of an Indian rebel," in ibid., 1: 20; "Auto of the march and halting places," in ibid., 1:22; "Auto of Alonso García," in ibid., 1:70; "Auto for passing muster, reviewing arms and horses, and others things taken on 29 September 1680," in ibid., 1:159; "Declaration of Juan de la Cruz," in ibid., 2:329–30.

48. "Letter from Father Fray Antonio de Sierra to the father visitador," in ibid., 1:59.

49. "Auto of Alonso García," in ibid., 1:66; "Letter of the governor and captain-general, Don Antonio de Otermín, from New Mexico," in ibid., 1:98. See Barbara De Marco, "Voices from the Archives, Part 2: Francisco de Ayeta's 1693 Retrospective on the 1680 Pueblo Revolt," *Romance Philology* 53, pt. 2 (Spring 2000): 449–508.

50. "Letter of the governor of El Parral, Don Bartolomé de Estrada, to the viceroy," in *Revolt of the Pueblo Indians*, Hackett and Shelby, 1:45.

51. "Auto of Antonio de Otermín," in ibid., 1:122; "Another letter of the same [Don Bartolomé de Estrada] of La Nueva Vizcaya," in ibid., 1:133–34; Daniel T. Reff, "The 'Predicament of Culture' and Spanish Missionary Accounts of the Tepehuan and Pueblo Revolts," *Ethnohistory* 42:1 (Winter 1995): 63–90; Jane C. Sanchez, "Spanish-Indian Relations During the Otermín Administration, 1677–1683," *New Mexico Historical Review* 58 (January 1983): 133–51.

52. "Muster roll, Place of El Ancón de Fray García, November 7–10, 1681," in *Revolt of the Pueblo Indians*, Hackett and Shelby, 1:201.

53. "March of the army from El Paso to La Isleta," in ibid., 2:208–12.

54. "Auto and letter, La Isleta, December 10, 1681," in ibid., 2:224–25; "Continuation of the march," in ibid., 2:231; "Declaration of the lieutenant general of cavalry," in ibid., 2:259–60.

55. "Letter of Juan Domínguez de Mendoza to Antonio de Otermín," in ibid., 2:220; "Continuation of the march," in ibid., 2:227; "Declaration of the lieutenant general of cavalry," in ibid., 2:259–60.

56. "Declaration of Sargento Mayor Luís de Quintana," in ibid., 2:291; "Opinion of Fray Francisco de Ayeta," in ibid., 2:307–8; Fray Sylvestre Vélez de Escalante to Fray Juan Agustín Morfi, in *The Spanish Archives of New Mexico*, 2 vols., ed. Ralph Emerson Twitchell, 2:267–80 (New York: Arno Press, 1976).

57. For friars' letters during the resettlement of New Mexico, see Espinosa, *Pueblo Indian Revolt of 1696*, 75–290. For the secular perspective, see John L. Kessell and Rick Hendricks, eds., *By Force of Arms: The Journals of Don Diego de Vargas, 1691–1693* (Albuquerque: University of New Mexico Press, 1992); John L. Kessell, Rick Hendricks, and Meredith Dodge, eds., *To The Royal Crown Restored: The Journals of Don Diego de Vargas, New Mexico,*

1692–1694 (Albuquerque: University of New Mexico Press, 1995); John L. Kessell, Rick Hendricks, and Meredith Dodge, eds., Blood on the Boulders: The Journals of Don Diego de Vargas, New México, 1694–1697, 2 vols. (Albuquerque: University of New Mexico Press, 1998); John L. Kessell, Rick Hendricks, Meredith Dodge, and Larry D. Miller, eds., That Disturbances Cease: The Journals of Don Diego de Vargas, New Mexico, 1697–1700 (Albuquerque: University of New Mexico Press, 2000).

58. Hackett and Shelby, Revolt of the Pueblo Indians, 1:xxiv–clxxxiii; Oakah L. Jones, Jr., Pueblo Warriors and Spanish Conquest (Norman: University of Oklahoma Press, 1966). For a study of Spanish military advantages and technology see John F. Guilmartin, Jr., "The Cutting Edge: An Analysis of the Spanish Invasion and Overthrow of the Inca Empire, 1532–1539," in Transatlantic Encounters: Europeans and Andeans in the Sixteenth Century, ed. Kenneth J. Andrien and Rolena Adorno, 40–69 (Berkeley: University of California Press, 1991).

Chapter Six

1. For analyses of Spanish religious imperatives in the Americas, see Robert L. Kapitzke, Religion, Power, and Politics in Colonial St. Augustine (Gainesville: University Press of Florida, 2001), esp. 8–66; Anthony Pagden, Lords of All the World: Ideologies of Empire in Spain, Britain, and France, c.1500–c.1800 (New Haven: Yale University Press, 1995), esp. 37–102.

2. Norris, "The Franciscans in New Mexico, 1692–1754: Toward a New Assessment," 152–53n.6.

3. Rick Hendricks and Gerald Mandell, "Francisco de Lima, Portuguese Merchants of Parral, and the New Mexico Trade, 1638–1675," New Mexico Historical Review 77 (2002): 263, 266, 268–70, 274–75; Oakah L. Jones, Jr., "San José del Parral: Colonial Trade of Parralenses with Nuevo México and El Paso del Rio del Norte," The Journal of Big Bend Studies 13 (2001): 16–18; María Luisa Pérez-González, "Royal Roads in the Old and the New World: The Camino de Oñate and Its Importance in the Spanish Settlement of New Mexico," Colonial Latin American Historical Review 7 (1998): 213. Hendricks and Mandell indicate that travel was more frequent along New Mexico's Royal Road than France V. Scholes has suggested. Regardless, New Mexico's trade and communication was less frequent, reliable, and regular than Florida's. See Bushnell, Situado and Sabana, 51–52, 113–16.

SELECTED BIBLIOGRAPHY

Manuscripts

Jeannette Thurber Connor Papers. P. K. Yonge Library of Florida History, University of Florida, Gainesville, Florida.

Woodbury Lowery Collection. P. K. Yonge Library of Florida History, University of Florida, Gainesville, Florida.

France Vinton Scholes Collection. Zimmerman Library, University of New Mexico, Albuquerque, New Mexico.

John Batterson Stetson Collection. P. K. Yonge Library of Florida History, University of Florida, Gainesville, Florida.

Primary Sources

Andrews, Evangeline Walker, and Charles McLean Andrews, eds. *Jonathan Dickinson's Journal or, God's Protecting Providence; Being a Narrative of a Journey from Port Royal in Jamaica to Philadelphia between August 23, 1696 and April 1, 1697*. New Haven: Yale University Press, 1945.

Benavides, Fray Alonso. *Benavides' Memorial of 1630*. Translated by Peter P. Forrestal. Washington, D.C.: Academy of American Franciscan History, 1954.

Bennett, Charles E. *A Harvest of Reluctant Souls: The Memorial of Fray Alonso de Benavides, 1630*. Edited and translated by Baker H. Morrow. Niwot, Colorado: University Press of Colorado, 1996.

———. *Laudonnière and Fort Caroline: History and Documents*. Tuscaloosa: University of Alabama Press, 2001.

———. ed. and trans. *Settlement of Florida*. Gainesville: University of Florida Press, 1968.

Bloom, Lansing B. "A Glimpse of New Mexico in 1620." *New Mexico Historical Review* 111 (1928): 357–80.

———. "The Royal Order of 1620 to Custodian Fray Estéban de Perea." *New Mexico Historical Review* 5 (1930): 288–98.

———. "Fray Estevan de Perea's *Relacion*." *New Mexico Historical Review* 8 (1933): 211–35.

Boyd, Mark F., Hale G. Smith, and John W. Griffin, ed., *Here They Once Stood: The Tragic End of the Apalachee Missions*. Gainesville: University Press of Florida, [1951] 1999.

———. "Further Consideration of the Apalachee Missions." *The Americas* 9 (1953.): 459–79.

Cabeza de Vaca, Alvar Núñez. *His Account, His Life, and the Expedition of Pánfilo de Narváez*. Edited and translated by Rolena Adorno and Patrick C. Pautz. Lincoln: University of Nebraska Press, 1999.

———. *The Narrative of Cabeza de Vaca*. Edited and translated by Rolena Adorno and Patrick C. Pautz. Lincoln: University of Nebraska Press, 2003.

Chamberlin, Robert, trans. *Requerimiento*. Washington, D.C.: Carnegie Endowment of Washington, 1948.

Clayton, Lawrence A., Vernon James Knight, Jr., and Edward C. Moore, eds. *The De Soto Chronicles: The Expedition of Hernando de Soto to North America in 1539–1543*. 2 vols. Tuscaloosa: University of Alabama Press, 1993.

Connor, Jeanette Thurber, ed. and trans. *Colonial Records of Spanish Florida*. 2 vols. Deland: The Florida State Historical Society, 1925, 1930.

Cordoba, Fray Pedro de. *Doctrina Cristiana y Cartas*. Santo Domingo: Ediciones de la Fundación Corripio, Inc., [1986] 1988.

d'Escalante Fontaneda, Hernando. *Memoir of D.o d'Escalante [sic] Fontaneda Respecting Florida. Written in Spain about the Year 1575*. Edited by David O. True et al. Translated by Buckingham Smith. Coral Gables, Florida: University of Miami Press, 1944.

De Marco, Barbara. "Voices from the Archives, Part 1: Testimony of the Pueblo Indians in the 1680 Pueblo Revolt." *Romance Philology* 53, pt. 2 (Spring 2000): 375–448.

———. "Voices from the Archives, Part 2: Francisco de Ayeta's 1693 Retrospective on the 1680 Pueblo Revolt." *Romance Philology* 53, pt. 2 (Spring 2000): 449–508.

Espinosa, J. Manuel. *The Pueblo Indian Revolt of 1696 and the Franciscan Missions in New Mexico: Letters of the Missionaries and Related Documents*. Norman: University of Oklahoma Press, 1988.

Habig, Marion, ed. *St. Francis of Assisi, Writings and Early Biographies: English Omnibus of the Sources for the Life of St. Francis*. Chicago: Franciscan Herald Press, 1973.

Hackett, Charles Wilson, ed. and trans. *Historical Documents Relating to New Mexico, Nueva Vizcaya, and Approaches Thereto, to 1773*. 3 vols. Washington, D.C.: The Carnegie Institution of Washington, 1923.

Hackett, Charles W., and Carmion C. Shelby, eds. and trans. *Revolt of the Pueblo Indians of New Mexico and Otermin's Attempted Reconquest, 1680–1682*. 2 vols. Albuquerque: University of New Mexico Press, 1942.

Hammond, George P., and Agapito Rey, eds. and trans. *Obregón's History of 16th Century Explorations in Western America: Chronicle, Commentary, or Relation of the Ancient and Modern Discoveries in New Spain and New Mexico, Mexico, 1584*. Los Angeles: Wetzel Publishing Co., Inc., 1928.

———. *Narratives of the Coronado Expedition, 1540–1542*. Albuquerque: University of New Mexico Press, 1940.

―――. *Don Juan de Oñate, Colonizer of New Mexico, 1595–1628.* 3 vols.
Albuquerque: University of New Mexico Press, 1953.

―――. *The Rediscovery of New Mexico, 1580–1594: The Explorations of
Chamuscado, Espejo, Castaño de Sosa, Morlete, and Leyva de Bonilla and
Humaña.* Albuquerque: University of New Mexico Press, 1966.

Hann, John H. "The Chacato Revolt Inquiry," *Florida Archaeology* 7 (1993):
32, 36–53.

―――. ed. and trans. "Church Furnishings, Sacred Vessels and Vestments Held
by the Missions of Florida: Translation of Two Inventories." *Florida
Archaeology* 2 (1986): 147–64.

―――. ed. and trans. "Heathen Acuera, Murder, and a Potano Cimarrona: The
St. Johns River and the Alachua Prairie in the 1670s." *Florida Historical
Quarterly* (1992): 451–74.

―――. ed. and trans. "1630 Memorial of Fray Francisco Alonso de Jesus on
Spanish Florida's Missions and Natives." *The Americas* 50 (1993): 85–105.

―――. ed. and trans. "Translation of Alonso de Leturiondo's Memorial to the
King of Spain."
Florida Archaeology 2 (1986): 165–225.

―――. ed. and trans. "Translation of Governor Rebolledo's 1657 Visitation of
Three Florida Provinces and Related Documents." *Florida Archaeology* 2
(1986): 81–145.

―――. "Visitation Records of 1677–1678," *Florida Archaeology* 7 (1993):

―――. ed. and trans. "Visitations and Revolts in Florida, 1656–1695." *Florida
Archaeology* 7 (1993): 1–296.

Hodge, Frederick Webb, George P. Hammond, and Agapito Rey, eds. and trans.
Fray Benavides' Revised Memorial of 1634. Albuquerque: University of New
Mexico Press, 1945.

Kessell, John L., and Rick Hendricks, eds. *The Spanish Missions of New Mexico I:
Before 1680.* New York and London: Garland Publishing, 1991.

―――. *By Force of Arms: The Journals of Don Diego de Vargas, 1691–1693.*
Albuquerque: University of New Mexico Press, 1992.

Kessell, John L., Rick Hendricks, and Meredith Dodge, eds. *To The Royal Crown
Restored: The Journals of Don Diego de Vargas, New Mexico, 1692–1694.*
Albuquerque: University of New Mexico Press, 1995.

―――. *Blood on the Boulders: The Journals of Don Diego de Vargas, New
Mexico, 1694–1697.* 2 vols. Albuquerque: University of New Mexico
Press, 1998.

Kessell, John L., Rick Hendricks, Meredith Dodge, and Larry D. Miller, eds.
*That Disturbances Cease: The Journals of Don Diego de Vargas, New
Mexico, 1697–1700.* Albuquerque: University of New Mexico
Press, 2000.

Labouret, Henri, and Paul Rivet, eds. *Le Royaume d'Arda et son Èvangèlisation au
XVII siècle.* Paris: Institut D'ethnologie, Université de Paris, 1929.

Las Casas, Bartolomé de. *A Short Account of the Destruction of the Indies.* Edited and translated by Nigel Griffen. London: Penguin, 1992.

———. *In Defense of the Indians: The Defense of the most Reverend Lord, Don Fray Bartolomé de las Casas, of the Order of Preachers, Late Bishop of Chiapa, Against the Persecutors and Slanderers of the Peoples of the New World Discovered Across the Seas,* edited and translated by Stafford Poole. DeKalb: Northern Illinois University Press, 1974.

Laudonnière, René de. *Three Voyages.* Edited and translated by Charles E. Bennett. Gainesville: University Presses of Florida, 1975.

Lawson, Sarah, ed. and trans. *A Foothold in Florida: The Eye-Witness Account of Four Voyages made by the French to that Region and Their Attempt at Colonisation, 1562–1568.* Somerset, England: Castle Cary Press, 1992.

Lopez de Gauna, Martin. "Ynstruccion a Peralta por Vi-Rey." Transcribed by Lansing B. Bloom. Translated by Ireno L. Chaves. *New Mexico Historical Review* 4 (1929): 178–87.

Milanich, Jerald T., and William C. Sturtevant, eds. *Francisco Pareja's 1613 Confessionario: A Documentary Source for Timucuan Ethnography.* Tallahassee: Division of Archives, History, and Records Management, Florida Department of State, 1972.

Oré, Luis Gerónimo de. *The Martyrs of Florida, 1513–1616.* Translated by Maynard Geiger. New York: Joseph F. Wagner, Inc., 1936.

Pareja, Fray Francisco. *Catechismo y breve exposicion de la doctrina christiana; muy util y necessaria, asi para los Españoles como para los naturals, en lengua Castellana, y Timuquana, en modo de preguntas, y respuestas.* Mexico: en casa de la viuda de Pedro Balli, por C. A. Cesar, 1612.

———. *Arte de la Lengua Timucuana compuesto en 1614 por el Pedro Francisco Pareja y publicado conforme al ejemplar original único.* Edited by Lucien Adam and Julien Vinson. Paris: Maisonneuve Frères et Ch. Leclerc, Éditeurs, 1886.

Pérez de Villagrá, Gaspar. *History of New Mexico.* Translated by Gilberto Espinosa. Los Angeles: The Quivira Society, 1933.

Quinn, David B., ed. *New American World: A Documentary History of North America to 1612.* 5 vols. New York: Arno Press and Hector Bye, Inc., 1979.

Robertson, James Alexander, ed. and trans. *True Relation of the Hardships Suffered by Governor Fernando de Soto & Certain Portuguese Gentlemen During the Discovery of the Province of Florida. Now Newly Set Forth by a Gentleman of Elvas.* 2 vols. Deland: The Florida State Historical Society, 1933.

Salmerón, Gerónimo de Zárate. *Relaciones.* Translated by Alicia Milich. Albuquerque: Horn and Wallace Publishers, 1966.

Snow, David K., ed. *The Native American and Spanish Colonial Experience in the Greater Southwest: Introduction to the Documentary Records.* New York and London: Garland Publishing, 1992.

———. ed. *The Native American and Spanish Colonial Experience in the Greater Southwest, II.* New York and London: Garland Publishing, 1992.

Solís de Merás, Gonzalo. *Memorial of Pedro Menéndez de Avilés, Adelantado, Governor and Captain-General of Florida.* Translated by Jeannette Thurber Connor. Deland, Florida: The Florida State Historical Society, 1923.

Thomas, David Hurst, Jr., ed. *Ethnology of the Indians of Spanish Florida.* New York and London: Garland Publishing, Inc., 1991.

———. ed. *The Missions of Spanish Florida.* New York and London: Garland Publishing, Inc., 1991.

Twitchell, Ralph Emerson, ed. *The Spanish Archives of New Mexico.* 2 vols. New York: Arno Press, 1976.

Tyler, S. Lyman, and H. Darrel Taylor, eds. and trans. "The Report of Fray Alonso de Posada in Relation to Quivira and Teguayo." *New Mexico Historical Review* 33 (1958): 285–314.

Wenhold, Lucy. "A Seventeenth Century Letter of Gabriel Diaz Vara Calderón, Bishop of Cuba, Describing the Indian Missions of Florida." *Smithsonian Miscellaneous Collections* vol. 95, no. 16. Washington, D.C.: Smithsonian Institution Press, 1936.

Worth, John E. "Fontandeda Revisted: Five Descriptions of Sixteenth-Century Florida." *Florida Historical Quarterly* (1995): 339–52.

———. *The Struggle for the Georgia Coast: An Eighteenth-Century Spanish Retrospective on Guale and Mocama.* Anthropological Papers no. 75. New York: American Museum of Natural History, 1995.

Secondary Sources

Adams, E. Charles. *The Origin and Development of the Pueblo Katsina Cult.* Tucson: University of Arizona Press, 1991.

Adelman, Jeremy, and Stephen Aron. "From Borderlands to Borders: Empires, Nation-States, and the Peoples in Between in North American History." *American Historical Review* 104 (June 1999): 814–41.

Adler, Michael A., ed. *The Prehistoric Pueblo World, A.D. 1150–1350.* Tucson: University of Arizona Press, 1996.

Anderson, Gary Clayton. *The Indian Southwest, 1580–1830: Ethnogenesis and Reinvention.* Norman: University of Oklahoma Press, 1999.

Anderson, H. Allen. "The Encomienda in New Mexico, 1598–1680." *New Mexico Historical Review* 60 (1985): 353–77.

Andreoli, Thomas E., et al. *Cecil Essentials of Medicine.* 3rd ed. Philadelphia: W. B. Saunders Company, 1993.

Andrien, Kenneth J., and Rolena Adorno, eds. *Transatlantic Encounters: Europeans and Andeans in the Sixteenth Century.* Berkeley: University of California Press, 1991.

Axtell, James. *After Columbus: Essays in the Ethnohistory of Colonial North America.* Oxford: Oxford University Press, 1988.

———. *Beyond 1492: Encounters in Colonial North America.* Oxford: Oxford

University Press, 1992.

——. The Indians' New South: Cultural Change in the Colonial Southeast. Baton Rouge and London: Louisiana State University Press, 1997.

——. The Invasion Within: The Contest of Cultures in Colonial North America. New York and Oxford: Oxford University Press, 1985.

——. Natives and Newcomers: The Cultural Origins of North America. New York and Oxford: Oxford University Press, 2001.

——. "Some Thoughts on the Ethnohistory of Missions." Ethnohistory 29 (1982): 35–41.

Baker, Brenda J., and Lisa Kealhofer, eds. Bioarchaeology of Native American Adaptation in the Spanish Borderlands. Gainesville: University Press of Florida, 1996.

Barker, Alex W., and Timothy R. Pauketat, eds. Lords of the Southeast: Social Inequality and the Native Elites of Southeastern North America. Anthropological papers of the American Anthropological Association, no. 3, 1992.

Barrett, Elinore M. Conquest and Catastrophe: Changing Rio Grande Pueblo Settlement Patterns in the Sixteenth and Seventeenth Centuries. Albuquerque: University of New Mexico Press, 2002.

——. "The Geography of the Rio Grande Pueblos in the Seventeenth Century." Ethnohistory 49 (Winter 2002): 123–69.

Bayer, Laura, et al. Santa Ana: The People, the Pueblo, and the History of Tamaya. Albuquerque: University of New Mexico Press, 1994.

Beninato, Stefanie. "Popé, Pose-yemu, and Naranjo: A New Look at Leadership in the Pueblo Revolt of 1680." New Mexico Historical Review 65 (October 1990): 417–35.

Benton, Lauren. "Making Order Out of Trouble: Jurisdictional Politics in the Spanish Colonial Borderlands." Law and Social Inquiry: Journal of the American Bar Foundation 26 (2001): 373–401.

Bitterli, Urs. Cultures in Conflict: Encounters between European and Non-European Cultures, 1492–1800. Translated by Ritchie Robertson. Cambridge: Polity Press, 1989.

Blake, Kevin S., and Jeffery S. Smith. "Pueblo Mission Churches as Symbols of Permanence and Identity." Geographical Review 90 (2000): 359–80.

Bolton, Herbert E. The Spanish Borderlands: A Chronicle of Old Florida and the Southwest. 1921. Reprint with an introduction by Albert L. Hurtado. Albuquerque: University of New Mexico Press, 1996.

Bowden, Henry Warner. American Indians and Christian Missions: Studies in Cultural Conflict. Chicago: Chicago University Press, 1981.

Boxer, C. R. The Church Militant and Iberian Expansion, 1440–1700. Baltimore: The Johns Hopkins University Press, 1978.

Bray, Warwick, ed. The Meeting of Two Worlds: Europe and the Americas, 1492–1650. Oxford: Oxford University Press for the British Academy, 1993.

Brooks, James F. Captives and Cousins: Slavery, Kinship, and Community in the

Southwest Borderlands. Chapel Hill: University of North Carolina Press for
    the Omohundro Institute of Early American History and Culture, 2002.
Brugge, David M. "Pueblo Factionalism and External Relations." *Ethnohistory* 16
    (Spring 1969): 191–200.
Bunting, Bainbridge. *Early Architecture in New Mexico*. Albuquerque: University
    of New Mexico Press, 1976.
Bushnell, Amy Turner. "A Peripheral Perspective." *Historical Archaeology* 31
    (1997): 18–23.
———. "Missions and Moral Judgment," *OAH Magazine of History* 14 (Summer
    2000): 21–22.
———. "Patricio de Hinachuba: Defender of the Word of God, The Crown of
    the King, and the Little Children of Ivitachuco." *American Indian Culture
    and Research Journal* 3 (1979): 1–21.
———. *Situado and Sabana: Spain's Support System for the Presidio and Mission
    Provinces of Florida*. American Museum of Natural History, Anthropology
    Papers, no.74. Athens: University of Georgia Press, 1994.
———. "'That Demonic Game': The Campaign to Stop Indian *Pelota* Playing in
    Spanish Florida, 1675–1684." *The Americas* 35 (1978): 1–19.
Calloway, Colin G., ed. *New Directions in American Indian History*. Norman:
    University of Oklahoma Press, 1988.
Cervantes, Fernando. *The Devil in the New World: The Impact of Diabolism in
    New Spain*. New Haven: Yale University Press, 1994.
Chaplin, Joyce E. *Subject Matter: Technology, the Body, and Science on the Anglo-
    America Frontier, 1500–1676*. Cambridge and London: Harvard University
    Press, 2001.
Chávez, Angélico. "Pohé-yemo's Representative and the Pueblo Revolt of 1680."
    New Mexico Historical Review 42 (1967): 85–126.
Chavez, Thomas. "But Were They All Natives?" *El Palacio* 86 (Winter 1980–81): 32.
Christian, William A., Jr. *Apparitions in Late Medieval and Renaissance Spain*.
    Princeton: Princeton University Press, 1981.
———. *Local Religion in Sixteenth-Century Spain*. Princeton: Princeton
    University Press, 1981.
Clendinnen, Inga. *Ambivalent Conquests: Maya and Spaniard in Yucatán,
    1517–1570*. Cambridge: Cambridge University Press, 1987.
———. "Disciplining the Indians: Franciscan Ideology and Missionary Violence
    in Sixteenth-Century Yucatán." *Past and Present* 94 (February 1982): 27–48.
———. "Ways to the Sacred: Reconstructing 'Religion' in Sixteenth-Century
    Mexico." *History and Anthropology* 5 (1990): 105–141.
Comaroff, John, and Jean Comaroff. *Ethnography and the Historical Imagination*.
    Boulder: Westview Press, 1992.
Conkling, Robert. "Legitimacy and Conversion in Social Change: The Case of
    French Missionaries and the Northeastern Algonkian." *Ethnohistory* 21
    (1974): 1–24.
Cook, David Noble. *Born to Die: Disease and New World Conquest, 1492–1650*.

Cambridge: Cambridge University Press, 1998.

Cordell, Linda S. *Prehistory of the Southwest.* San Diego: Academic Press, 1984.

Creamer, Winifred. "Re-Examining the Black Legend: Contact Period Demography in the Rio Grande Valley of New Mexico." *New Mexico Historical Review* 69 (1994): 263–78.

Cronan, William. *Changes in the Land: Indians, Colonists, and the Ecology of New England.* New York: Hill and Wang, 1983.

Crosby, Alfred W. *The Columbian Exchange: Biological and Cultural Consequences of 1492.* Westport, Connecticut: Greenwood Press, 1972.

———. *Ecological Imperialism: The Biological Expansion of Europe, 900–1900.* Cambridge: Cambridge University Press, 1986.

Cruz, Anne J., and Mary Elizabeth Perry, eds. *Culture and Control in Counter-Reformation Spain.* Minneapolis: University of Minnesota Press, 1992.

Cuello, José. "Beyond the 'Borderlands' Is the North of Colonial Mexico: A Latin-Americanist Perspective to the Study of the Mexican North and the United States Southwest." *Proceedings of the Pacific Coast Council in Latin American Studies* 9 (1982):1–24.

Cutter, Charles R. "The Administration of Law in Colonial New Mexico." *Journal of the Early Republic* 18 (1998): 99–139.

———. "Judicial Punishment in Colonial New Mexico." *Western Legal History* 8 (1995): 114–29.

———. *The Protector de Indios in Colonial New Mexico, 1659–1821.* Albuquerque: University of New Mexico Press, 1986.

Daniel, E. Randolph. *The Franciscan Concept of Mission in the High Middle Ages.* Lexington: University Press of Kentucky, 1975.

Daniels, Christine, and Michael V. Kennedy, eds. *Negotiated Empires: Centers and Peripheries in the Americas, 1500–1820.* New York and London: Routledge, 2002.

Deagan, Kathleen A., ed. *America's Ancient City: Spanish St. Augustine, 1565–1763.* New York and London: Garland Publishing, Inc., 1991.

Diamond, Jared. *Guns, Germs, and Steel: The Fates of Human Societies.* New York: W.W. Norton and Co., 1999.

Dickason, Olive Patricia. "Campaigns to Capture Young Minds: A Look at Early Attempts in Colonial Mexico and New France to Remold Amerindians." *Historical Papers* (1987): 44–66.

Dobyns, Henry F. "Puebloan Historic Demographic Trends." *Ethnohistory* 49 (Winter 2002): 171–204.

———. *Their Number Become Thinned: Native American Population Dynamics in Eastern America.* Knoxville: The University of Tennessee Press, 1983.

Dozier, Edward P. *The Pueblo Indians of North America.* Prospect Heights, Illinois: Waveland Press, 1983.

Edgerton, Samuel Y. *Theaters of Conversion: Religious Architecture and Indian Artisans in Colonial Mexico.* Albuquerque: University of New Mexico Press, 2001.

Eggan, Fred. *Social Organization of the Western Pueblos*. Chicago: University of
Chicago Press, 1950.

Ehrmann, W.W. "The Timucua Indians of Sixteenth Century Florida." *Florida
Historical Quarterly* 18 (1940): 168–91.

Eire, Carlos. *From Madrid to Purgatory: The Art and Craft of Dying in Sixteenth-
Century Spain*. Cambridge: Cambridge University Press, 1995.

Elliot, J. H. *Spain and Its New World, 1500–1700: Selected Essays*. New Haven: Yale
University Press, 1989.

Ellis, Florence Hawley. *A Reconstruction of the basic Jemez Pattern of Social
Organization, with Comparisons to Other Tanoan Social Structures*.
University of New Mexico Publications in Anthropology, no. 11.
Albuquerque: University of New Mexico Press, 1964.

———. *San Gabriel del Yungue: As Seen by an Archaeologist*. Santa Fe: Sunstone
Press, 1989.

Ewan, Charles R. "Continuity and Change: De Soto and the Apalachee."
Historical Archaeology 30 (1996): 41–53.

Fenton, William N. *Factionalism at Taos Pueblo, New Mexico*. Bureau of American
Ethnology, Bulletin 164, Anthropological Papers, no. 56. Washington, D.C.:
United States Government Printing Office, 1957.

Fletcher, Richard. *Moorish Spain*. Berkeley and Los Angeles: University of
California Press, 1992.

French, David H. *Factionalism at Isleta Pueblo*. American Ethnological Society,
Monograph 14. New York, 1948.

Gallay, Alan. *The Indian Slave Trade: The Rise of the English Empire in the
American South, 1670–1717*. New Haven: Yale University Press, 2002.

Gannon, Michael V. *The Cross in the Sand: The Early Catholic Church in Florida,
1513–1870*. Gainesville: University Presses of Florida, 1965.

Geiger, Maynard. "The Franciscan Conquest of Florida, 1573–1618." Ph.D. diss.,
The Catholic University of America, 1937.

Granberry, Julian. *A Grammar and Dictionary of the Timucua Language*. 3rd ed.
Tuscaloosa: University of Alabama Press, 1993.

Gray, Edward G., and Norman Fiering, eds. *The Language Encounter in the
Americas, 1492–1800*. New York and Oxford: Berghahn Books, 2000.

Greenblatt, Stephen. *Marvelous Possessions: The Wonder of the New World*.
Chicago: University of Chicago Press, 1991.

Griffin, John W. *Fifty Years of Southeastern Archaeology: Selected Works of John W.
Griffin*. Edited by Patricia C. Griffin. Gainesville: University Press of
Florida, 1996.

Griffiths, Nicholas, and Fernando Cervantes, eds. *Spiritual Encounters:
Interactions between Christianity and Native Religions in Colonial America*.
Lincoln: University of Nebraska Press, 1999.

Gruzinski, Serge. *The Conquest of Mexico: The Incorporation of Indian Societies
into the Western World, 16th–18th Centuries*. Translated by Eileen Corrigan.
Cambridge and Oxford: Polity Press, 1993.

Gutiérrez, Ramón A. *When Jesus Came, the Corn Mothers Went Away: Marriage, Sexuality, and Power in New Mexico, 1500–1846.* Stanford: Stanford University Press, 1991.

Guy, Donna J., and Thomas E. Sheridan, eds. *Contested Ground: Comparative Frontiers on the Northern and Southern Edges of the Spanish Empire.* Tucson: University of Arizona Press, 1998.

Haas, Jonathan, and Winifred Creamer. "Warfare Among the Pueblos: Myth, History, and Ethnography." *Ethnohistory* 44 (Spring 1997): 235–61.

Hall, Thomas D. *Social Change in the Southwest, 1350–1880.* Lawrence, Kansas: University Press of Kansas, 1989.

Hanke, Lewis. *All Mankind is One: A Study of the Disputation between Bartolomé de las Casas and Juan Ginés de Sepúlveda in 1550 on the Intellectual and Religious Capacity of the American Indians.* DeKalb: Northern Illinois University Press, 1974.

———. *History of Latin American Civilization.* 2 vols. Boston: Little, Brown, 1973.

———. "The 'Requerimiento' and its Interpreters." *Revista de historia de América* 1 (1938): 25–34.

———. *The Spanish Struggle for Justice in the Conquest of America.* Philadelphia: University of Pennsylvania Press, 1949.

Hanlon, Don. "The Spanish Mission Church in Central New Mexico: A Study in Architectural Morphology." *Anthropologica* 34 (1992): 203–29.

Hann, John H. *A History of the Timucua Indians and Missions.* Gainesville: University Press of Florida, 1996.

———. *Apalachee: The Land Between the Rivers.* Gainesville: University Press of Florida, 1988.

———. "Demographic Patterns and Changes in Mid-Seventeenth Century Timucua and Apalachee." *Florida Historical Quarterly* 64 (April 1986): 371–92.

———. "Political Leadership Among the Natives of Spanish Florida." *Florida Historical Quarterly* 71 (1992): 188–208.

———. "Summary Guide to Spanish Florida Missions and *Visitas* with Churches in the Sixteenth and Seventeenth Centuries." *The Americas* 46 (1990): 417–513.

———. "Twilight of the Mocamo and Guale Aborigines as Portrayed in the 1695 Spanish Visitation." *Florida Historical Quarterly* (1987): 1–24.

Hann, John H., ed. and trans. "Apalachee Counterfeiters in St. Augustine." *Florida Historical Quarterly* 67 (1988): 52–68.

Hefner, Robert W., ed. *Conversion to Christianity: Historical and Anthropological Perspectives on a Great Transformation.* Berkeley: University of California Press, 1993.

Hendricks, Rick, and Gerald Mandell. "Francisco de Lima, Portuguese Merchants of Parral, and the New Mexico Trade, 1638–1675." *New Mexico Historical Review* 77 (2002): 261–93.

Henige, David P. *Numbers From Nowhere: The American Indian Contact Population Debate.* Norman: University of Oklahoma Press, 1998.

Hoffman, Ronald, Mechal Sobel, and Fredrika J. Teute, eds. *Through a Glass*

Darkly: Reflections on Personal Identity in Early America. Chapel Hill: University of North Carolina Press for the Omohundro Institute of American History and Culture, 1997.

Howell, Todd L. "Identifying Leaders at Hawikku." *Kiva* 62 (1996): 61–82.

———. "Tracking Zuni Gender and Leadership Roles Across the Contact Period." *Journal of Anthropological Research* 51 (1995): 125–47.

Hudson, Charles M. ed. *Black Drink: A Native American Tea*. Athens: The University of Georgia Press, 1979.

———.*The Southeastern Indians*. Knoxville: University of Tennessee Press, 1976.

Hudson, Charles, and Carmen Chaves Tesser, eds. *The Forgotten Centuries: Indians and Europeans in the American South, 1521–1704*. Athens: University of Georgia Press, 1994.

Ivey, Jake. "Ahijados: The Rite of Communion and Mission Status on the Northern Frontier in the Seventeenth Century." *Catholic Southwest* 11 (2000): 7–26.

Ivey, James E. "The Baroque in New Mexico, 1620–1630." *Catholic Southwest* 9 (1998): 9–23.

———. "Convento Kivas in the Missions of New Mexico." *New Mexico Historical Review* 73 (1998): 121–52.

———. "'The Greatest Misfortune of All': Famine in the Province of New Mexico, 1667–1672." *Journal of the Southwest* 36 (1994): 76–100.

———. *"In the Midst of Loneliness": The Architectural History of the Salinas Missions*. Santa Fe: The National Park Service, 1988.

Jackson, Robert H., ed. *New Views of Borderlands History*. Albuquerque: University of New Mexico Press, 1998.

John, Elizabeth A. H. *Storms Brewed in Other Men's Worlds: The Confrontation of Indians, Spanish, and French in the Southwest, 1540–1795*. 2nd ed. Norman: University of Oklahoma Press, 1996.

Jones, B. Calvin. "Southern Cult Manifestations at the Lake Jackson Site, Leon County, Florida: Salvage Excavation of Mound 3." *Midcontinental Journal of Archaeology* 7 (1982): 3–44.

Jones, B. Calvin, John Hann, and John F. Scarry. "San Pedro y San Pablo de Patale: A Seventeenth-Century Spanish Mission in Leon County, Florida." *Florida Archaeology* 5 (1991): 1–201.

Jones, Oakah L., Jr. *Los Paisanos: Spanish Settlers on the Northern Frontier of New Spain*. Norman: University of Oklahoma Press, 1979.

———. *Pueblo Warriors and Spanish Conquest*. Norman: University of Oklahoma Press, 1966.

———. "San José del Parral: Colonial Trade of Parralenses with Nuevo México and El Paso del Río del Norte." *The Journal of Big Bend Studies* 13 (2001): 11–25.

Kamen, Henry. *Spain, 1469–1714: A Society of Conflict*. 2nd ed. London and New York: Longman Group UK Ltd., 1991.

Kapitzke, Robert L. *Religion, Power, and Politics in Colonial St. Augustine*. Gainesville: University Press of Florida, 2001.

Kenagy, Suzanne G. "Stepped Cloud and Cross: The Intersection of Pueblo and European Visual Symbolic Systems." *New Mexico Historical Review* 64 (July 1989): 325–40.

Kessell, John L. "Esteban Clemente: Precursor of the Pueblo Revolt." *El Palacio* 86 (Winter 1980–81): 16–17.

———. *Kiva, Cross, and Crown: The Pecos Indians and New Mexico, 1540–1840.* Tucson: Southwest Parks and Monuments Association, 1987.

———. "Restoring Seventeenth-Century New Mexico, Then and Now." *Historical Archaeology* 31 (1997): 46–54.

———. *Spain in the Southwest: A Narrative History of Colonial New Mexico.* Norman: University of Oklahoma Press, 2002.

Kessell, John L., and Rick Hendricks, eds. *The Spanish Missions of New Mexico, I: Before 1680.* New York and London: Garland Publishing, 1991

Kicza, John E. "Patterns in Early Spanish Overseas Expansion." *William and Mary Quarterly,* 3rd ser., 49 (April 1992): 229–53.

———. ed. *The Indian in Latin American History: Resistance, Resilience, and Acculturation.* Wilmington, Del.: Scholarly Resources, Inc., 2000.

Kimball, Geoffrey. "A Grammatical Sketch of Apalachee." *International Journal of American Linguistics* 53 (April 1987): 136–74.

———. "An Apalachee Vocabulary." *International Journal of American Linguistics* 54 (1988): 387–98.

King, Archdale A. *Liturgy of the Roman Church.* Milwaukee, Wisconsin: The Bruce Publishing Co, 1957.

Klauser, Theodor. *A Short History of the Western Liturgy: An Account and Some Reflections.* Translated by John Halliburton. London: Oxford University Press, 1969.

Knaut, Andrew L. *The Pueblo Revolt of 1680: Conquest and Resistance in Seventeenth-Century New Mexico.* Norman: University of Oklahoma Press, 1995.

Krech, Shepard III. *The Ecological Indian: Myth and History.* New York: W.W. Norton and Co., 1999.

Kubler, George. *The Religious Architecture of New Mexico in the Colonial Period and since the American Occupation.* Albuquerque: University of New Mexico Press, 1972.

Kupperman, Karen Ordahl, ed. *America in European Consciousness, 1493–1750.* Chapel Hill: University of North Carolina Press for the Institute of Early American History and Culture, 1995.

Kwachka, Patricia B., ed. *Perspectives on the Southeast: Linguistics, Archaeology, and Ethnohistory.* Athens: University of Georgia Press, 1994.

Lamar, Howard, and Leonard Thompson, eds. *The Frontier in History: North American and Southern Africa Compared.* New Haven: Yale University Press, 1981.

Langer, Erik, and Robert H. Jackson. *The New Latin American Mission History.* Lincoln and London: University of Nebraska Press, 1995.

Larsen, Clark Spencer, ed. *Bioarchaeology of Spanish Florida: The Impact of*

Colonialism. Gainesville: University Press of Florida, 2001.

Larson, Lewis H. *Aboriginal Subsistence Technology on the Southeastern Coastal Plain During the late Prehistoric Period.* Gainesville: University Presses of Florida, 1980.

LeBlanc, Steven A. *Prehistoric Warfare in the American Southwest.* Salt Lake City: University of Utah Press, 1999.

Levine, Frances. *Our Prayers Are in This Place: Pecos Pueblo Identity over the Centuries.* Albuquerque: University of New Mexico Press, 1999.

Levine, Frances, and Anna LaBauve. "Examining the Complexity of Historic Population Decline: A Case Study of Pecos Pueblo, New Mexico." *Ethnohistory* 44 (1997): 75–112.

Lockhart, James. *The Nahuas After the Conquest: A Social and Cultural History of the Indians of Central Mexico, Sixteenth through Eighteenth Centuries.* Stanford: Stanford University Press, 1992.

Loucks, Lana Jill. "Political and Economic Interactions Between Spaniards and Indians: Archaeological and Ethnohistorical Perspectives of the Mission System in Florida." Ph.D. diss., University of Florida, 1979.

Lyon, Eugene. *The Enterprise of Florida: Pedro Menèndez de Avilés and the Spanish Conquest of 1565–1568.* Gainesville: University Presses of Florida, 1976.

———. ed. *Pedro Menéndez de Avilés.* New York: Garland Press, 1995.

MacCameron, Robert. "Environmental Change in Colonial New Mexico." *Environmental History Review* 18 (1994): 17–39.

MacCormack, Sabine. "'The Heart Has Its Reasons': Predicaments of Missionary Christianity in Early Colonial Peru." *Hispanic American Historical Review* 63 (1985): 443–66.

———. *Religion in the Andes: Vision and Imagination in Early Colonial Peru.* Princeton: Princeton University Press, 1991.

MacKay, John Alexander. *The Other Spanish Christ: A Study in the Spiritual History of Spain and South America.* New York: The Macmillan Co., 1993.

Magnaghi, Russell M. "Plains Indians in New Mexico: The Genizaro Experience." *Great Plains Quarterly* 10 (1990): 86–95.

Matter, Robert A. "Mission Life in Seventeenth-Century Florida." *The Catholic Historical Review* 67 (1981): 401–20.

———. *Pre-Seminole Florida: Spanish Soldiers, Friars, and Indian Missions, 1513–1763.* New York and London: Garland Publishers, 1990.

McAlister, Lyle N. *Spain and Portugal in the New World, 1492–1700.* Minneapolis: University of Minnesota Press, 1984.

McEwan, Bonnie G., ed. *The Spanish Missions of La Florida.* Gainesville: University Press of Florida, 1993.

———. *Indians of the Greater Southeast: Historical Archaeology and Ethnohistory.* Gainesville: University Press of Florida, 2000.

McNeill, William H. *Plagues and Peoples.* Garden City, New York: Anchor Press, 1976.

Merrell, James H. *The Indians' New World: Catawbas and Their Neighbors from European Contact Through the Era of Removal.* New York: W.W. Norton and Co., 1989.

——. "Some Thoughts on Colonial Historians and American Indians." *William and Mary Quarterly*, 3rd ser., 46 (1989): 94–119.

Merrill, William L. *Rarámuri Souls: Knowledge and Social Process in Northern Mexico.* Washington and London: Smithsonian Institution Press, 1988.

Merrill, William L., Edward J. Ladd, and T. J. Ferguson. "The Return of the Ahayu:da: Lessons for Repatriation from Zuni Pueblo and the Smithsonian Institution." *Current Anthropology* 34 (December 1993): 523–67.

Milanich, Jerald T. *Archaeology of Precolumbian Florida.* Gainesville: University Press of Florida, 1994.

——. *Laboring in the Fields of the Lord: Spanish Missions and Southeastern Indians.* Washington and London: Smithsonian Institution Press, 1999.

Milanich, Jerald, and Samuel Proctor, eds. *Tacachale: Essays on the Indians of Florida and Southeastern Georgia during the Historic Period.* Gainesville: University Press of Florida, 1978.

Miller, Christopher L., and George R. Hamell. "A New Perspective on Indian-White Contact: Cultural Symbols and Colonial Trade." *The Journal of American History* 73 (September 1986): 311–28.

Mills, Kenneth. "The Limits of Religious Coercion in Mid-Colonial Peru." *Past and Present* 145 (1996): 84–121.

——. *Idolatry and Its Enemies: Colonial Andean Religion and Extirpation, 1640–1750.* Princeton: Princeton University Press, 1997.

Mindeleff, Victor. *A Study of Pueblo Architecture in Tusayan and Cibola.* Washington and London: Smithsonian Institution Press, 1989.

Minge, Ward Alan. *Acoma: Pueblo in the Sky.* Albuquerque: University of New Mexico Press, 1991.

Mitchell, Timothy. *Passional Culture: Emotion, Religion, and Society in Southern Spain.* Philadelphia: University of Pennsylvania Press, 1990.

Montgomery, Ross Gordon, Watson Smith, and John Otis Brew. *Franciscan Awatovi.* Papers of the Peabody Museum of American Archaeology and Ethnology, Harvard University, vol. 36. Cambridge: The Peabody Museum, 1949.

Moorman, John. *A History of the Franciscan Order From Its Origins to the Year 1517.* Oxford: Clarendon Press, 1968.

Morales, Francisco, O.F.M. *Ethnic and Social Background of the Franciscan Friars in Seventeenth Century Mexico.* Washington, D.C.: Academy of American Franciscan History, 1973.

——. ed. *Francisican Presence in the Americas: Essays on the Activities of the Franciscan Friars in the Americas, 1492–1900.* Potomac, MD: Academy of American Franciscan History, 1983.

Morgan, William N. *Precolumbian Architecture in Eastern North America.* Gainesville: University Press of Florida, 1999.

Morris, Brian. *Anthropological Studies of Religion: An Introductory Text.* Cambridge: Cambridge University Press, 1987.

Morrison, Kenneth M. "Baptism and Alliance: The Symbolic Mediation of

Religious Syncretism." *Ethnohistory* 37 (1990): 416–37.

Muldoon, James. *The Americas in the Spanish World Order: The Justification for Conquest in the Seventeenth Century*. Philadelphia: University of Pennsylvania Press, 1994.

Nalle, Sara T. *God in La Mancha: Religious Reform and the People of Cuenca, 1500–1650*. Baltimore: The Johns Hopkins University Press, 1992.

Nock, Arthur Darby. *Conversion: The Old and the New in Religion from Alexander the Great to Augustine of Hippo*. Oxford: Oxford University Press, 1933, reprint 1961.

Norris, Jim. "The Franciscans in New Mexico, 1692–1754: Toward a New Assessment." *The Americas* 51 (October 1994): 151–71.

O'Callaghan, Joseph F. *A History of Medieval Spain*. Ithaca: Cornell University Press, 1975.

Ortiz, Alfonso, ed. *New Perspectives on the Pueblos*. Albuquerque: University of New Mexico Press, 1972.

———. "Popay's Leadership: A Pueblo Perspective." *El Palacio* 86 (Winter 1980–1981): 18–22.

———. *The Tewa World: Space, Time, Being, and Becoming in a Pueblo Society*. Chicago and London: University of Chicago Press, 1969.

Pagden, Anthony. *Lords of All the World: Ideologies of Empire in Spain, Britain, and France, c.1500–c.1800*. New Haven: Yale University Press, 1995.

Palkovich, Ann M. "Historic Population of the Eastern Pueblos: 1540–1910." *Journal of Anthropological Research* 41 (1985): 401–26.

Parsons, Elsie Clews. *Pueblo Indian Religion*. 2 vols. Lincoln: University of Nebraska Press, [1939] 1996.

Payne, Stanley G. *Spanish Catholicism: An Historical Overview*. Madison: The University of Wisconsin Press, 1984.

Pearson, Fred Lamar, Jr. "Spanish-Indian Relations in Florida, 1602–1675: Some Aspects of Selected *Visitas*." *Florida Historical Quarterly* 52 (1974): 261–73.

———. "Timucuan Rebellion of 1656: The Rebolledo Investigation and the Civil-Religious Controversy." *Florida Historical Quarterly* 61 (1983): 260–80.

Pérez-González, María Luisa. "Royal Roads in the Old and the New World: The *Camino de Oñate* and Its Importance in the Spanish Settlement of New Mexico." *Colonial Latin American Historical Review* 7 (1998): 191–218.

Perry, Mary Elizabeth and Anne J. Cruz, eds. *Cultural Encounters: The Impact of the Inquisition in Spain and the New World*. Los Angeles: University of California Press, 1991.

Phelan, John Leddy. *The Millennial Kingdom of the Franciscans in the New World: A Study of the Writings of Gerónimo de Mendieta, 1525–1604*. Berkeley and Los Angeles: University of California Press, 1956.

———. *The People and the King: The Comunero Revolution in Columbia, 1781*. Madison: University of Wisconsin Press, 1978.

Preucel, Robert W., ed. *Archaeologies of the Pueblo Revolt: Identity, Meaning, and Renewal in the Pueblo World*. Albuquerque: University of New Mexico

Press, 2002.

Rabasa, José. *Writing Violence on the Northern Frontier: The Historiography of Sixteenth-Century New Mexico and Florida and the Legacy of Conquest.* Durham and London: Duke University Press, 2000.

Rafael, Vicente L. "Confession, Conversion, and Reciprocity in Early Tagalog Colonial Society." *Comparative Studies in Society and History* 29 (1987): 320–39.

———. *Contracting Colonialism: Translation and Christian Conversion in Tagalog Society Under Early Spanish Rule.* Durham: Duke University Press, 1993.

Ramenofsky, Ann F. *Vectors of Death: The Archaeology of European Contact.* Albuquerque: University of New Mexico Press, 1987.

———. "The Problem of Introduced Infectious Diseases in New Mexico: AD 1540–1680." *Journal of Anthropological Research* 52 (1996): 161–84.

Ramirez, Susan, ed. *Indian-Religious Relations in Colonial Spanish America.* Foreign and Comparative Studies/Latin American ser. 9. Maxwell School of Citizenship and Public Affairs, Syracuse University, 1989.

Reff, Daniel T. "Contextualizing Missionary Discourse: The Benavides Memorials of 1630 and 1634." *Journal of Anthropological Research* 50 (1994): 51–67.

———. "The Predicament of Culture and Spanish Missionary Accounts of the Tepehuan and Pueblo Revolts." *Ethnohistory* 42 (Winter 1995): 63–90.

Reitz, Elizabeth J., and C. Margaret Scarry. *Reconstructing Historic Subsistence with an Example from Sixteenth-Century Spanish Florida.* Special Publication Series, no. 3. Glassboro, New Jersey: Society for Historical Archaeology, 1985.

Ricard, Robert. *The Spiritual Conquest of Mexico: An Essay on the Apostate and the Evangelizing Methods of the Mendicant Orders in New Spain: 1523–1572.* Translated by Lesley Byrd Simpson. Berkeley: University of California Press, 1966.

Richter, Daniel K. "Iroquois versus Iroquois: Jesuit Missions and Christianity in Village Politics, 1642–1686." *Ethnohistory* 32 (1985): 1–16.

Riley, Carroll L. *Rio del Norte: People of the Upper Rio Grande from Earliest Times to the Pueblo Revolt.* Salt Lake City: University of Utah Press, 1995.

———. *The Kachina and the Cross: Indians and Spaniards in the Early Southwest.* Salt Lake City: University of Utah Press, 1999.

Riley, Carroll L., and Joni L. Manson. "The Cibola-Tiguex Route: Continuity and Change in the Southwest." *New Mexico Historical Review* 58 (1983): 347–67.

Robson, Michael. *St. Francis of Assisi: The Legend and the Life.* London: Geoffrey Chapman, 1997.

Rodack, Madeline Turrell. "Adolph Bandelier's History of the Borderlands." *Journal of the Southwest* 30 (1988): 35–120.

Rodríguez, Sylvia. "Procession and Sacred Landscape in New Mexico." *New Mexico Historical Review* 77 (2002): 1–26.

Ronda, James P. "'We Are Well As We Are'": An Indian Critique of Seventeenth-Century Christian Missions." *William and Mary Quarterly,* 3rd ser. 34

(1977): 66–82.

Ruhl, Donna L. "Oranges and Wheat: Spanish Attempts at Agriculture in *La Florida*." *Historical Archaeology* 31 (1997): 36–45.

Salmon, Roberto Mario. *Indian Revolts in Northern New Spain: A Synthesis of Resistance, 1680–1786*. Lanham, Maryland: University Press of America, 1991.

Sanchez, Jane C. "Spanish-Indian Relations During the Otermín Administration, 1677–1683." *New Mexico Historical Review* 58 (January 1983): 133–51.

Sánchez, Joseph P. "Introduction: Juan de Oñate and the Founding of New Mexico, 1598–1609." *Colonial Latin American Historical Review* 7 (1998): 89–107.

———. "Nicolás de Aguilar and the Jurisdiction of Salinas in the Province of New Mexico, 1659–1662." *Revista Complutense de Historia de América* 22 (1996): 139–59.

———. *The Rio Abajo Frontier, 1540–1692: A History of Early Colonial New Mexico*. 2nd ed. Albuquerque: Albuquerque Museum, 1996.

Sando, Joe. *Pueblo Nations: Eight Centuries of Pueblo Indian History*. Santa Fe, New Mexico: Clear Light, 1992.

Saunders, Rebecca. "Mission-Period Settlement Structure: A Test of the Model at San Martín de Timucua." *Historical Archaeology* 30 (1996): 24–36.

Scarry, John F., ed. *Political Structure and Change in the Prehistoric Southeastern United States*. Gainesville: University Press of Florida, 1996.

Schaafsma, Polly, ed. *Kachinas in the Pueblo World*. Albuquerque: University of New Mexico Press, 1994.

Scholes, France V. "Church and State in New Mexico, 1610–1650." *New Mexico Historical Review* 11 (1936): 9–76, 145–78, 283–94, 297–349; 12 (January 1937): 78–106.

———. "Civil Government and Society in New Mexico in the Seventeenth Century." *New Mexico Historical Review* 10 (April 1935): 71–111.

———. "The First Decade of the Inquisition in New Mexico." *New Mexico Historical Review* 10 (July 1935): 195–241.

———. "Notes on the Jemez Missions in the Seventeenth Century." *El Palacio* 44 (1938): 61–71, 93–102.

———. "Problems in the Early Ecclesiastical History of New Mexico." *New Mexico Historical Review* 7 (1932): 32–74.

———. "The Supply Service of the New Mexican Missions in the Seventeenth Century." *New Mexico Historical Review* 5 (1930): 93–115, 186–210, 386–404.

———. "Troublous Times in New Mexico, 1659–1670." *New Mexico Historical Review* 12 (1937): 134–74, 380–452; 13 (1938): 63–84; 15 (1940): 249–68, 369–417; 16 (July 1941): 15–40, 313–27.

Scholes, France V., and Lansing B. Bloom. "Friar Personnel and Mission Chronology, 1598–1629." *New Mexico Historical Review* 19 (1944): 319–36; 20 (1945): 58–82.

Schroeder, Susan, ed. *Native Resistance and the Pax Colonial in New Spain*. Lincoln: University of Nebraska Press, 1998.

Schwartz, Stuart B. *The Iberian Mediterranean and Atlantic Traditions on the*

Formation of Columbus As a Colonizer. Minneapolis: University of Minnesota Press, 1986.

Scully, Vincent. Pueblo: Mountain, Village, Dance. 2nd ed. Chicago: University of Chicago Press, 1989.

Sedgwick, Mary K. Acoma, the Sky City: A Study in Pueblo-Indian History and Civilization. Cambridge: Harvard University Press, 1927.

Shapiro, Gary, and Bonnie G. McEwan. "Archaeology at San Luis: The Apalachee Council House." Florida Archaeology 6 (1992): 1–173.

Shapiro, Gary, and Richard Vernon. "Archaeology at San Luis Part Two: The Church Complex." Florida Archaeology 6 (1992): 177–278.

Simmons, Marc. The Last Conquistador: Juan de Oñate and the Settling of the Far Southwest. Norman: University of Oklahoma Press, 1991.

———. "The Pueblo Revolt: Why Did It Happen?" El Palacio 86 (Winter 1980–81): 11–15.

———. "Settlement Patterns and Village Plans in Colonial New Mexico." Journal of the West 8 (1969): 7–21.

Smith, Bruce D., ed. The Mississippian Emergence. Washington and London: Smithsonian Institution Press, 1990.

Smith, Watson. When Is a Kiva? And Other Questions about Southwestern Archaeology. Tucson: The University of Arizona Press, 1990.

Snow, David A., and Richard Machalek. "The Sociology of Conversion." American Review of Sociology 10 (1984): 167–90.

Spicer, Edward H. Cycles of Conquest: The Impact of Spain, Mexico, and the United States on the Indians of the Southwest, 1533–1960. Tucson: University of Arizona Press, 1962.

———. "Spanish-Indian Acculturation in the Southwest." American Anthropologist 56 (August 1954): 663–84.

Spielmann, Katherine A. "Late Prehistoric Exchange Between the Southwest and Southern Plains." Plains Anthropologist 28 (1983): 257–72.

Spielmann, Katherine A., Margaret J. Schoeninger, and Katherine Moore. "Plains-Pueblo Interdependence and Human Diet at Pecos Pueblo, New Mexico." American Antiquity 55 (1990): 745–65.

Spiess, Lincoln Bruce. "Church Music in Seventeenth-Century New Mexico." New Mexico Historical Review 11 (1965): 5–21.

Staski, Edward. "Change and Inertia on the Frontier: Archaeology at the Paraje de San Diego, Camino Real, in Southern New Mexico." International Journal of Historical Archaeology 2 (1998): 21–44.

Stevens-Arroyo, Anthony. "The Inter-Atlantic Paradigm: The Failure of Spanish Medieval Colonization of the Canary and Caribbean Islands." Comparative Studies in Sociology and History 35 (July 1993): 515–43.

Sturtevant, William C. "Spanish-Indian Relations in Southeastern North America." Ethnohistory 9 (1962): 41–94.

Swanton, John R. Early History of the Creek Indians and Their Neighbors. Gainesville: University Press of Florida, [1922] 1998.

———. *The Indians of the Southeastern United States*. Washington: Smithsonian Institution Press, 1979.

Taylor, Mark C., ed. *Critical Terms for Religious Studies*. Chicago: Chicago University Press, 1998.

Taylor, William B. *Magistrates of the Sacred: Priests and Parishioners in Eighteenth-Century Mexico*. Stanford: Stanford University Press, 1996.

Taylor, William B., and Franklin Pease G.Y., eds. *Violence, Resistance, and Survival in the Americas: Native Americans and the Legacy of Conquest*. Washington and London: Smithsonian Institution Press, 1994.

Thomas, David Hurst, Jr., ed. *Columbian Consequences: Archaeological and Historical Perspectives on the Spanish Borderlands*. 3 vols. Washington and London: Smithsonian Institution Press, 1990.

Titiev, Mischa. *Old Oraibi: A Study of the Hopi Indians of Third Mesa*. Albuquerque: University of New Mexico Press, [1944] 1992.

Todorov, Tzvetan. *The Conquest of America*. Translated by Richard Howard. New York: Harper and Row, 1984.

Toulouse, Joseph H., Jr. *The Mission of San Gregorio de Abó: A Report on the Excavation and Repair of a Seventeenth-Century New Mexico Mission*. Monographs of the School of American Research, no. 13. Albuquerque: University of New Mexico Press, 1949.

Trexler, Richard C. *Naked Before the Father: The Reunification of Francis of Assisi*. Humana Civilitas: Studies and Sources Relating to the Middle Ages and the Renaissance, vol. 9. New York: Peter Lang, 1989.

Trigg, Heather B. "The Ties That Bind: Economic and Social Interactions in Early–Colonial New Mexico, A.D. 1598–1680." *Historical Archaeology* 37 (2003): 65–84.

Trigger, Bruce G. "Early Native North American Responses to European Contact: Romantic versus Rationalistic Interpretations." *Journal of American History* 77 (March 1991): 1195–1215.

———. "Ethnohistory: Problems and Prospects." *Ethnohistory* 29 (1982): 1–19.

———. "Ethnohistory: The Unfinished Edifice." *Ethnohistory* 33 (1986): 253–67.

Van Oss, Adriaan C. *Catholic Colonialism: A Parish History of Guatemala, 1524–1821*. Cambridge: Cambridge University Press, 1986.

Verano, John W., and Douglas H. Ubelaker, eds. *Disease and Demography in the Americas: Changing Patterns Before and After 1492*. Washington and London: Smithsonian Institution Press, 1994.

Vivian, Gordon. *Gran Quivira: Excavations in a 17th Century Jumano Pueblo*. Archaeological Research Series, no. 8, National Park Service, U.S. Department of the Interior, 1979.

Weber, David J. *The Idea of the Spanish Borderlands*. New York: Garland Publishing, Inc., 1991.

———. ed. *New Spain's Far Northern Frontier: Essays on Spain in the American West, 1540–1821*. Dallas: Southern Methodist University Press, 1979.

———. *The Spanish Frontier in North America*. New Haven: Yale University

Weber, David, and Jane M. Rausch, eds. *Where Cultures Meet: Frontiers in Latin American History*. Wilmington, Del: Scholarly Resources, Inc., 1994.

Webster, Jill R. *Els Menorets: The Franciscans in the Realms of Aragon from St. Francis to the Black Death*. Studies and texts 114. Toronto: Pontifical Institute of Mediaeval Studies, 1993.

Weisman, Brent Richards. *Excavations on the Franciscan Frontier: Archaeology at the Fig Springs Mission*. Gainesville: University Press of Florida, 1992.

White, Richard. *The Middle Ground: Indians, Empires, and Republics in the Great Lakes Region, 1650–1815*. Cambridge: Cambridge University Press, 1991.

White, Leslie. *The Pueblo of San Felipe*. Memoirs of the Anthropological Association, no.38. Menasha, Wisconsin: American Anthropological Association, 1932.

———. *The Pueblo of Santa Ana, New Mexico*. American Anthropological Memoirs, no. 60. New York: American Anthropological Association, 1969.

———. *The Pueblo of Santo Domingo, New Mexico*. Memoirs of the American Anthropological Association, no. 43. Menasha, Wisconsin: American Anthropological Association, 1935.

———. *The Pueblo of Sia, New Mexico*. Smithsonian Institution Bureau of American Ethnology, Bulletin 184. Washington, D.C.: U.S. Government Printing Office, 1962.

Wilcox, David R., and W. Bruce Masse, eds. *The Protohistoric Period in the North American Southwest, AD 1450–1700*. Anthropological Research Papers, no. 24. Tempe: Arizona State University, 1981.

Wilson, John P. *Quarai*. Tucson: Southwest Parks & Monuments Association, 1999.

Worth, John E. *The Struggle for the Georgia Coast: An Eighteenth-Century Spanish Retrospective on Guale and Mocama*. American Museum of Natural History, Anthropological Papers, no. 75. Athens: University of Georgia Press, 1995.

———. *Timucuan Chiefdoms of Spanish Florida*. 2 vols. Gainesville: University of Florida Press, 1998.

———. "The Timucuan Missions of Spanish Florida and the Rebellion of 1656." Ph.D. diss., University of Florida, 1992.

Wright, A. D. *Catholicism and Spanish Society Under the Reign of Philip II, 1555–1598, and Philip III, 1598–1621*. Lewiston, Queenston, and Lampeter: The Edwin Mellen Press, 1991.

Wright, Barton. *Pueblo Cultures*. Institute of Religious Iconography, State University of Groningen, sec. 10, fasc. 4. Leiden: E. J. Brill, 1986.

Wright, J. Leitch. *The Only Land They Knew: The Tragic Story of the American Indians in the Old South*. New York: The Free Press, 1981.

INDEX